Health and Performance through Sports at All Ages 2.0

Health and Performance through Sports at All Ages 2.0

Editor

Gianpiero Greco

Basel • Beijing • Wuhan • Barcelona • Belgrade • Novi Sad • Cluj • Manchester

Editor
Gianpiero Greco
Department of Translational
Biomedicine and
Neuroscience (DiBraiN)
University of Study of Bari
Bari
Italy

Editorial Office
MDPI
St. Alban-Anlage 66
4052 Basel, Switzerland

This is a reprint of articles from the Special Issue published online in the open access journal *Journal of Functional Morphology and Kinesiology* (ISSN 2411-5142) (available at: www.mdpi.com/journal/jfmk/special_issues/7627X62P2W).

For citation purposes, cite each article independently as indicated on the article page online and as indicated below:

Lastname, A.A.; Lastname, B.B. Article Title. *Journal Name* **Year**, *Volume Number*, Page Range.

ISBN 978-3-7258-0584-6 (Hbk)
ISBN 978-3-7258-0583-9 (PDF)
doi.org/10.3390/books978-3-7258-0583-9

Contents

About the Editor

Gianpiero Greco

Gianpiero Greco has a PhD in Neuroscience and Translational Medicine. He is a Professor of Exercise and Sport Sciences and Research Methodology at the University of Bari. He has more than 80 publications in impacted journals to his credit. He aims to improve psychophysical well-being and human performance through physical activity and sport in healthy and unhealthy populations. His research involves the general population of all age groups, including students, athletes, workers, and the tactical population.

Preface

Sports participation offers numerous health benefits, including improved cardiovascular health, enhanced musculoskeletal strength, and weight management. Physical and sports activity positively impacts adults' mental and physical health and behaviours, the physical fitness of children and adults with behavioural problems, the cognitive and social-emotional domains, and adolescents' body image. Engageing in sports contributes to healthy ageing by preserving cognitive function, mobility, and independence for older adults. Additionally, sports participation among children and adolescents promotes healthy growth and development, instills lifelong habits of physical activity, and reduces the risk of obesity and related health issues.

The articles in this reprint contribute to expanding our knowledge in this field with new scientific evidence to meet the needs of people of all ages who practice physical activity and sports.

Gianpiero Greco
Editor

Journal of
Functional Morphology and Kinesiology

MDPI

Editorial

Special Issue "Health and Performance through Sports at All Ages 2.0"

Gianpiero Greco

Department of Translational Biomedicine and Neuroscience (DiBraiN), University of Study of Bari, 70124 Bari, Italy; gianpiero.greco@uniba.it

This Special Issue, "Health and Performance through Sports at All Ages 2.0", aimed to investigate the impact of physical activity and sport on health and human performance across all age groups. Previous research has shown that engaging in sports activities offers numerous health benefits, including improved cardiovascular health, enhanced musculoskeletal strength, and weight management [1]. Physical and sports activity positively impacts the mental and physical health and behaviors of adults [2], the physical fitness of children [3] and adults with behavioral problems [4], the cognitive and social–emotional domains [4,5], and the body image of adolescents [5]. For older adults, engaging in sports activities contributes to healthy aging by preserving cognitive function, mobility, and independence [6]. Additionally, sports participation among children and adolescents promotes healthy growth and development, instils lifelong habits of physical activity, and reduces the risk of obesity and related health issues [7].

During childhood and adolescence, physical activity is crucial for healthy growth and development. Regular exercise helps children build strong muscles and bones, maintain a healthy weight, and develop essential motor skills and coordination [8]. Moreover, participation in sports and physical activities fosters social skills, such as teamwork, leadership, and communication, which are essential for overall development [9].

Physical activity remains essential in adulthood for maintaining health and optimizing performance. Regular exercise reduces the risk of chronic diseases, such as heart disease, diabetes, and certain cancers [1]. It also helps manage weight, improve cardiovascular health, and enhance muscular strength and endurance [10]. Additionally, staying active promotes mental well-being, reduces stress, and improves sleep quality, leading to a better overall quality of life [11].

As individuals age, physical activity becomes even more critical for maintaining health and independence. Regular exercise helps older adults preserve muscle mass and bone density, reduce the risk of falls and fractures, and manage chronic conditions, such as arthritis and osteoporosis [12]. Moreover, staying physically active in old age promotes cognitive function, reduces the risk of dementia, and enhances overall mobility and quality of life [13].

In addition to its impact on health, physical activity plays a vital role in optimizing performance across all age groups. Participation in sports and physical activities enhances athletic performance, improves motor skills and coordination, and fosters a competitive spirit [7]. Moreover, regular exercise helps individuals set and achieve goals, build resilience, and overcome challenges, both on and off the field [14].

Despite the benefits of physical activity, several barriers and challenges can hinder participation at all ages. These may include lack of time, access to facilities, motivation, and physical limitations [15]. Moreover, societal factors such as socioeconomic status, cultural norms, and environmental factors can also influence levels of physical activity across different age groups [16,17].

check for updates

Citation: Greco, G. Special Issue "Health and Performance through Sports at All Ages 2.0". *J. Funct. Morphol. Kinesiol.* **2024**, *9*, 36. https://doi.org/10.3390/jfmk9010036

Received: 11 February 2024
Accepted: 21 February 2024
Published: 23 February 2024

The articles included in this Special Issue have contributed to expanding our knowledge in this field with new scientific evidence to satisfy the needs of the population of all ages practicing physical activity and sports.

Nineteen manuscripts were submitted for consideration to this Special Issue, and all of them were subjected to the rigorous *JFMK* review process. In total, ten papers were finally accepted for publication and inclusion in this Special Issue (nine articles and one systematic review). The contributions are listed below:

1. Grigoletto, A.; Mauro, M.; Toselli, S. Evaluation of the Effectiveness of a Nordic Walking and a Resistance Indoor Training Program: Anthropometric, Body Composition, and Functional Parameters in the Middle-Aged Population. J. Funct. Morphol. Kinesiol. 2023, 8, 79. https://doi.org/10.3390/jfmk8020079;
2. Bongiovanni, T.; Rossi, A.; Genovesi, F.; Martera, G.; Puleo, G.; Orlandi, C.; Spedicato, M.; Iaia, F.M.; Del Vescovo, R.; Gallo, S.; et al. How Do Football Playing Positions Differ in Body Composition? A First Insight into White Italian Serie A and Serie B Players. J. Funct. Morphol. Kinesiol. 2023, 8, 80. https://doi.org/10.3390/jfmk8020080;
3. Karatrantou, K.; Papavasiliou, T.; Batatolis, C.; Vasilopoulou, T.; Ioakimidis, P.; Gerodimos, V. A Chair-Based Music–Kinetic Combined Exercise Program as an Alternative Approach for Increasing Health, Functional Capacity, and Physical Fitness Indices in Middle-Aged Pre-Menopausal Women. J. Funct. Morphol. Kinesiol. 2023, 8, 81. https://doi.org/10.3390/jfmk8020081;
4. Jagomast, T.; Mohr, T.; Axt, P.N.; Mortensen, K.; Brinkmann, F.; Weckmann, M.; Ring, G.; Reppel, M.; Drömann, D.; Franzen, K.F. Effects of Physical Activity in the High School Curriculum on Cardiovascular Health, Cognitive and Physical Performance. J. Funct. Morphol. Kinesiol. 2023, 8, 101. https://doi.org/10.3390/jfmk8030101;
5. Tsartsapakis, I.; Gerou, M.; Zafeiroudi, A.; Kellis, E. Transversus Abdominis Ultrasound Thickness during Popular Trunk–Pilates Exercises in Young and Middle-Aged Women. J. Funct. Morphol. Kinesiol. 2023, 8, 110. https://doi.org/10.3390/jfmk8030110;
6. Crawford, D.A.; Heinrich, K.M.; Haddock, C.K.; Poston, W.S.C.; Day, R.S.; Kaipust, C.; Skola, B.; Wakeman, A.J.; Kunkel, E.; Bell, A.; et al. A Single, Multimodal Exercise Tolerance Test Can Assess Combat Readiness in Army-ROTC Cadets: A Brief Report. J. Funct. Morphol. Kinesiol. 2023, 8, 152. https://doi.org/10.3390/jfmk8040152;
7. Grigoletto, A.; Mauro, M.; Toselli, S. Differences in Body Composition and Maturity Status in Young Male Volleyball Players of Different Levels. J. Funct. Morphol. Kinesiol. 2023, 8, 162. https://doi.org/10.3390/jfmk8040162;
8. Rodrigues, F.; Jacinto, M.; Antunes, R.; Monteiro, D.; Mendes, D.; Matos, R.; Amaro, N. Comparing the Effects of Multicomponent and Concurrent Exercise Protocols on Muscle Strength in Older Adults. J. Funct. Morphol. Kinesiol. 2024, 9, 3. https://doi.org/10.3390/jfmk9010003;
9. Greco, G.; Centrone, C.; Poli, L.; Silva, A.F.; Russo, L.; Cataldi, S.; Giustino, V.; Fischetti, F. Impact of Coastal Walking Outdoors and Virtual Reality Indoor Walking on Heart Rate, Enjoyment Levels and Mindfulness Experiences in Healthy Adults. J. Funct. Morphol. Kinesiol. 2024, 9, 11. https://doi.org/10.3390/jfmk9010011;
10. Olasagasti-Ibargoien, J.; Castañeda-Babarro, A.; León-Guereño, P.; Uria-Olaizola, N. Barriers to Physical Activity for Women with Physical Disabilities: A Systematic Review. J. Funct. Morphol. Kinesiol. 2023, 8, 82. https://doi.org/10.3390/jfmk8020082.

In Contribution 1, the authors wanted to investigate new strategies to combat sedentary behavior in the middle-aged population by making use of green spaces. They compared the effectiveness of a period of outdoor training (Nordic walking) with indoor resistance training in a non-clinical middle-aged population based on anthropometric characteristics, body composition, and functional parameters. The Nordic walking group showed a higher elevation in muscle mass and a higher decrease in fat parameters than the indoor resistance training group. However, these two types of training could represent a good strategy to remain active and prevent sedentary behaviors.

The authors of Contribution 2 investigated how playing positions differ in specific body composition variables in professional soccer players concerning specific field zones and tactical lines. These authors analyzed the following positions: goalkeepers (GKs), central backs (CBs), fullbacks (FBs), central midfielders (MIDs), wide midfielders (WMs), attacking midfielders (AMs), second strikers (SSs), external strikers (ESs), and central forwards (CFs), as well as their field zones (central and external) and tactical lines (defensive, middle, and offensive). The GKs and CFs were the tallest and heaviest players, with no differences from each other. Likewise, the GKs and CFs, along with the CBs, were apparently more muscular (for both the upper and lower limbs) and fatter at the same time compared with the other roles. Overall, players of the defensive line (e.g., the CBs and FBs), along with those playing in central field zones (e.g., the CBs, MIDs, AMs, SSs, and CFs), were significantly superior in almost all anthropometric and body composition variables to those of middle and offensive line and external zones, respectively.

In Contribution 3, the authors considered the chairs that have been widely used as cheap, easily accessible, safe, and effective training means in different settings (e.g., in gyms, houses, workplaces, and in rehabilitation). These authors investigated the effectiveness of a 10-week chair-based music–kinetic-integrated combined exercise program (aerobic dance, flexibility, coordination, and strength exercises with body weight or auxiliary means) on the health, functional capacity, and physical fitness indicators of middle-aged pre-menopausal women. The exercise group showed significantly reductions in body fat, blood pressure, the time during the timed up-and-go test, heart rate, and the rate of perceived exertion, while increasing respiratory function, flexibility, balance, maximal handgrip strength, and endurance. These authors concluded that the chair-based combined music–kinetic exercise program was effective and could be safely used in different settings to improve health, functional capacity, and physical fitness in middle-aged women.

Although it is well-known that cardiovascular health at a young age has implications for preventing cardiovascular disease and is associated with improved physical and cognitive performance during the aging process [1], the authors of Contribution 4 wanted to address the problem of physical activity interventions at school that are overlooked. They compared groups of high school students, stratified by the level of physical activity in their high school curriculum and downtime. Regarding cognitive skills, extracurricular physical activity improved the number of connection tests in male participants. For physical performance, female students with a sports-focused curriculum were faster in the 3 km run. Concerning arterial stiffness, the measurements yielded a lower mean arterial pressure and aortic pulse wave velocity in male students with a sports-focused curriculum. These authors suggested that extracurricular physical activity and enrolment in a sports-focused curriculum may be associated with lower cardiovascular risk due to lower levels of arterial stiffness and better physical and cognitive abilities.

It Is also known that the transversus abdominis is a core muscle that contributes to functional mobility and lumbar stability. In Contribution 5, the authors aimed to compare the changes in transversus abdominis thickness during different Pilates exercises (basic position, hundred, hip roll, side plank, and dead bug) and identify the exercise that elicited the greatest transversus abdominis activation. Their findings suggested that the dead bug exercise is the most effective for enhancing transversus abdominis activation among the Pilates exercises that were tested. The basic position and the hundred exercises can be used as warm-up exercises before performing more challenging exercises, such as the hip roll, the side plank, and the dead bug. The sequence of exercises can be similar for both young and middle-aged women.

In Contribution 6, the authors, through their research on tactical populations, sought to design and evaluate a single, multimodal exercise tolerance test capable of serving as a time-efficient proxy measure of combat readiness. It is well known that the Army Combat Fitness Test is a multi-event assessment battery designed to determine the combat readiness of U.S. Army personnel. Unfortunately, for Reserve Officers' Training Corps programs, the logistical demands of collegiate life make repeated administration of the Army Combat

Fitness Test challenging. The findings suggested that the multimodal exercise tolerance test has the potential to provide a means to monitor progress, identify areas for improvement, and guide informed decision making regarding the individualization of cadet combat training plans.

Another interesting piece of research in this Special Issue was carried out on one of the most played sports, namely volleyball, which is an intermittent team sport that requires specific anthropometrical and physical characteristics for winning performance. The authors of Contribution 7 evaluated the maturity status of the young male players of eight volleyball teams and observed differences in anthropometric characteristics and body composition. Their findings showed that young volleyball players classified as "early" seemed to show anthropometric characteristics linked to better performance at the tournament (higher height, upper arm and calf muscle area, fat mass percentage, and total fat-free mass). The authors suggested that the results of the study could have practical implications for talent selection, but further studies are needed to better evaluate the effect of maturity status on the characteristics of volleyball players.

A study on the elderly was carried out by the authors of Contribution 8, which compared the effects of a multicomponent exercise program and a concurrent exercise program on muscle strength in community-dwelling elderly subjects. These authors found that while both the multicomponent and concurrent exercise programs were effective in improving muscle strength in community-dwelling older adults, the multicomponent exercise group exhibited superior outcomes compared to the concurrent exercise group across the physical fitness measures. These findings suggest that a multicomponent exercise program may be more beneficial for enhancing muscle strength in this population.

As has been shown by Contribution 1, outdoor exercise in a green space is beneficial for peoples' well-being. However, limited studies have compared outdoor and virtual reality indoor physical activities, especially in coastal settings. Therefore, the authors of Contribution 9 assessed the impact of outdoor coastal walking and indoor walking in a virtual reality simulation with a similar environment on physiological and psychological variables in healthy adults. Their findings suggested that physical activity in immersive technology may lead to physiological loads comparable to those in the outdoor environment. Outdoor walking is more enjoyable than indoor walking and virtual reality indoor walking, but it exhibits a mindfulness response comparable to virtual reality indoor walking. Therefore, virtual reality indoor walking could be an alternative to outdoor walking for those who cannot engage in outdoor activities for various reasons.

Finally, the systematic review of Contribution 10 aimed to identify the barriers faced by women with physical disabilities in practicing sports. The barriers to physical activity for women with physical disabilities are multiple and complex, and span multiple dimensions. This review identified different barriers, including (i) personal barriers such as age, fatigue, loneliness, lifestyle, or simply being a woman may limit participation in any physical activity; (ii) motivation and other psychological factors such as fear, the perception of not being able to engage in physical activity, or a negative self-perception; (iii) any management barriers, such as poor accessibility or lack of adaptations to sports centers, lack of transport to sports facilities, lack of communication between professionals, and poor organizational management; (iv) very often, training staff are not adequately trained to adapt physical activity or programs to users' needs; (v) the financial costs of sporting activities as this barrier can have a crucial impact on participation in sport; (vi) men received more support from family and friends than women; and (vii) social attitudes towards people with disabilities: people with disabilities who perceive stereotyping to a high degree also perceive a lower quality of life. Disabled people's participation in physical activity is directly related to some specific barriers that seem to differ according to their gender. Therefore, the success of participation in physical activities depends not only on the user's concern but also on an inclusive social environment.

In conclusion, sports participation provides numerous health benefits and contributes to improved performance throughout the lifespan [18–20]. Incorporating regular physical activity through sports engagement is essential for promoting overall health, optimizing performance, and addressing age-related challenges. Future research should continue to explore the specific mechanisms underlying the relationship between sports participation and health outcomes, with a focus on developing tailored and adapted interventions to encourage lifelong physical activity engagement.

Given the great success of the second edition of this Special Issue, we have launched a third edition, for which we hope to receive contributions focusing on the effects of sports and physical activity on health and human performance across all age groups.

Conflicts of Interest: The authors declare no conflicts of interest.

References

1. Warburton, D.E.; Nicol, C.W.; Bredin, S.S. Health benefits of physical activity: The evidence. *CMAJ Can. Med. Assoc. J.* **2006**, *174*, 801–809. [CrossRef] [PubMed]
2. Posadzki, P.; Pieper, D.; Bajpai, R.; Makaruk, H.; Könsgen, N.; Neuhaus, A.L.; Semwal, M. Exercise/physical activity and health outcomes: An overview of Cochrane systematic reviews. *BMC Public Health* **2020**, *20*, 1724. [CrossRef] [PubMed]
3. Greco, G.; Cataldi, S.; Fischetti, F. Effectiveness of a Short After-School Intervention on Physical Fitness in School-Aged Children. *J. Theor. Res. Educ.* **2019**, *14*, 143–164. [CrossRef]
4. Fischetti, F.; Cataldi, S.; Di Terlizzi, P.; Greco, G. Multilateral methodology in physical education improves coping skills, resilience and physical fitness in drug addicts. *J. Hum. Sport Exerc.* **2020**, *15*, 367–379. [CrossRef]
5. Latino, F.; Greco, G.; Fischetti, F.; Cataldi, S. Multilateral training improves body image perception in female adolescents. *J. Hum. Sport Exerc.* **2019**, *14*, S927–S936. [CrossRef]
6. Marmeleira, J. Physical activity and cognitive function in the elderly: A review. *Eur. Rev. Aging Phys. Act.* **2010**, *7*, 1–12.
7. Faigenbaum, A.D.; Lloyd, R.S.; MacDonald, J.; Myer, G.D. Citius, Altius, Fortius: Beneficial effects of resistance training for young athletes: Narrative review. *Br. J. Sports Med.* **2016**, *50*, 3–7. [CrossRef] [PubMed]
8. Janssen, I.; LeBlanc, A.G. Systematic review of the health benefits of physical activity and fitness in school-aged children and youth. *Int. J. Behav. Nutr. Phys. Act.* **2010**, *7*, 40. [CrossRef] [PubMed]
9. Eime, R.M.; Young, J.A.; Harvey, J.T.; Charity, M.J.; Payne, W.R. A systematic review of the psychological and social benefits of participation in sport for adults: Informing development of a conceptual model of health through sport. *Int. J. Behav. Nutr. Phys. Act.* **2013**, *10*, 135. [CrossRef] [PubMed]
10. Kohl, H.W., 3rd; Craig, C.L.; Lambert, E.V.; Inoue, S.; Alkandari, J.R.; Leetongin, G.; Kahlmeier, S.; Lancet Physical Activity Series Working Group. The pandemic of physical inactivity: Global action for public health. *Lancet* **2012**, *380*, 294–305. [CrossRef] [PubMed]
11. Rebar, A.L.; Stanton, R.; Geard, D.; Short, C.; Duncan, M.J.; Vandelanotte, C. A meta-analysis of the effect of physical activity on depression and anxiety in non-clinical adult populations. *Health Psychol. Rev.* **2015**, *9*, 366–378. [CrossRef] [PubMed]
12. Nelson, M.E.; Rejeski, W.J.; Blair, S.N.; Duncan, P.W.; Judge, J.O.; King, A.C.; Macera, C.A.; Castaneda-Sceppa, C. Physical activity and public health in older adults: Recommendation from the American College of Sports Medicine and the American Heart Association. *Med. Sci. Sports Exerc.* **2007**, *39*, 1435–1445. [CrossRef] [PubMed]
13. Bherer, L.; Erickson, K.I.; Liu-Ambrose, T. A review of the effects of physical activity and exercise on cognitive and brain functions in older adults. *J. Aging Res.* **2013**, *2013*, 657508. [CrossRef] [PubMed]
14. Hillman, C.H.; Erickson, K.I.; Kramer, A.F. Be smart, exercise your heart: Exercise effects on brain and cognition. *Nat. Rev. Neurosci.* **2008**, *9*, 58–65. [CrossRef] [PubMed]
15. Bauman, A.E.; Reis, R.S.; Sallis, J.F.; Wells, J.C.; Loos, R.J.; Martin, B.W.; Lancet Physical Activity Series Working Group. Correlates of physical activity: Why are some people physically active and others not? *Lancet* **2012**, *380*, 258–271. [CrossRef] [PubMed]
16. Sallis, J.F.; Bull, F.; Guthold, R.; Heath, G.W.; Inoue, S.; Kelly, P.; Oyeyemi, A.L.; Perez, L.G.; Richards, J.; Hallal, P.C. Progress in physical activity over the Olympic quadrennium. *Lancet* **2016**, *388*, 1325–1336. [CrossRef] [PubMed]
17. Ding, D.; Ramirez Varela, A.; Bauman, A.E.; Ekelund, U.; Lee, I.-M.; Heath, G.; Katzmarzyk, P.T.; Reis, R.; Pratt, M. Towards better evidence-informed global action: Lessons learnt from the Lancet series and recent developments in physical activity and public health. *Br. J. Sports Med.* **2020**, *54*, 462–468. [CrossRef] [PubMed]
18. Kramer, A. An overview of the beneficial effects of exercise on health and performance. In *Physical Exercise for Human Health*; Springer: Singapore, 2020; pp. 3–22.
19. Westerbeek, H.; Eime, R. The physical activity and sport participation framework—A policy model toward being physically active across the lifespan. *Front. Sports Act. Living* **2021**, *3*, 90. [CrossRef]
20. Malm, C.; Jakobsson, J.; Isaksson, A. Physical activity and sports—Real health benefits: A review with insight into the public health of Sweden. *Sports* **2019**, *7*, 127. [CrossRef]

Journal of
Functional Morphology and Kinesiology

MDPI

Article

Impact of Coastal Walking Outdoors and Virtual Reality Indoor Walking on Heart Rate, Enjoyment Levels and Mindfulness Experiences in Healthy Adults

Gianpiero Greco [1], Claudio Centrone [1], Luca Poli [1], Ana Filipa Silva [2,3,4], Luca Russo [5], Stefania Cataldi [1,*], Valerio Giustino [6,†] and Francesco Fischetti [1,†]

1 Department of Translational Biomedicine and Neuroscience (DiBraiN), University of Study of Bari, 70124 Bari, Italy; gianpiero.greco@uniba.it (G.G.); claudio.centrone@uniba.it (C.C.); luca.poli@uniba.it (L.P.); francesco.fischetti@uniba.it (F.F.)
2 Sports and Leisure School, Polytechnic Institute of Viana do Castelo, 4900-347 Viana do Castelo, Portugal; anafilsilva@gmail.com
3 Research Center in Sports Performance, Recreation, Innovation and Technology (SPRINT), 4960-320 Melgaço, Portugal
4 The Research Centre in Sports Sciences, Health Sciences and Human Development (CIDESD), 5001-801 Vila Real, Portugal
5 Department of Human Sciences, Università Telematica degli Studi IUL, 50122 Florence, Italy; l.russo@iuline.it
6 Sport and Exercise Sciences Research Unit, Department of Psychology, Educational Science and Human Movement, University of Palermo, 90144 Palermo, Italy; valerio.giustino@unipa.it
* Correspondence: stefania.cataldi@uniba.it
† These authors contributed equally to this work.

Abstract: Outdoor exercise is beneficial for psychophysical well-being. Limited studies have compared outdoor and virtual reality (VR) indoor physical activities, especially in coastal settings. Therefore, this study aimed to assess the impact of outdoor coastal walking and indoor walking in a VR simulation with a similar environment on physiological and psychological variables in healthy adults. A total of 26 subjects (14 M and 12 F, age 25.2 ± 2.5 years) voluntarily participated in this crossover randomized controlled and counterbalanced study and were allocated under three conditions: VR indoor walking (INVR), outdoor walking (OUT) and standard indoor walking (IN). IN and INVR conditions were performed on a treadmill (speed 4.5 km/h) and the OUT was performed on a seaside pedestrian road. The same outdoor environment was displayed in the visor during the INVR. Heart rate ($HR_{mean/max}$), physical activity enjoyment (PACES-It) and state of mindfulness for physical activity (SMS-PA) were assessed at the end of each condition. The OUT condition showed significantly greater PACES-It scores and HR_{mean} than IN and INVR ($p < 0.001$) and greater SMS-PA scores and HR_{max} than IN ($p < 0.01$ and $p < 0.05$, respectively). No significant differences were found between OUT and INVR regarding HR_{max} and SMS-PA scores ($p > 0.05$). Findings suggest that physical activity in an immersive technology may lead to physiological loads comparable to the outdoor environment. OUT is more enjoyable than IN and INVR but exhibits a mindfulness response comparable to INVR. Therefore, INVR could be an alternative to OUT for those who cannot engage in outdoor activities for various reasons.

Keywords: VR; technology; physical activity; physical fitness; exercise adherence

check for updates

Citation: Greco, G.; Centrone, C.; Poli, L.; Silva, A.F.; Russo, L.; Cataldi, S.; Giustino, V.; Fischetti, F. Impact of Coastal Walking Outdoors and Virtual Reality Indoor Walking on Heart Rate, Enjoyment Levels and Mindfulness Experiences in Healthy Adults. *J. Funct. Morphol. Kinesiol.* **2024**, *9*, 11. https://doi.org/10.3390/jfmk9010011

Academic Editor: Olivier Hue

Received: 23 November 2023
Revised: 19 December 2023
Accepted: 22 December 2023
Published: 29 December 2023

1. Introduction

In the aftermath of the COVID-19 pandemic, the global workforce witnessed a substantial transition towards remote and digital work models. However, this shift has inadvertently given rise to a concerning surge in sedentary behaviors, posing a significant threat to individual well-being [1]. As the boundaries between personal and professional spaces blur, people increasingly find themselves immersed in prolonged periods of screen time, often seated for extended hours. This sedentary lifestyle has been associated with various health issues, including musculoskeletal problems, obesity, and cardiovascular concerns [1]. A sedentary lifestyle, characterized by prolonged periods of sitting and a decline in physical activity (PA) levels, is intricately linked to psychological and social well-being. Scientific evidence indicates that sedentary behavior is associated with an increased risk of mental health issues, including heightened stress, anxiety, and depression [2]. Furthermore, the social ramifications of a sedentary lifestyle are notable. Reduced physical activity can contribute to social isolation [3] and a diminished quality of life, affecting interpersonal relationships and overall social engagement. Consequently, addressing this emergent challenge requires a comprehensive approach that not only acknowledges the convenience of remote work but also actively promotes PA and ergonomic practices to safeguard the health and well-being of the workforce in this evolving professional landscape.

The surrounding environment, particularly the natural outdoors, has proven to play a vital role in improving relaxation levels and enhancing the overall enjoyment of PA [4]. Connecting with nature and engaging in outdoor exercises not only helps individuals break away from the monotony of indoor settings but also provides a refreshing and invigorating experience that positively impacts their mental state [5]. Researchers have found that being in nature can significantly reduce stress levels, improve mood, and boost cognitive function [6]. PA, therefore, becomes a crucial factor in making the most of the outdoor natural environment's benefits [7]. Engaging in various outdoor activities, be they hiking, cycling, running, or simply taking a walk in the park, brings numerous advantages across different aspects of an individual's life. A previous study has shown that outdoor activities have a positive impact on the social, psychological, and physiological well-being of individuals [7]. Not only do these activities promote physical health, but they also contribute to a sense of community and connectedness as people often engage in outdoor exercises with friends, family, or in group settings [8]. Moreover, outdoor activities have demonstrated preventive effects in both young and elderly populations, helping to reduce the risk of various health conditions [7].

An aspect insufficiently explored within expectancy-value theories linked to PA is enjoyment, synonymous with intrinsic motivation [9]. Enjoyment represents a positive emotional state encompassing sensations like pleasure, liking, and fun [10]. Previous studies, both correlational and descriptive, have suggested a potential association between enjoyment and youth engagement in PA [9,11]. It is known that social interactions, either directly or indirectly, enhance enjoyment, especially in entertainment services like online games [12]. As the game and entertainment industries dominate virtual reality (VR), increased social interactions among VR users are anticipated to boost enjoyment and usage intentions [13].

Mindfulness is an important factor for enhancing PA as well: in fact, there is a positive relationship between dispositional mindfulness and PA, particularly with psychological factors related to PA [14]. Mindfulness-based interventions demonstrated a greater probability of effectiveness when specifically customized for PA, targeting psychological aspects linked to engaging in physical exercises [14]. Elevated levels of mindfulness during PA could aid individuals in addressing challenges related to self-control, self-regulation, and body image concerns. This, in turn, may amplify internal motivation, contributing to sustained PA and heightened trait mindfulness. Consequently, it is crucial to assess mindfulness during PA and utilize dependable and valid measurement instruments for this purpose [15].

As technology continues to advance, innovative solutions have emerged to tackle sedentary behavior and motivate people to lead active lifestyles. Exergames, a combination of exercise and gaming, have gained popularity due to their effectiveness in increasing motivation and changing sedentary habits [16–18]. These interactive games often require physical movements, making exercise more engaging and enjoyable for individuals [17]. Furthermore, the integration of augmented reality (AR) and VR in physical exercise has shown promising results in terms of enhancing the overall exercise experience [19]. AR and VR technologies offer immersive and interactive workout environments that capture users' attention and provide novel ways to engage in PA [17]. AR and VR represent distinct immersive technologies. While VR creates entirely artificial environments, isolating users from the real world, AR overlays digital information onto the real world, enhancing the user's perception. VR often involves dedicated headsets, offering deep immersion, whereas AR can be experienced through various devices, blending digital content with the real environment [20].

A previous study has shown that exercising with AR and VR has positive effects on both PA levels and psychological well-being [19]. The virtual settings can make workouts more interesting and challenging, encouraging individuals to participate more frequently and maintain their exercise routines [19]. In particular, virtual reality has shown significant potential to improve exercise outcomes due to an increase in training session frequency and has been found to enhance muscular strength [19]. Moreover, the use of VR has demonstrated promising results in reducing chronic pain for certain individuals, making it a valuable tool in rehabilitation and pain management [21].

As of today, only a few studies have examined the difference between outdoor activities and indoor activities that incorporate AR and VR technologies [22,23], and none of them have specifically explored the coastal environment. Therefore, this study aimed to assess the impact of outdoor coastal walking (OUT) and indoor walking in a VR simulation (INVR) with a similar environment on some physiological (i.e., heart rate) and psychological (i.e., enjoyment levels and mindfulness experiences) measures in healthy adults. We hypothesized that all measured variables of the INVR condition would have values similar to the OUT condition.

2. Materials and Methods

2.1. Participants

A total of 26 healthy adults (age, 25.2 ± 2.5 years; body mass, 67.7 ± 8.6 kg; body height, 171.0 ± 10.0 cm; BMI, 23.1 ± 2.4 kg/m^2; gender, 12 females and 14 males) voluntarily participated in the study carried out in June 2023. Participants were recruited from the University of Bari (Italy) and included students in the bachelor's degree and master's degree courses in Sports Science aged between 19 and 30 years. The exclusion criteria were as follows: (i) refusal to participate in the study, (ii) symptoms or signs of musculoskeletal disorders or other severe lower extremity injuries, (iii) presence of acute or chronic disease, and (iv) failure to attend the study protocol.

To establish the sample size needed for the study, an a priori power analysis [24] with an assumed type I error of 0.05 and a type II error rate of 0.20 (80% statistical power) was calculated and revealed that 13 participants in total would be sufficient to observe medium effect sizes "within-subjects".

Before the study, the participants signed the informed consent document, which provided detailed explanations of the activities and tests that would be administered during the study and the possibility of retiring at any time. This study was conducted in accordance with the Declaration of Helsinki and approved by the Ethics Committee of Bari University (protocol code 0015637 | 16 February 2023).

2.2. Study Design

A randomized controlled crossover study was used (within-subjects repeated-measures design). This study design was employed to assess the acute effects of each walking condition on participants' physiological and psychological variables. Each subject underwent each condition in a random and counterbalanced order.

Participants were randomly assigned to three walking conditions: (1) indoor walking with virtual reality (INVR) in the coastal environment, (2) outdoor coastal walking (OUT), or (3) standard indoor walking (IN). The randomization was performed by Research Randomizer, a program published on a publicly accessible official website (www.randomizer.org, accessed on 1 June 2023). The three conditions and all assessments were conducted at the same time of the day to minimize possible circadian-related effects—between 9 a.m.

and 12 a.m. with a 2-day washout period between trials. This timeframe was chosen to minimize the impact of external temperatures during the OUT session. Moreover, the subjects were asked to avoid strenuous PA and caffeine intake in the 24 h preceding each condition and during the data collection.

Participant characteristics and all outcome measures obtained after each walking condition were assessed by Researcher 1, who was blinded to treatment allocations. The interventions and assessments were performed in the same coastal environment and indoor gym at the University Sports Center in Bari (Italy). Researcher 2 conducted the interventions and was not involved in the subject assessment. Both researchers were instructed not to communicate with subjects about study goals or treatments.

Figure 1 shows a flow chart of the randomized allocation of participants to the three conditions.

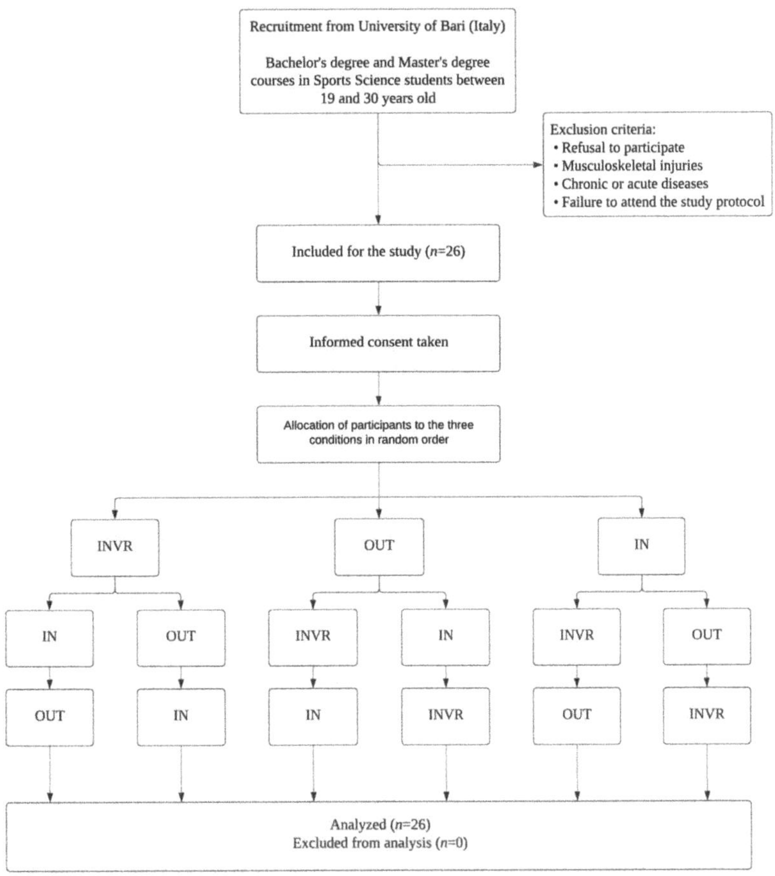

Figure 1. Randomized allocation of participants to the three conditions (indoor walking with virtual reality (INVR), outdoor coastal walking (OUT), standard indoor walking (IN)).

2.3. Intervention Protocol

Before the experiment, participants were asked not to engage in any strenuous activity for at least 30 min. During this time, participants filled out the informed consent form. Subsequently, each participant performed their assigned walking condition according to randomization, wearing an HR monitoring wearable device.

To create the INVR condition, the same walking path as the OUT condition (Figure 2) was recorded using the Samsung New Gear 360 to produce a 360-degree video. During the INVR sessions, participants wore VR headsets and headphones, with a Samsung Galaxy S20 FE phone placed inside the headsets, providing them with an immersive virtual reality experience of the recorded outdoor walking path. The 360-degree video was recorded at the same speed of 4.5 km/h used for indoor sessions. This speed was chosen based on previous studies that used a similar setting [23].

Figure 2. Coastal pathway used for the outdoor coastal walking (OUT) and indoor walking with virtual reality (INVR) sessions.

The OUT condition was performed by walking outside on a coastal-view pathway (Figure 2). Each participant walked for 6 min at a predetermined speed of 4.5 km/h.

The IN condition was performed on a treadmill at 4.5 km/h speed. No headphones or other equipment were worn during this session, except for the HR monitor.

Immediately after the end of each walking condition, which lasted 6 min each, participants were measured for HR (average and maximum) and subjective ratings of enjoyment and mindfulness by answering the Physical Activity Enjoyment Scale (PACES-it) [25] and State of Mindfulness Scale for Physical Activity (SMS-PA) [26] questionnaires, respectively.

2.4. Measures

2.4.1. Heart Rate

During the walking sessions, the participants' heart rate was continuously monitored using a wearable device (Polar® Ignite 2; Polar Electro Oy: Kempele, Finland), worn on the left wrist. After each test, the average HR (HR_{mean}) and maximum HR (HR_{max}) were recorded. Previous studies [27,28] have demonstrated the validity of this type of tracker for accurately assessing heart rate in adults.

2.4.2. Physical Activity of Enjoyment Scale—Italian Version (PACES-it)

The Physical Activity Enjoyment Scale (PACES) is a questionnaire that measures an individual's subjective enjoyment of PA [25,29]. It consists of 16 items with scores given on a 5-point Likert scale, from 1 (completely disagree) to 5 (completely agree): 9 items are positive (for example: "it energizes me") and 7 items are negative (for example "It's boring") (Cronbach alpha 0.78 to 0.89) [30]. The PACES assesses various dimensions of enjoyment, including positive affect, psychological engagement and satisfaction with the activity [31,32]. It is a widely used tool in research and helps researchers understand individuals' perceptions and attitudes toward PA, providing insights into the motivational factors that influence exercise behavior. PACES-It was administrated to the participants at the end of each session.

2.4.3. State of Mindfulness Scale for Physical Activity (SMS-PA)

The State Mindfulness Scale for Physical Activity (SMS-PA) is an adapted version of the State Mindfulness Scale, focusing specifically on mindfulness during PA [33]. It was developed to capture the breadth of physical experiences during PA that were not adequately captured by the original scale. The SMS-PA measures the extent to which individuals attend to their physical exertion, muscular engagement, and bodily movements during PA. This scale consists of 12 items, with 6 items assessing mindfulness of the mind (thoughts and emotions) and 6 items assessing mindfulness of the body (movement, body sensations, muscle engagement). After each condition, the participants rate their agreement with each item on a 5-point scale ranging from 0 to 4, indicating the level of mindfulness experienced.

The SMS-PA is applicable for use with youth aged ten and older, and adaptations in Italian have also been developed (Cronbach alpha 0.85 to 0.90) [26]. It is intended to be completed immediately following participation in PA, providing insights into individuals' mindfulness experiences during that specific activity.

2.5. Statistical Analysis

Statistical analyses were conducted using the JASP software v. 0.17.2.1 (JASP Team, 2023; jasp-stats.org). Data were presented as mean (M) values and standard deviations (SD) and were checked for assumptions of sphericity via Mauchly's test. If the sphericity assumption was violated, the Greenhouse–Geisser correction was used.

The Shapiro–Wilk test was used to test the normality of all variables. One-way ANOVA with repeated measures was applied to detect any differences between the three conditions. If there was a significant difference between the conditions, then a post hoc test with Bonferroni's correction was conducted to identify the significant comparison.

Eta squared (η^2) was used to estimate the magnitude of the difference within groups and defined as follows: small: $\eta^2 < 0.06$, moderate: $0.06 \leq \eta^2 < 0.14$, and large: $\eta^2 \geq 0.14$ effect size (ES). Cohen's d ES was calculated for the post hoc tests. The criteria to interpret the magnitude of Cohen's d were as follows: small: $0.20 \leq d < 0.50$, moderate: $0.50 \leq d < 0.79$, and large: $d \geq 0.80$ ES [34]. The statistical significance level was set a priori at $p \leq 0.05$.

3. Results

All twenty-six participants who took part in the study were subjected to all three walking conditions and none of them reported injuries throughout the duration of the research. Table 1 shows all the changes experienced by participants between the three walking conditions.

Table 1. Changes found among the three walking conditions.

Variables	INVR	OUT	IN
HR mean (bpm)	99.8 ± 12.4 ^{a***}	108.6 ± 7.7 ^{a***,b***}	99.9 ± 8.8 ^{b***}
HR max (bpm)	112.7 ± 17.4	118.1 ± 8.5 ^{b*}	110.0 ± 9.0 ^{b*}
PACES-It (scores)	51.7 ± 17.2 ^{a***}	69.6 ± 7.8 ^{a***,b***}	53.3 ± 12.3 ^{b***}
SMS-PA (scores)	33.0 ± 9.1	36.4 ± 7.8 ^{b**}	31.9 ± 6.1 ^{b**}

Data are reported as mean ± SD. Abbreviations: INVR, Indoor Walking with Virtual Reality; OUT, Outdoor Walking; IN, Indoor Walking; HR, Heart Rate; PACES, Physical ACtivity Enjoyment Scale; SMS-PA, State of Mindfulness Scale for Physical Activity. [a] Significant difference between INVR and OUT; [b] significant difference between OUT and IN. * $p < 0.05$; ** $p < 0.01$; *** $p < 0.001$.

One-way ANOVA with repeated measures found significant "within-subjects effects" for all the outcomes measures: HR_{mean} (F = 10.456, $p < 0.001$, $\eta^2 = 0.295$, large ES), HR_{max} (F = 4.048, $p = 0.035$, $\eta^2 = 0.139$, moderate ES), PACES-It (F = 21.861, $p < 0.001$, $\eta^2 = 0.467$, large ES), SMS-PA (F = 5.345, $p = 0.008$, $\eta^2 = 0.176$, large ES). Mauchly's test of sphericity for HR_{mean} and HR_{max} indicated that the assumption of sphericity was violated ($p < 0.05$), and thus Greenhouse–Geisser correction was used.

Bonferroni's post hoc test showed that HR_{mean} was significantly higher during the OUT compared to IN ($t = -3.934$, $p < 0.001$, $d = 0.881$, large ES) and INVR ($t = -3.986$, $p < 0.001$, $d = 0.893$, large ES) sessions (Figure 3).

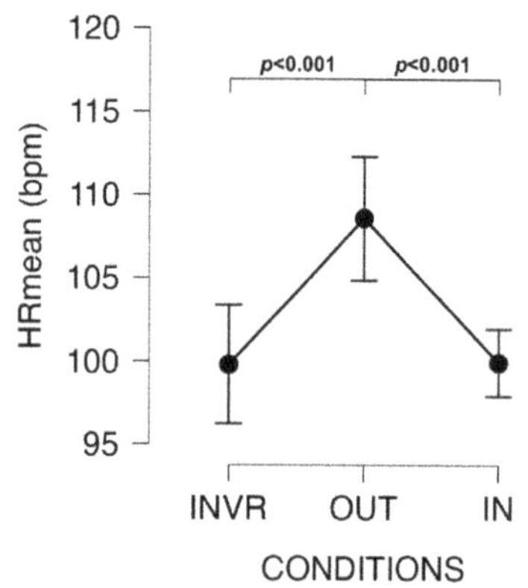

Figure 3. Changes in HRmean among conditions.

Greater HR_{max} was found in the OUT than IN ($t = -2.791$, $p = 0.022$, $d = 0.654$, moderate ES) sessions. HR_{max} was not significantly different in OUT compared to the INVR ($p > 0.05$) session (Figure 4).

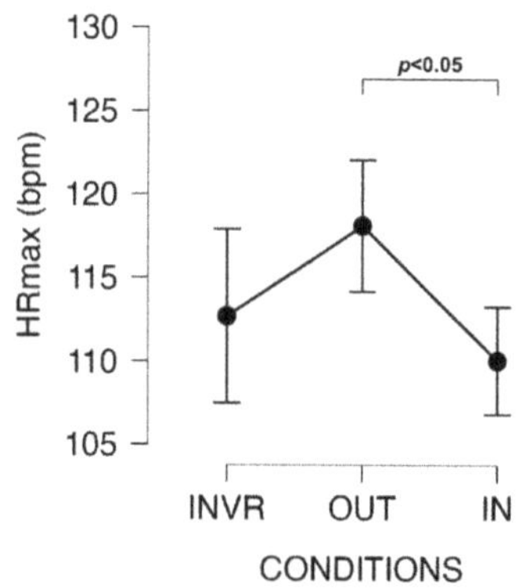

Figure 4. Changes in HRmax among conditions.

The level of enjoyment measured by PACES-It was also significantly higher in the OUT session compared to the others (OUT vs. IN: $t = -5.452$, $p < 0.001$, $d = 1.251$, large ES; OUT vs. INVR: $t = -5.966$, $p < 0.001$, $d = 1.369$, large ES) (Figure 5).

Greater SMS-PA scores were found in the OUT than IN sessions ($t = -3.143$, $p = 0.008$, $d = 0.589$, moderate ES). SMS-PA score was not significantly different in OUT compared to the INVR ($p > 0.05$) session (Figure 6).

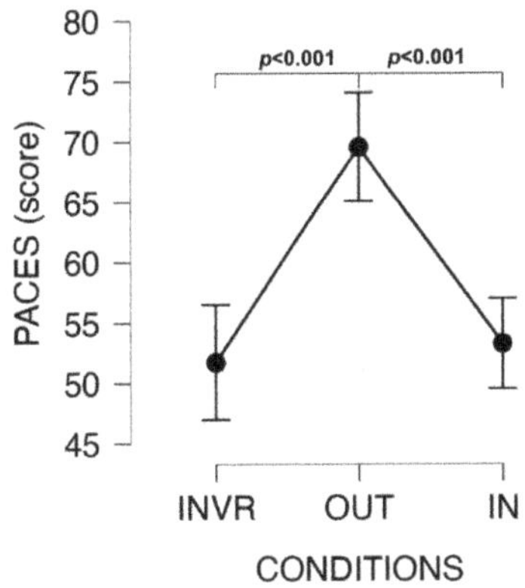

Figure 5. Changes in PACES scores among conditions.

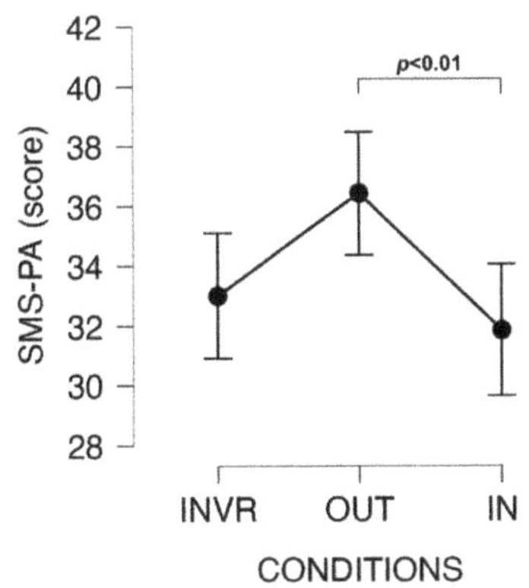

Figure 6. Changes in SMS-PA scores among conditions.

4. Discussion

The study embarked on a meticulous exploration, probing the intricate impacts of three distinct walking conditions—namely INVR (indoor walking with virtual reality), OUT (outdoor coastal walking) and IN (indoor walking)—on psychological and physiological measures within a cohort of healthy adults. This endeavor aimed to unravel nuanced differences in heart rate (HR), enjoyment levels, and mindfulness experiences engendered by these diverse walking scenarios. The primary hypothesis postulated that the INVR condition would manifest values akin to the OUT condition across all variables under scrutiny. This hypothesis was substantiated, albeit selectively, finding confirmation in the case of HRmax and SMS measures. Intriguingly, no statistically significant differences were unearthed between the INVR and OUT conditions in these particular facets, signifying a degree of physiological equivalence.

Conversely, when we delve into HRmean and PACES measures, a different narrative emerges. These metrics exhibited lower values in both the IN and INVR conditions in comparison to the OUT condition. This highlights a palpable distinction in cardiovascular and experiential dimensions when engaging in indoor as opposed to outdoor walking. Participants showcased markedly higher HRmean values during OUT, lending credence to the notion that the natural outdoor environment poses distinctive physical demands, culminating in heightened cardiovascular exertion during outdoor ambulation. This is an observation that echoes extant research [35–37], reiterating the unique physiological implications of traversing natural terrains.

However, the absence of significant differences in HRmax between INVR and OUT introduces a compelling dimension to the discourse. It implies that the immersive virtual reality experience, an emblem of cutting-edge technology, can, to some extent, emulate the physiological responses induced by outdoor walking. While this substantiates the idea that technology-mediated indoor activities can approximate the physiological benefits of outdoor endeavors, distinctions were indeed detected between OUT and IN. The greater cardiovascular exertion associated with outdoor environments [35] became manifest in the higher value of OUT, reinforcing the irreplaceable facets of natural settings in PA.

Transitioning from the physiological to the experiential, enjoyment levels emerged as a pivotal parameter. IN and INVR were consistently reported as less enjoyable compared to OUT. This underscores a crucial psychological facet; participants derived heightened pleasure and satisfaction from the natural outdoor setting of OUT, indicating a potential intrinsic motivation embedded in outdoor activities. The immersive virtual reality experience during INVR, and the standard indoor environment of IN, were perceived as less enjoyable, potentially influencing motivation and adherence to PA. This aligns seamlessly with the findings of a parallel study [23], which reported significantly higher enjoyment during outdoor walking compared to indoor walking sessions with VR. Consequently, our study reinforces the intrinsic allure of the natural outdoor setting of OUT, postulating it as more enjoyable and, by extension, more conducive to sustaining PA over time.

Acknowledging the documented mindfulness benefits of self-paced outdoor walking [38–40] and the profound impact of VR-based exercise on mindfulness [41,42], our study aligns with these precepts. Mindfulness experiences showed no significant differences between OUT and INVR, suggesting that both environments facilitated a comparable state of mindfulness. This implies that the immersive virtual reality experience of INVR effectively engendered mindfulness, mirroring the serene and natural ambiance of coastal walking outdoors.

This study represents a noteworthy stride in unraveling the multifaceted dynamics of different walking conditions on both physiological and psychological facets. The confirmation of certain hypotheses, such as the physiological equivalence between INVR and OUT in specific parameters, is intriguing and opens avenues for further exploration. The consistent theme of outdoor walking being more enjoyable aligns with broader trends in PA research, emphasizing the pivotal role of natural environments in promoting sustained engagement. While the study, like any scientific endeavor, is not without limitations, it provides a robust foundation for future research endeavors that can build upon these insights, refining our understanding of how the choice of walking environment intertwines with the intricate tapestry of human health and well-being.

Expanding on the broader implications of this research, the study fundamentally underscores the need for a nuanced understanding of the interplay between technology-mediated indoor PA and the irreplaceable allure of outdoor environments. In an era dominated by virtual experiences and technology-driven leisure, the study offers a critical lens for the potential of immersive virtual reality in approximating the physiological responses and mindfulness benefits associated with outdoor walking. The findings suggest that, while technology can emulate certain aspects of the outdoor experience, the intrinsic joy and satisfaction derived from natural settings remain unparalleled.

The implications of these findings extend beyond the realms of academic inquiry into the practical domains of public health and well-being. Understanding the psychological and physiological nuances of different walking conditions can inform the design and implementation of interventions aimed at promoting PA. For instance, individuals constrained by factors such as inclement weather, lack of access, or time limitations may find a viable alternative in immersive virtual reality experiences. However, the study also cautions against a one-size-fits-all approach, highlighting the superior enjoyment associated with outdoor walking [23]. Thus, urban planning, workplace wellness programs, and health policies should consider the role of outdoor spaces in fostering PA and mental well-being.

Moreover, the study sheds light on the importance of mindfulness in the context of PA. The comparable mindfulness experiences between outdoor walking and virtual reality-based indoor walking suggest that technology, when designed with a mindful intent, can contribute to mental well-being. This insight is particularly relevant in a society grappling with sedentary lifestyles and stress-related health issues. Integrating mindfulness practices into technology-mediated PA could present a holistic approach to health promotion [22,26].

The longitudinal implications of different walking conditions constitute another area ripe for exploration. While the study provides a snapshot of acute effects, understanding the sustained impact of outdoor walking, indoor walking, and virtual reality-based activities can inform more robust recommendations for individuals and communities. Longitudinal studies tracking participants over extended periods could elucidate the enduring benefits and potential habituation to different walking modalities.

Finally, this study navigates the intersection of technology, PA, and well-being, unraveling layers of complexity in how different walking conditions shape our physiological responses, enjoyment levels, and mindfulness experiences. As society grapples with evolving patterns of PA and increasing reliance on technology, these insights become pivotal signposts. They guide us in harnessing the potential of immersive virtual reality for health promotion while underscoring the timeless allure and benefits of natural outdoor environments. The study, therefore, beckons further exploration, inviting researchers, policymakers, and practitioners to embark on a journey of deeper understanding and innovative interventions at the nexus of human movement and well-being.

Strengths and Limitations

The study's reliance on a relatively small sample size, drawn exclusively from university sports science students, introduces a potential source of bias, limiting the generalizability of the results to a broader population. The predominantly homogeneous participant cohort may not fully represent diverse demographic groups, affecting the external validity of the findings. While the cross-over design is pragmatic for short-term analyses, it complicates the observation of long-term effects, making it challenging to draw conclusions about sustained impacts over time. The novelty associated with participants' first-time use of the visor may have induced emotional arousal, potentially influencing physiological parameters. The study recognizes this as a potential confounding factor. Due to the specific conditions of the study and the unique sample, caution is warranted in generalizing the findings to broader populations or different settings. The study, by incorporating virtual reality technology, might introduce a bias toward technology-mediated activities, and the findings may not fully capture the preferences and responses of individuals less accustomed to such technology. The study, while providing valuable insights, may lack a real-world context. Participants' experiences in a controlled study environment might differ from their experiences in their daily lives. The study primarily focuses on acute effects, and while this provides a snapshot, it may not fully capture the sustained impact and habituation to different walking modalities over an extended period. The study acknowledges the potential for participant bias due to the small and specific sample, emphasizing the need for future research with broader participant diversity. The caution against a one-size-fits-all approach, while valid, adds complexity to the applicability of the study's findings to diverse populations and contexts.

On the other hand, during in this study a meticulous exploration of three distinct walking conditions was conducted, providing a detailed analysis of their impacts on psychological and physiological measures. The research question addressed a pertinent issue, examining the effects of different walking conditions on both physiological (heart rate) and psychological (enjoyment, mindfulness) aspects, crucial for overall well-being. The inclusion of virtual reality (INVR) as one of the walking conditions adds innovation to the study, reflecting contemporary trends in technology and its potential impact on PA and well-being. The study confirmed certain hypotheses, such as the physiological equivalence between INVR and OUT in specific parameters, contributing valuable insights to the understanding of how technology-mediated indoor activities compare to outdoor experiences. It contributes substantially to the existing body of knowledge on the interplay between walking conditions and human well-being, emphasizing the importance of natural environments in promoting sustained engagement. The study not only focused on physiological measures but also delved into psychological factors such as enjoyment and mindfulness, providing a holistic view of the impact of different walking conditions. The cross-over design offered insight into the short-term effects of different walking conditions. With this study design, the influence of confounding variables was reduced because each subject acted as his or her own control; moreover, it produced rapid responses to the research question because counterbalanced randomization could show cause and effect [43]. Thus, our study sought to bring novelty to the field of research.

Physical activity with virtual reality (VR) can serve as a compelling alternative to outdoor physical activity, especially in circumstances where outdoor engagement is challenging or limited. VR offers an immersive and interactive experience that simulates outdoor environments, providing users with a dynamic and engaging workout. This alternative is particularly beneficial in adverse weather conditions, urban settings with limited green spaces, or situations where individuals face time constraints. Moreover, VR can cater to diverse preferences by offering various virtual landscapes and activities, making it adaptable to different fitness levels and interests. Incorporating gamification elements further enhances motivation, making VR-based physical activity an appealing substitute for outdoor exercises. However, it is essential to balance this with the understanding that the intrinsic benefits of natural settings cannot be entirely replaced. Therefore, the use of VR should be strategic, considering individual preferences, accessibility, and the overarching goal of promoting sustained physical activity and well-being.

Finally, while the study makes significant strides in unraveling the dynamics of different walking conditions, it is crucial to interpret its findings within the context of these strengths and limitations. Future research should aim to address these limitations for a more comprehensive understanding of the interplay between technology-mediated indoor activities and the allure of outdoor environments on human well-being.

5. Conclusions

To the best of our knowledge, this is the first study that provides new insights into the physiological and psychological effects of different walking conditions, including those in coastal environments. OUT has greater HR_{mean} values with respect to INVR and IN, but HR_{max} did not differ significantly between OUT and INVR. This suggests that PA in an immersive environment may lead to physiological loads comparable to the outdoor setting. OUT emerges as an enjoyable and engaging alternative to IN and INVR. Also, the immersive virtual reality experience of INVR presents a comparable mindfulness response to the OUT, supporting its potential use in PA interventions. Thus, both OUT and INVR offer similar levels of mindfulness experiences, highlighting the benefits of incorporating outdoor coastal walking and virtual reality-enhanced indoor walking in PA interventions. These findings imply the need to provide diverse and stimulating environments to enhance enjoyment and motivation for PA and improve individual well-being and health.

Author Contributions: Conceptualization, G.G. and C.C.; methodology, G.G., C.C. and L.P.; software, L.P.; validation, G.G. and L.P.; formal analysis, L.R. and A.F.S.; investigation, C.C. and L.P.; resources, S.C., V.G. and F.F.; data curation, G.G., C.C. and L.P.; writing—original draft preparation, G.G. and C.C.; writing—review and editing, G.G., S.C., V.G. and F.F.; visualization, L.R. and A.F.S.; supervision, G.G., V.G. and F.F. All authors have read and agreed to the published version of the manuscript.

Funding: This research received no external funding.

Institutional Review Board Statement: This study was conducted in accordance with the Declaration of Helsinki and approved by the Ethics Committee of Bari University (protocol code 0015637 | 16 February 2023).

Informed Consent Statement: Informed consent was obtained from all parents of the participants involved in the study.

Data Availability Statement: The data presented in this study are available on request from the first author.

Conflicts of Interest: The authors declare no conflict of interest.

References

1. Cancello, R.; Soranna, D.; Zambra, G.; Zambon, A.; Invitti, C. Determinants of the Lifestyle Changes during COVID-19 Pandemic in the Residents of Northern Italy. *Int. J. Environ. Res. Public Health* **2020**, *17*, 6287. [CrossRef] [PubMed]
2. Huang, Y.; Li, L.; Gan, Y.; Wang, C.; Jiang, H.; Cao, S.; Lu, Z. Sedentary Behaviors and Risk of Depression: A Meta-Analysis of Prospective Studies. *Transl. Psychiatry* **2020**, *10*, 26. [CrossRef] [PubMed]
3. Werneck, A.O.; Collings, P.J.; Barboza, L.L.; Stubbs, B.; Silva, D.R. Associations of Sedentary Behaviors and Physical Activity with Social Isolation in 100,839 School Students: The Brazilian Scholar Health Survey. *Gen. Hosp. Psychiatry* **2019**, *59*, 7–13. [CrossRef] [PubMed]
4. Kruize, H.; Van Kamp, I.; Van Den Berg, M.; Van Kempen, E.; Wendel-Vos, W.; Ruijsbroek, A.; Swart, W.; Maas, J.; Gidlow, C.; Smith, G.; et al. Exploring Mechanisms Underlying the Relationship between the Natural Outdoor Environment and Health and Well-Being—Results from the PHENOTYPE Project. *Environ. Int.* **2020**, *134*, 105173. [CrossRef] [PubMed]
5. Das, A.; Gailey, S. Green Exercise, Mental Health Symptoms, and State Lockdown Policies: A Longitudinal Study. *J. Environ. Psychol.* **2022**, *82*, 101848. [CrossRef] [PubMed]
6. Bélanger, M.; Gallant, F.; Doré, I.; O'Loughlin, J.L.; Sylvestre, M.-P.; Abi Nader, P.; Larouche, R.; Gunnell, K.; Sabiston, C.M. Physical Activity Mediates the Relationship between Outdoor Time and Mental Health. *Prev. Med. Rep.* **2019**, *16*, 101006. [CrossRef] [PubMed]
7. Manferdelli, G.; La Torre, A.; Codella, R. Outdoor Physical Activity Bears Multiple Benefits to Health and Society. *J. Sports Med. Phys. Fit.* **2019**, *59*, 868–879. [CrossRef] [PubMed]
8. Riley-Jacome, M.; Gallant, M.P.; Fisher, B.D.; Gotcsik, F.S.; Strogatz, D.S. Enhancing Community Capacity to Support Physical Activity: The Development of a Community-Based Indoor–Outdoor Walking Program. *J. Prim. Prev.* **2010**, *31*, 85–95. [CrossRef]
9. Motl, R.W.; Dishman, R.K.; Saunders, R.; Dowda, M.; Felton, G.; Pate, R.R. Measuring Enjoyment of Physical Activity in Adolescent Girls. *Am. J. Prev. Med.* **2001**, *21*, 110–117. [CrossRef]
10. Scanlan, T.K.; Simons, J.P. The Construct of Sport Enjoyment. In *Motivation in Sport and Exercise*; Human Kinetics: Champaign, IL, USA, 1992.
11. Sallis, J.F.; Prochaska, J.J.; Taylor, W.C.; Hill, J.O.; Geraci, J.C. Correlates of Physical Activity in a National Sample of Girls and Boys in Grades 4 through 12. *Health Psychol.* **1999**, *18*, 410–415. [CrossRef]
12. Chen, V.H.-H.; Duh, H.B.-L.; Phuah, P.S.K.; Lam, D.Z.Y. Enjoyment or Engagement? Role of Social Interaction in Playing Massively Mulitplayer Online Role-Playing Games (MMORPGS). In *Entertainment Computing—ICEC 2006*; Harper, R., Rauterberg, M., Combetto, M., Eds.; Lecture Notes in Computer Science; Springer: Berlin/Heidelberg, Germany, 2006; Volume 4161, pp. 262–267, ISBN 978-3-540-45259-1.
13. Lee, J.; Kim, J.; Choi, J.Y. The Adoption of Virtual Reality Devices: The Technology Acceptance Model Integrating Enjoyment, Social Interaction, and Strength of the Social Ties. *Telemat. Inform.* **2019**, *39*, 37–48. [CrossRef]
14. Schneider, J.; Malinowski, P.; Watson, P.M.; Lattimore, P. The Role of Mindfulness in Physical Activity: A Systematic Review. *Obes. Rev.* **2019**, *20*, 448–463. [CrossRef] [PubMed]
15. Baceviciene, M.; Jankauskiene, R.; Balciuniene, V. Mindfulness, Physical Activity and Sports Participation: Validity Evidence of the Lithuanian Translation of the State Mindfulness Scale for Physical Activity 2 in Physically Active Young Adults. *Behav. Sci.* **2023**, *13*, 820. [CrossRef] [PubMed]
16. Bice, M.R.; Ball, J.W.; McClaran, S. Technology and Physical Activity Motivation. *Int. J. Sport Exerc. Psychol.* **2016**, *14*, 295–304. [CrossRef]
17. González-González, C.; Río, N.G.; Navarro-Adelantado, V. Exploring the Benefits of Using Gamification and Videogames for Physical Exercise: A Review of State of Art. *Int. J. Interact. Multimed. Artif. Intell.* **2018**, *5*, 46–52. [CrossRef]
18. Greco, G.; Poli, L.; Clemente, F.M.; Francesco, F.; Cataldi, S. The Effectiveness of New Digital Technologies in Increasing Physical Activity Levels and Promoting Active and Healthy Ageing: A Narrative Review. *Health Soc. Care Community* **2023**, *2023*, 2803620. [CrossRef]
19. Ng, Y.-L.; Ma, F.; Ho, F.K.; Ip, P.; Fu, K. Effectiveness of Virtual and Augmented Reality-Enhanced Exercise on Physical Activity, Psychological Outcomes, and Physical Performance: A Systematic Review and Meta-Analysis of Randomized Controlled Trials. *Comput. Hum. Behav.* **2019**, *99*, 278–291. [CrossRef]
20. Kim, J.-H.; Kim, M.; Park, M.; Yoo, J. Immersive Interactive Technologies and Virtual Shopping Experiences: Differences in Consumer Perceptions between Augmented Reality (AR) and Virtual Reality (VR). *Telemat. Inform.* **2023**, *77*, 101936. [CrossRef]
21. Gromala, D.; Tong, X.; Choo, A.; Karamnejad, M.; Shaw, C.D. The Virtual Meditative Walk: Virtual Reality Therapy for Chronic Pain Management. In Proceedings of the 33rd Annual ACM Conference on Human Factors in Computing Systems, Seoul, Republic of Korea, 18–23 April 2015; ACM: New York, NY, USA, 2015; pp. 521–524.

22. Mavrantza, A.M.; Bigliassi, M.; Calogiuri, G. Psychophysiological Mechanisms Underlying the Effects of Outdoor Green and Virtual Green Exercise during Self-Paced Walking. *Int. J. Psychophysiol.* **2023**, *184*, 39–50. [CrossRef]
23. Plante, T.G.; Cage, C.; Clements, S.; Stover, A. Psychological Benefits of Exercise Paired with Virtual Reality: Outdoor Exercise Energizes Whereas Indoor Virtual Exercise Relaxes. *Int. J. Stress Manag.* **2006**, *13*, 108–117. [CrossRef]
24. Faul, F.; Erdfelder, E.; Lang, A.-G.; Buchner, A. G*Power 3: A Flexible Statistical Power Analysis Program for the Social, Behavioral, and Biomedical Sciences. *Behav. Res. Methods* **2007**, *39*, 175–191. [CrossRef] [PubMed]
25. Carraro, A.; Young, M.C.; Robazza, C. A contribution to the validation of the physical activity enjoyment scale in an Italian sample. *Soc. Behav. Pers. Int. J.* **2008**, *36*, 911–918. [CrossRef]
26. Bisagni, D.; Bisagni, M.; Vaccaro, M. Mindfulness and Psychological Flexibility in Sport Practice: Validation of the Italian Version of the SMS-PA and the Sports Version of the AAQ-II. *Psicoter. Cogn. Comport.* **2018**, *24*, 153–173.
27. Budig, M.; Keiner, M.; Stoohs, R.; Hoffmeister, M.; Höltke, V. Heart Rate and Distance Measurement of Two Multisport Activity Trackers and a Cellphone App in Different Sports: A Cross-Sectional Validation and Comparison Field Study. *Sensors* **2021**, *22*, 180. [CrossRef] [PubMed]
28. Jagim, A.R.; Koch-Gallup, N.; Camic, C.L.; Kroening, L.; Nolte, C.; Schroeder, C.; Gran, L.; Erickson, J.L. The Accuracy of Fitness Watches for the Measurement of Heart Rate and Energy Expenditure during Moderate Intensity Exercise. *J. Sports Med. Phys. Fit.* **2021**, *61*, 205–211. [CrossRef] [PubMed]
29. Kendzierski, D.; DeCarlo, K.J. Physical Activity Enjoyment Scale: Two Validation Studies. *J. Sport Exerc. Psychol.* **1991**, *13*, 50–64. [CrossRef]
30. Carraro, A. Valutare Il Piacere Nelle Attività Motorie: Il PACES-It. In *Giornale Italiano della Ricerca Educativa*; Pensa MultiMedia Editore srl: Lecce, Italy, 2012; pp. 259–265.
31. Mullen, S.P.; Olson, E.A.; Phillips, S.M.; Szabo, A.N.; Wójcicki, T.R.; Mailey, E.L.; Gothe, N.P.; Fanning, J.T.; Kramer, A.F.; McAuley, E. Measuring Enjoyment of Physical Activity in Older Adults: Invariance of the Physical Activity Enjoyment Scale (Paces) across Groups and Time. *Int. J. Behav. Nutr. Phys. Act.* **2011**, *8*, 103. [CrossRef] [PubMed]
32. Teques, P.; Calmeiro, L.; Silva, C.; Borrego, C. Validation and Adaptation of the Physical Activity Enjoyment Scale (PACES) in Fitness Group Exercisers. *J. Sport Health Sci.* **2020**, *9*, 352–357. [CrossRef]
33. Cox, A.E.; Ullrich-French, S.; French, B.F. Validity Evidence for the State Mindfulness Scale for Physical Activity. *Meas. Phys. Educ. Exerc. Sci.* **2016**, *20*, 38–49. [CrossRef]
34. Cohen, J. A Power Primer. *Psychol. Bull.* **1992**, *112*, 155–159. [CrossRef]
35. Boldina, A.; Chung, H.C.; Santos, A.M.C.; Steemers, K. Active Urbanism: Heart Rate and Oxygen Consumption Comparison When Walking on Imitation Steppingstones versus a Plain Surface. *Cities Health* **2023**, *7*, 398–415. [CrossRef]
36. Fuegen, K.; Breitenbecher, K.H. Walking Outdoors Increases Heart Rate but Not Perceived Exertion. *Ecopsychology* **2022**, *14*, 215–225. [CrossRef]
37. Li, C.; Lee, C.-W.; Tsang, K.T. Outdoor Walking Better? Environmental Elements of Cardiorespiratory Fitness Training Trails. *Front. Sports Act. Living* **2023**, *4*, 1036777. [CrossRef] [PubMed]
38. Bigliassi, M.; Galano, B.M.; Lima-Silva, A.E.; Bertuzzi, R. Effects of Mindfulness on Psychological and Psychophysiological Responses during Self-paced Walking. *Psychophysiology* **2020**, *57*, e13529. [CrossRef] [PubMed]
39. Djernis, D.; Lerstrup, I.; Poulsen, D.; Stigsdotter, U.; Dahlgaard, J.; O'Toole, M. A Systematic Review and Meta-Analysis of Nature-Based Mindfulness: Effects of Moving Mindfulness Training into an Outdoor Natural Setting. *Int. J. Environ. Res. Public Health* **2019**, *16*, 3202. [CrossRef] [PubMed]
40. Bailey, A.W.; Allen, G.; Herndon, J.; Demastus, C. Cognitive Benefits of Walking in Natural versus Built Environments. *World Leis. J.* **2018**, *60*, 293–305. [CrossRef]
41. Arpaia, P.; D'Errico, G.; De Paolis, L.T.; Moccaldi, N.; Nuccetelli, F. A Narrative Review of Mindfulness-Based Interventions Using Virtual Reality. *Mindfulness* **2022**, *13*, 556–571. [CrossRef]
42. O'Connor, S.; Mayne, A.; Hood, B. Virtual Reality-Based Mindfulness for Chronic Pain Management: A Scoping Review. *Pain Manag. Nurs.* **2022**, *23*, 359–369. [CrossRef]
43. Jones, B.; Kenward, M.G. *Design and Analysis of Cross-Over Trials*, 3rd ed.; Chapman and Hall: London, UK, 2014.

Journal of
Functional Morphology and Kinesiology

MDPI

Article

Differences in Body Composition and Maturity Status in Young Male Volleyball Players of Different Levels

Alessia Grigoletto [1], Mario Mauro [2,*] and Stefania Toselli [2,*]

1 Department of Biomedical and Neuromotor Science, University of Bologna, Via Selmi 3, 40126 Bologna, Italy; alessia.grigoletto2@unibo.it
2 Department of Life Quality Studies, University of Bologna, 47921 Rimini, Italy
* Correspondence: mario.mauro4@unibo.it (M.M.); stefania.toselli@unibo.it (S.T.)

Abstract: Volleyball is an intermittent team sport that requires specific anthropometrical and physical characteristics for winning performance. The present study aimed to evaluate the maturity status of the young male players of eight volleyball teams, and to observe differences in anthropometric characteristics and body composition. Ninety-four male adolescent volleyball players were recruited during a national tournament carried out in Treviso (Italy). Anthropometric characteristics such as weight, stature, skinfold thicknesses, circumferences and diameters, and bioelectrical impedance were measured. The biological maturation was estimated for all players. Each team was classified as a higher or lower lever according to its tournament ranking. A two-way ANOVA compared team levels and players' maturity status. Considering the maturity offset, 62 boys were classified as "on time", 20 as "late", and 12 as "early". Three clubs presented many boys with "early" as the maturity offset, and two of these finished the tournament in the first position. Young volleyball players classified as "early" seemed to show anthropometric characteristics linked to better performance at the tournament (higher height, upper arm and calf muscle area, fat mass percentage, and total fat-free mass). The results of the present study could have practical implications for talent selection, but further studies are needed to better evaluate the effect of maturity status on the characteristics of volleyball players.

Keywords: sports; anthropometric characteristics; body composition; maturity status; young volleyball players

Citation: Grigoletto, A.; Mauro, M.; Toselli, S. Differences in Body Composition and Maturity Status in Young Male Volleyball Players of Different Levels. *J. Funct. Morphol. Kinesiol.* **2023**, *8*, 162. https://doi.org/10.3390/jfmk8040162

Academic Editor: Roland Van den Tillaar

Received: 23 October 2023
Revised: 15 November 2023
Accepted: 21 November 2023
Published: 23 November 2023

1. Introduction

Volleyball is an intermittent sport that requires high-intensity performance of an intermittent nature, i.e., frequent short bouts of high-intensity exercise followed by periods of low-intensity activity and brief rest periods [1–3]. Suitable anthropometric and body composition characteristics and high technical and tactical skills are needed to succeed in this sport [4,5]. The frequent jumps that are usually performed during a volleyball match require specific characteristics, such as thinness and explosive muscle power. Among anthropometric variables, leg length, arm span, and height differ between high-level players, along with physical skill, such as coordination in agility tests and vertical jumps [6,7]. Height, arm span, and upper and lower body power have been identified as key factors for performance in both male and female adolescent volleyball players [8,9]. However, few studies have discussed volleyball players' physical and functional characteristics, particularly during adolescence. In addition, the available literature principally focuses on female volleyball players [10,11], but there are far fewer studies on males.

Regarding adolescence, the influence of maturity status on physical and physiological characteristics has attracted increased scientific interest, considering its relevance for sports performance. Biological maturation can be defined as the timing and tempo of progress to achieving a mature state [12]. The physical development of young players is strongly influenced by maturity status, especially as regards their body composition and physical capacities [13–15].

Understanding the role of maturity in physical characteristics and performance in youth athletes during adolescence is essential, since this period coincides with the selection of players. Sport is selective, chiefly during adolescence, and often occurs along a maturity-related gradient. Many studies have analyzed the influence of maturity status on physical, physiological, and performance characteristics in soccer, basketball, or handball players [13,14,16–19], but less information exists on male volleyballers. Albaladejo-Saura and colleagues reported that volleyball players with a more advanced state of maturation exhibited higher values of height, arm span, sitting height, bone diameters, muscle perimeters and fat, muscle and bone masses, and better performance achieved in medicine ball throwing and in countermovement jump (CMJ) than their chronological age peers [20]. Since variables such as height, sitting height, leg length, and muscle circumference have a high correlation with performance in physical fitness tests related to volleyball requirements, the best values obtained by volleyball players with an advanced maturity status testify how this state represents a competitive advantage in the sport performance of volleyball during adolescence.

To our knowledge, no previous studies were carried out about bioelectrical impedance vectorial analysis (BIVA) and young volleyball players. Therefore, the present study aims to (a) compare the prevalence of maturity status among volleyball players of the teams that have reached different positions in the ranking of a national tournament, and (b) investigate the relationship between maturity status and anthropometric, performance, and body composition parameters and BIVA. These two aspects are strongly connected with talent selection.

It was hypothesized that players who reached a higher position in the ranking would exhibit differences in maturity status and their anthropometric and body composition profile. In particular, people with an early maturation could have better results in the final racking, and they could show higher values for some anthropometric characteristics, such as stature, circumferences, and lower value of fat mass in comparison with boys classified as on time or with a late maturation.

2. Materials and Methods

2.1. Participants and Study Design

This is an observational study assessed between the 17th and 18th of June 2022, during the National Tournament "0.13 Torneo Città di Treviso", organized in Treviso (Italy) from the volleyball society Volley Treviso. Eight teams of 22 were randomly selected to be measured during the study: Volley Treviso, La Piave Volley, Kosmos Volley, Pallavolo Sestese, Cisanonembro'thers, Gas Sales Bluenergy Piacenza, Virtus Fano, and VT Personal Time. A total of 94 young male volleyball players were evaluated (Volley Treviso: 11, La Piave Volley: 12, Kosmos Volley: 11, Pallavolo Sestese: 12, Cisanonembro'thers: 9, Gas Sales Bluenergy Piacenza: 12, Virtus Fano: 13, VT Personal Time: 14). Figure 1 shows the study design. All the evaluations were assessed within a Treviso sports center where a private room was set up for specific environmental features such as a temperature between 22 °C and 24 °C and air humidity between 50 and 60%.

The volume of the weekly workouts of each team was collected from all coaches, and each player trained for about 6 h per week (four workouts of 90 min each). In each training unit, 45 min was spent on strength and conditioning and coordinative capabilities, whereas 45 min was spent on technical–tactical skills. No diet information was collected.

Participants were informed and volunteered to decide to participate in the study. Their parents were informed and provided written consent. This study was in accordance with the Declaration of Helsinki and approved by the Bioethics Committee of the University of Bologna (N. prot. 25027).

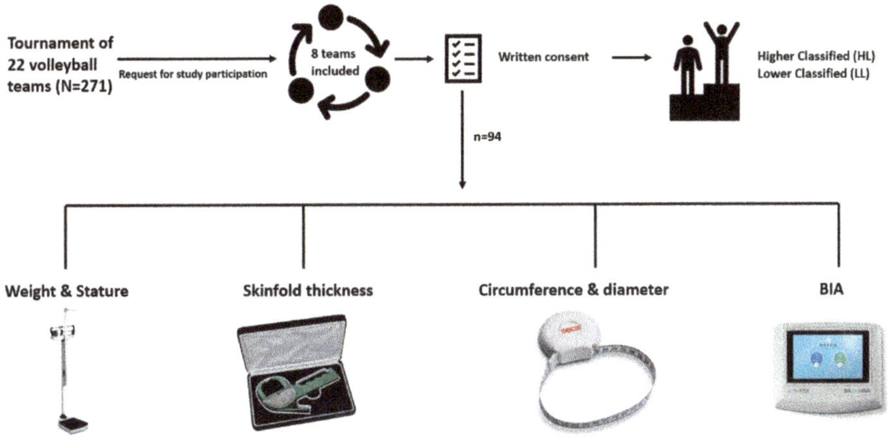

Figure 1. Study design.

2.2. Anthropometry

A trained operator collected all the anthropometric measurements, such as weight, height, circumferences, and skinfold thickness, according to standardized procedures [21]. The mean value of three measurements was gathered. Weight was measured to the nearest 0.1 kg using a calibrated analogue scale. Height and sitting height were collected at the nearest 0.1 cm using a stadiometer (GPM, Zurich, Switzerland). The body mass index (BMI) was calculated as the ratio between weight (kg) and squared stature converted in meters (m).

Circumferences (relaxed and contracted upper arm, waist, hip, calf) were measured to the nearest 0.1 cm with a non-stretchable tape. The upper arm circumference was taken on the subject in a standing position, at the mid-point between the shoulder acromion and the olecranon process point, with the participant's elbow relaxed along the body side (stretched evaluation) or to be flexed 90o with palm facing upward (contracted evaluation); the waist circumference was taken on the subject in a standing position with close feet and arm along the trunk, at the minimum abdominal circumference line, between the inferior margin of the last rib and the iliac crest. The hip circumference was taken on the subject in a standing position with close feet and arms along the trunk, at the highest point of the glutes; the calf circumference was taken at the bulkiest calf point, with the participant in a standing position (calf muscles stretched).

Diameters (humerus and femur) were taken to the nearest 0.1 cm with a sliding caliper, both on the left side of the body. The humerus and femoral widths were taken, respectively, between the own lateral and medial epicondyles, with the participant's elbow and knee flexed 90°.

Skinfold thicknesses (biceps, triceps, subscapular, supraspinal, suprailiac, thigh, medial, and lateral calf) were measured to the nearest 1 mm using a Lange skinfold caliper on the left side of the body (Beta Technology Inc., Houston, TX, USA) at the following sites: triceps and biceps, vertically at the midpoint between the acromion process and the olecranon process, respectively, at the posterior and anterior upper arm face; subscapular, at an angle of 45″ to the lateral side of the body, about 20 mm below the tip of the scapula; suprailiac, about 20 mm above the iliac crest (in the axillary line); supraspinal, about 20 mm above the iliac spine; calf, vertically at the bulkiest calf point both medially and laterally.

Then, body composition parameters such as fat-free mass (FFM), fat mass (FM), and percentage of fat mass (%F) were estimated according to the equation developed by Slaughter et al. [22]. According to Frisancho's equations, many body areas were estimated, such as the total area of the upper arm (TUA) and of the lower limb (TCA), muscle area of the upper arm (UMA) and lower limb (CMA), and fat area of the arm (UFA) and lower limb (CFA) [23]. In addition, calf and arm fat indexes (FCI and UFI) were derived.

2.3. Maturity Status

Mirwald and colleagues developed a specific equation for boys to estimate the years from the peak height velocity (PHV), which is an important index of adolescent growth [24]. Maturity offset represents the time before or after the PHV; by subtracting the age at PHV from chronological age, it is possible to estimate the year from PHV.

$$\begin{aligned}\text{MO} = {} & -9.236 + 0.0002708(\text{leg length} * \text{sitting height}) - 0.001663(\text{age} * \text{leg } 1007216 \\ & (\text{age} * \text{sitting height}) + 0.02292(\text{weight}/\text{height}).\end{aligned}$$

Children who are not yet in their adolescent growth spurt often have a lower approximation of the age at PHV (APHV) and those who have already passed their adolescent growth spurt are often higher [12]. For this reason, age-specific Z-score was used to classify the young athletes. Based on the age-specific standardized Z-score of the predicted APHV, boys were classified as later ($Z > 1$), on time ($-1.0 \leq Z \leq 1.0$), and earlier $Z < 1.0$ maturing [25].

2.4. Bioelectric Impedance Vector Analysis (BIVA)

Bioelectric impedance analysis (BIA) was used to measure impedance. An electric current was used with a frequency of 50 kHz (BIA 101 BIVA® PRO, Akern, Florence, Italy). The participants were in the supine position, with four electrical conductors; two electrodes were placed on the right hand and two on the right foot after cleaning the skin with alcohol [26,27]. Subjects were asked to put their lower limbs at an angle of 45° compared to the median line of the body and to put their upper limbs at an angle of 30° from the trunk. Athletes received the instruction to abstain from foods and liquids for ≥4 h before the test. BIVA was carried out using the classic methods, e.g., normalizing R (Ω) and Xc (Ω) for height in meters [28]. Both the elite male volleyball players' and the general adolescent male population's bioelectrical-specific ellipses were used as a reference to build the 50%, 75%, and 95% tolerance ellipses on the R/H–Xc/H graph. BIVA plots the parameters recorded in BIA (R, Xc, PhA) as a vector within a specific tolerance ellipse (specific profile for each sport and competitive level), and it allows the evaluation of soft tissues through patterns based on percentiles of their electrical characteristics. A BIVA vector that falls out of the 75% tolerance ellipses exhibits a different tissue impedance compared to the selected reference population, while vectors that fall in the 50% ellipse represent common impedance characteristics.

2.5. Statistical Analysis

The eight teams were divided into two groups (higher level, HL; lower level, LL) according to their final ranking at the tournament (teams that reached at least quarterfinals = HL, teams that lost before quarterfinals = LL). The mean and standard deviation (SD) of the two groups were calculated for each variable and the frequency of appearance (percentage) was determined for the maturity status. The distribution of the variables' residuals was verified with the Shapiro–Wilk test. When a variable presented a right-skewed curve, the logarithm transformation was applied to meet the normality distribution assumption. The two-tailed one-way analysis of variance (ANOVA) was performed to evaluate the differences between the two groups and among maturity statuses. When a variable's distribution could not meet the normality assumption, a non-parametric statistic test was performed (Mann–Whitney rank-sum and Kruskal–Wallis's rank tests). The probability of the type-I error was settled at <0.05. Finally, a post hoc Tukey evaluation was used to evaluate the difference between the final position at the tournament and between the maturity status when the Snedecor–Fisher statistical test probability value (*F*) was observed as significant.

3. Results

Table 1 shows the maturity status prevalence according to the tournament's final ranking. Three teams were classified as higher-level due to the results of the tournament, and five teams were classified as lower level. Teams with a worse ranking presented a higher number of boys with later maturity status, whereas the ratio of players who matured on time was similar (HL = 69.44%, LL = 63.79%).

Table 1. Prevalence of maturity status among teams classified as better and worse.

MS (Z ± 1)	Ranking Frequency		Δ Ranks		
	HL	LL	Z or χ^2	p	RR
E	7	5	1.529	0.126	2.256
OT	25	37	0.562	0.574	1.089
L	4	16	−1.901	0.05 *	0.403
Total	36	58	4.98	0.083	

Note. MS = maturity status, E = early, OT = on time, L = late, Z = the test of proportion Z, χ^2 = Pearson chi-squared test; p = p-value; RR = risk ratio; *, statistically significant; Δ difference.

Tables 2–4 show the mean and standard deviation of each variable for both the ranking group and the maturity status, and it reports the statistical comparisons between them and their interaction.

Table 2. General variable statistics according to MS ± 1 year and the final ranking of the tournament.

	HL			LL								
	E (n = 7)	OT (n = 25)	L (n = 4)	E (n = 5)	OT (n = 37)	L (n = 16)	Ranking		MS		Ranking * MS	
Variable	Mean (±SD)	Mean (±SD)	Mean (±SD)	Mean (±SD)	Mean (±SD)	Mean (±SD)	$F_{(1, 88)}$	P	$F_{(2, 88)}$	P	$F_{(2, 88)}$	P
Age (year) #	12.49 (0.81)	12.01 (0.37)	12.75 (0.51)	11.68 (1.82)	13.04 (0.26)	12.40 (0.85)	0.354	0.552	2.865	0.239	3.680	<0.001 *
Weight (Kg)	64.07 (7.97)	52.32 (9.29)	38.00 (4.00)	59.40 (13.99)	45.78 (7.99)	49.88 (9.19)	0.010	0.931	14.540	<0.001 *	1.910	0.154
Stature (cm)	175.89 (7.29)	161.79 (5.30)	148.98 (3.48)	162.36 (16.84)	155.83 (6.71)	159.91 (8.83)	1.580	0.212	13.330	<0.001 *	4.970	0.001 *
Trunk height (cm)	86.81 (3.21)	79.24 (2.65)	70.80 (1.60)	85.68 (8.30)	74.15 (1.46)	80.35 (4.24)	1.130	0.291	43.020	<0.001 *	1.130	0.327
Leg length (cm)	89.07 (5.30)	82.55 (3.74	78.18 (2.32))	76.68 (8.95)	81.68 (6.83)	79.56 (6.39)	5.720	0.019 *	0.800	0.454	5.710	0.005 *
BMI (kg/m^2)	20.64 (1.43)	19.99 (3.49)	17.13 (1.74)	22.24 (1.69)	19.18 (3.26)	19.37 (2.42)	1.730	0.192	4.860	0.010 *	1.560	0.216

Note: E = early, OT = on time, L = late, MS = maturity status, SD = standard deviation, F = Snedecor–Fischer statistic test, BMI = body mass index, %F = fat percentage, FM = fat mass, FFM = fat-free mass, R = resistance, Xc = reactance, PA = phase angle, * = statistical significant, # = Mann–Whitney rank-sum test and Kruskal–Wallis rank test.

Table 3. Anthropometric statistics according to MS ± 1 year and the final ranking of the tournament.

	HL			LL								
	E (n = 7)	OT (n = 25)	L (n = 4)	E (n = 5)	OT (n = 37)	L (n = 16)	Ranking		MS		Ranking * MS	
Variable	Mean (±SD)	Mean (±SD)	Mean (±SD)	Mean (±SD)	Mean (±SD)	Mean (±SD)	$F_{(1, 88)}$	P	$F_{(2, 88)}$	P	$F_{(2, 88)}$	P
str. Arm circ. (cm)	24.97 (2.68)	20.98 (2.12)	22.48 (2.18)	26.90 (2.72)	22.93 (2.96)	23.60 (2.54)	5.420	0.022 *	8.460	<0.001 *	0.230	0.796
con. Arm circ. (cm)	26.66 (2.34)	22.00 (1.92)	23.85 (2.34)	27.76 (2.40)	23.71 (3.01)	24.61 (2.68)	2.610	0.110	9.230	<0.001 *	0.180	0.832
Calf circ. (cm)	35.69 (1.99)	29.88 (0.38)	32.61 (2.44)	35.06 (3.77)	31.33 (3.65)	32.32 (2.40)	0.060	0.813	9.890	<0.001 *	0.630	0.533
Waist circ. (cm)	70.24 (6.69)	60.55 (1.97)	65.90 (5.87)	73.82 (5.82)	64.74 (6.42)	66.19 (5.22)	2.800	0.098	8.740	<0.001 *	0.860	0.428
Hip circ. (cm)	89.89 (6.60)	71.95 (7.48)	82.62 (6.51)	91.16 (8.20)	80.32 (7.21)	82.72 (6.27)	2.950	0.089	14.240	<0.001 *	2.030	0.137
Humeral diamet. (mm) #	6.79 (0.59)	6.15 (0.44)	6.34 (0.38)	6.50 (0.44)	6.62 (1.47)	6.43 (0.39)	0.001	0.991	6.015	0.050 *	0.740	0.595

Table 3. *Cont.*

	HL			LL								
	E (n = 7)	OT (n = 25)	L (n = 4)	E (n = 5)	OT (n = 37)	L (n = 16)	Ranking		MS		Ranking * MS	
Variable	**Mean (±SD)**	**Mean (±SD)**	**Mean (±SD)**	**Mean (±SD)**	**Mean (±SD)**	**Mean (±SD)**	$F_{(1, 88)}$	P	$F_{(2, 88)}$	P	$F_{(2, 88)}$	P
Femoral diamet. (mm) #	9.50 (0.58)	8.10 (0.48)	9.40 (1.28)	8.56 (0.85)	8.35 (0.60)	8.59 (0.55)	17.366	<0.001 *	12.647	0.001 *	5.610	<0.001 *
Triceps SK (mm)	10.14 (3.53)	9.25 (2.06)	12.44 (4.3)	16.40 (1.52)	12.31 (4.88)	11.68 (4.12)	5.680	0.019 *	1.160	0.318	3.950	0.023 *
Subscapular SK (mm)	9.29 (2.69)	6.00 (2.16)	10.40 (4.61)	11.20 (1.79)	9.94 (3.02)	8.82 (2.89)	4.400	0.039 *	2.870	0.062	5.600	0.005 *
Supraspinal SK (mm)	11.71 (5.68)	6.50 (2.65)	12.80 (7.05)	15.00 (3.32)	11.06 (4.37)	10.22 (5.10)	2.850	0.095	3.010	0.054	3.970	0.022 *
Suprailiac SK (mm)	13.00 (6.32)	9.25 (3.69)	14.40 (6.84)	16.60 (2.30)	14.31 (5.87)	11.95 (5.34)	2.510	0.117	1.150	0.320	3.350	0.039 *
Medial calf SK (mm)	10.86 (4.02)	11.25 (1.71)	12.68 (4.43)	15.60 (1.52)	13.44 (3.61)	12.65 (3.81)	4.440	0.038 *	0.170	0.846	2.060	0.133
Lateral calf SK (mm)	10.57 (2.15)	12.25 (1.26)	12.80 (3.54)	15.60 (1.34)	12.88 (3.40)	12.97 (2.87)	5.100	0.026 *	0.100	0.909	3.140	0.048 *
TUA (cm^2)	50.11 (10.41)	35.28 (7.22)	40.56 (7.90)	58.05 (11.83)	42.50 (10.82)	44.81 (9.81)	5.680	0.019 *	8.790	<0.001 *	0.260	0.768
UMA (cm^2)	38.11 (7.77)	26.13 (4.67)	27.66 (5.07)	38.11 (9.56)	29.25 (6.34)	31.88 (6.06)	1.950	0.166	9.140	<0.001 *	0.680	0.508
UFA (cm^2)	12.00 (4.77)	9.15 (2.78)	12.91 (5.02)	19.94 (2.90)	13.25 (6.26)	12.93 (5.58)	6.450	0.013 *	2.710	0.072	2.810	0.066
UFI (%)	23.59 (6.36)	25.59 (3.49)	31.20 (8.32)	34.82 (4.14)	30.10 (8.55)	28.15 (7.12)	3.980	0.049 *	0.320	0.729	5.100	<0.001 *
TCA (cm^2)	101.61 (11.08)	71.03 (1.80)	85.09 (12.66)	98.72 (20.35)	79.11 (17.11)	83.58 (12.16)	0.100	0.749	10.940	<0.001 *	0.730	0.483
CMA (cm^2)	67.23 (12.97)	40.31 (3.46)	48.74 (10.7)	51.62 (14.34)	43.09 (10.46)	47.33 (9.14)	2.670	0.106	9.480	<0.001 *	2.880	0.061
CFA (cm^2)	34.37 (8.26)	30.72 (1.80)	36.34 (10.83)	47.10 (7.34)	36.02 (10.22)	36.25 (8.98)	4.340	0.040 *	1.700	0.189	1.910	0.155
CFI (%)	34.06 (8.24)	43.31 (3.46)	42.57 (9.88)	48.32 (4.88)	45.64 (7.99)	43.27 (7.93)	5.980	0.016 *	0.470	0.624	3.240	0.044 *

Note: E = early, OT = on time, L = late, MS = maturity status, SD = standard deviation, F = Snedecor–Fischer statistic test, BMI = body mass index, circ = circumferences, str= stretched, con = contracted, SK = skinfold thickness, TUA = total upper area, UMA = upper muscle area, UFA = upper fat area, UFI = upper fat index, TCA = total calf area, CMA = calf mass area; CFA = calf fat area, CFI = calf fat index, * = statistical significant, # = Mann–Whitney rank-sum test and Kruskal–Wallis rank test

Table 4. Body composition statistics according to MS ± 1 year and the final ranking of the tournament.

	HL			LL								
	E (n = 7)	OT (n = 25)	L (n = 4)	E (n = 5)	OT (n = 37)	L (n = 16)	Ranking		MS		Ranking * MS	
Variable	**Mean (±SD)**	**Mean (±SD)**	**Mean (±SD)**	**Mean (±SD)**	**Mean (±SD)**	**Mean (±SD)**	$F_{(1, 88)}$	P	$F_{(2, 88)}$	P	$F_{(2, 88)}$	P
%F	18.54 (5.21)	14.79 (3.88)	21.23 (6.65)	25.56 (1.95)	20.87 (5.97)	19.40 (5.35)	6.510	0.012 *	2.160	0.121	4.900	0.010 *
FM (kg)	11.94 (3.79)	5.71 (2.05)	11.54 (5.49)	15.29 (4.09)	9.85 (4.06)	9.90 (3.99)	3.350	0.071	6.980	0.001 *	3.780	0.027 *
FFM (kg)	52.13 (6.88)	32.29 (2.32)	40.78 (5.13)	44.11 (10.05)	35.93 (5.05)	39.98 (6.70)	0.690	0.410	14.450	<0.001 *	2.590	0.081
R (Ω)	458.14 (50.11)	578.60 (74.45)	505.38 (54.37)	526.92 (43.87)	520.34 (71.54)	529.48 (63.68)	0.440	0.510	2.670	0.075	3.520	0.034 *
Xc (Ω)	61.66 (12.79)	68.63 (18.91)	61.72 (7.59)	59.70 (5.15)	61.21 (8.97)	63.21 (9.55)	0.570	0.453	0.460	0.631	0.840	0.437
PA #	7.73 (1.93)	6.50 (0.97)	6.74 (0.83)	6.48 (0.39)	6.61 (0.85)	6.78 (0.70)	0.318	0.572	3.022	0.221	1.880	0.106
R/H (Ω/cm)	260.88 (30.86)	388.98 (55.30)	428.79 (582.32)	329.06 (57.49)	335.26 (53.83)	333.65 (55.06)	0.100	0.758	0.390	0.681	0.350	0.708
Xc/H (Ω/cm)	34.89 (5.83)	46.03 (12.45)	38.18 (4.77)	37.20 (6.07)	39.45 (6.77)	39.74 (6.90)	0.240	0.627	3.270	0.043 *	2.180	0.119

Note: E = early, OT = on time, L = late, MS = maturity status, SD = standard deviation, F = Snedecor–Fischer statistic test, %F = fat percentage, FM = fat mass, FFM = fat free mass, R = resistance, Xc = reactance, PA = phase angle, * = statistical significant, # = Mann–Whitney rank-sum test and Kruskal–Wallis rank test.

Regarding the differences linked to the ranking position, better teams exhibited significantly higher values in leg length and femoral diameter and lower amounts of fat on the most informative skinfolds and fat percentage. On the contrary, boys who stopped before the quarterfinals showed significantly higher values in arm circumference, arm and calf skinfold thicknesses, and fat area or percentage on their lower and upper limbs (TUA, UFA, UFI, CFA, and CFI). Also, players clustered in the HL group showed a wider skeletal robustness in their lower limbs (femoral diameter).

Several statistically significant anthropometric differences were relative to maturity status. Boys classified as early showed better values in many important anthropometric characteristics such as height, weight, all the circumferences, and calf muscle area, and body composition parameters such as fat mass and fat-free mass than on-time and later youths.

Finally, regarding the interaction effect between ranking and maturity status, the earlier young players classified as higher-level showed significantly wider values in height, leg length, and femoral diameter than the earlier young players classified as lower level. In addition, the earlier boys ranked between the lower level presented higher values in parameters related to the local (triceps, subscapular, supraspinal, suprailiac, and lateral calf skinfolds, UFI, CFI) and total body fat mass (%F, FM) than earlier players classified in the first positions. Finally, although players who matured on time showed better characteristics in HL than LL teams in body composition (%F, FM), the LL players were taller and exhibited longer low limbs.

Bioimpedance Vector Analysis (BIVA)

Figures 2 and 3 show BIVA results regarding both the final ranking of the tournament (on the left) and the maturity status (on the right).

Figure 2 shows significant differences in BIVA vector distance according to the final ranking (Figure 2A) and between the boys classified as early and late (Figure 2B).

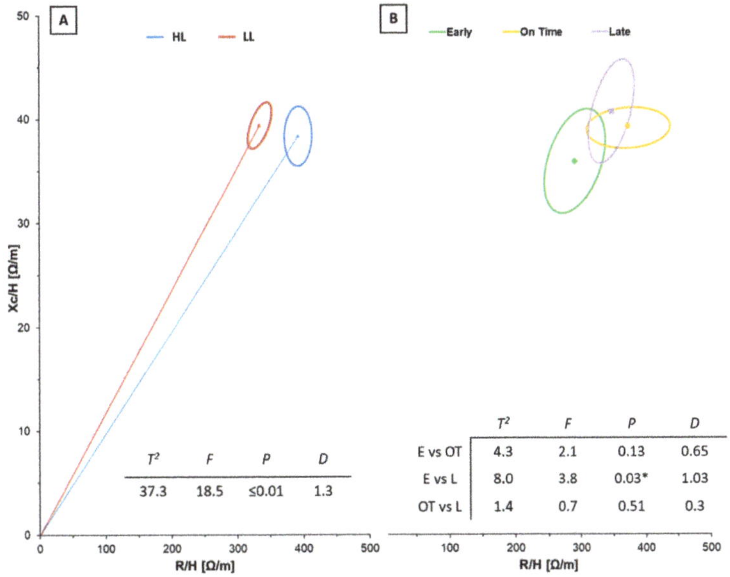

Figure 2. Paired graphs for the multivariate changes in classic resistance and reactance are shown depending on the ranking (**A**) and the maturity status (**B**). The mean vector displacements with 95%, confidence ellipses, and results of Hotelling's T^2 test are shown. E = early, OT = on time, L = late, HL= higher level, LL= lower level, * = statistical significant.

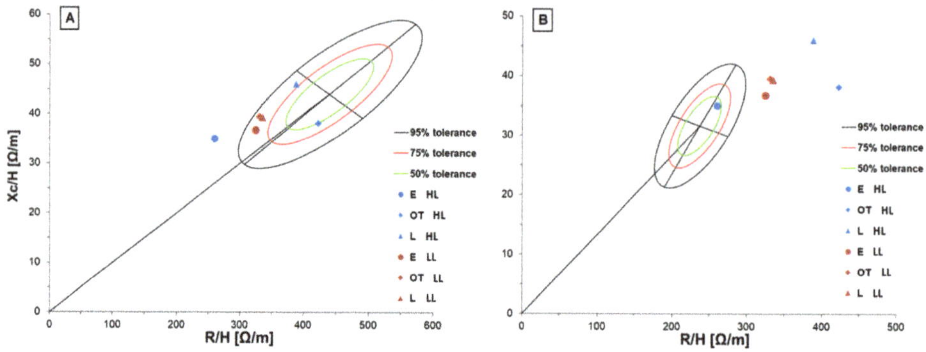

Figure 3. BIVA graphs for the multivariate changes in classical resistance and reactance are shown. The bioimpedance data are plotted on the tolerance ellipses of the general adolescent reference population (**A**) and of the elite volleyball players population (**B**). E = early, OT = on time, L = late, HL= higher level, LL= lower level.

Figure 3 shows different vector placements in the ellipses in accordance with the reference population. Compared to the general adolescent reference population (Figure 3A), only the boys who matured in an average manner were included in the 50% tolerance, while the early-matured boys exhibited a lower level of biological electric resistance. The early boys belonging to winning teams showed a wider displacement compared to leaner cell mass (left size vector position). In addition, they had a body composition more akin to the elite population of male adult volleyball players (Figure 3B). Differently, players of the HL teams who matured in an average manner or later exhibited the greatest BIVA differences compared to elite volleyball players (Figure 3B, blue triangle and diamond), especially in hydration and lean mass. As regards LL teams, all the maturity categories showed wide displacement against both the general adolescent population and the elite volleyball reference group. However, they were closer to the adolescent reference population than the adult elite volleyball players.

4. Discussion

The present study had two aims: (a) to compare the prevalence of maturity status among volleyball players of the teams that reached different positions in the ranking of a national tournament and (b) to investigate the relationship between maturity status and anthropometric and body composition parameters and BIVA. Our beginning hypotheses speculate that players who reached a higher position in the final ranking would exhibit differences in maturity status and their anthropometric profiles. Also, we believe that players who mature earlier show better body composition.

Many studies have been performed regarding the influence of maturity status on the body, physical performance, and physiological characteristics on the growing and scouting of adolescent soccer, basketball, or handball players, while less information exists on male volleyballers. The elite players have rapidly increased their physical demands in recent years, and, for this reason, recruiters and coaches put greater emphasis on physical fitness, and talent selection, from an early age [16,26]. In fact, in recent years, the identification of adolescent talent has gained increased interest from both the scientific community and sports managers [29]. The implementation of early talent identification programs could bring advantages to the teams that carry them out, both in economic and sporting terms [30].

Regarding the prevalence of maturity status, in the present study, significant differences were observed in the boys classified as late-maturing in comparison with those who were early or on time. In the teams that achieved higher ranking positions, only four boys were classified as late, while in the teams ranked between the lower levels, there were sixteen of them. This is in accordance with previous studies that demonstrated that maturity status has an important role in performance in adolescent males [21,31–34]. In fact, Romeo-Garcia and colleagues found that young male handball athletes who presented an early biological maturation achieved higher values in anthropometric characteristics and in physical tests [18]. They observed significant differences in basic measurements, such as weight, height, fat-free mass, BMI, and Cormic Index, and in some physical tests, such as medicine ball throw and squat jump, with the group of early maturers, who had the highest values. On the contrary, Toselli and colleagues did not find any differences in maturation category prevalences between elite and non-elite adolescent soccer teams from 11 to 14 years old [16]. However, having boys classified as late in the team reduces the possibility of winning and of demonstrating good performance in a short time. Despite this, the immediate advantage of premature maturation may not be associated with great future performance and talent expression. The role of coaches and trainers is fundamental for enhancing and scouting hidden talents.

According to the above-mentioned results, we found that teams that did not reach the quarterfinals showed higher values in several parameters linked to body fat and worse body composition. In fact, they exhibited higher values in several skinfold thicknesses, in body fat percentage, and in the fat area of the limbs. These results are in accordance with a previous study that investigated the effect of team level, maturation, and interaction in adolescent soccer players [16]. Many fat-related parameters differed between elite and non-elite players such as triceps, biceps, subscapular, suprailiac, and thigh skinfold thicknesses, and arm, thigh, and calf fat indexes. However, both young and adult volleyball players must make explosive movements and they may be powerful, agile, and rapid; for this reason, low body fat is required, particularly for young volleyball players [35]. Teams classified between the higher levels showed significantly higher values in leg length and femoral diameter, which are two important characteristics in volleyball. Height and leg length are fundamental in volleyball due to the height of the net (2.43 m for elite volleyball players, 2.15 m in U-13 competitions) [36].

Regarding differences due to maturity status, the present results are in line with a study conducted by Albaladejo-Saura et al. [20]. The authors found higher values in several anthropometric characteristics (such as height, diameters, trunk height, etc.), in volleyball players with a more advanced state of maturation, akin to what emerged in the present study. Among the anthropometric characteristics, the greatest differences between the two groups were found for skinfolds. This is in line with previous studies regarding soccer, which showed the importance of monitoring body fat, since appropriate levels of fat permit the players to move more effectively during training and games [37,38].

Regarding the results of the BIVA graphs, it is interesting to notice that early boys classified in the first positions had a body composition like the elite population of volleyball players, showing a lower level of resistance and leaner body. In addition, their vector characteristics differed against the general adolescent reference population. The premature growth of the muscle cells and the reduction of the inactive mass (fat mass) are relevant parameters in fast and power sports such as volleyball [2,28]. This could explain the better performance of these teams and could also be an important factor to consider and monitor the BIVA parameter changes over time for talent selection. At the same time, it is interesting to note that the boys in teams classified at lower levels had a similar position in both the BIA vector graphs, independent of maturity status. The boys classified on time and in the first position were plotted out from the tolerance ellipse of the elite volleyball players' population. This could be justified by the maturity status because they are near the PHV, which is a moment of big changes for the body. Also, this information could confirm that maturation in adolescence could widely affect changes in anthropometry and body composition, impacting physical performance and team scouting. Although only seven players out of thirty-six were classified as early-maturing in high-level teams, volleyball involves six players on the court for any action and two boys having improved body and physical characteristics could lead to winning.

Previous studies reported that the chance of selection for relatively younger soccer players was widely affected by maturation status, physical performance, and anthropometric characteristics, whereas relatively older athletes had a selection advantage independent of their maturity status [39,40]. It is difficult to provide an exhaustive comparison, but it seems that the influence of this aspect is the same in this sport.

The present study has several limitations. The study design included only one period of evaluation and longitudinal research with several follow-ups could enrich the specific literature. The teams were randomized and selected to be measured during the tournament, and it was not possible to evaluate all the teams involved. It could have been interesting to measure all the teams participating in the tournament to have a wider sample size and to collect more data for maturation state comparison. Also, the participants were only thirteen-year-old males; many investigations considering both sexes and different ages are suggested. In addition, it was not possible to collect information about the diet habits of the young male volleyball players. No data were given about the years of experience of the players, which could influence the final ranking, or about the time on the court of each player. Finally, physical tests (for example, jumping test or speed test) were not performed and no data related to match results and skills were collected. Future investigations could draw more complete study designs in order to evaluate the correlations between physical performance, match analysis, anthropometry and body composition, match level, and biological maturation.

5. Conclusions

In conclusion, in the present study, young male volleyball players classified as early had higher values of the anthropometric characteristics linked to better performance (represented by the final ranking of the tournament). In fact, among the eight teams, two of them that presented the most early maturing boys were ranked in the top places of the tournament (1st–8th place). Anthropometric characteristics, maturity status, and body composition variables significantly influenced the final ranking of the tournament. Further studies are needed to better evaluate this relationship in volleyball.

Author Contributions: Conceptualization, A.G. and S.T.; methodology, A.G., S.T. and M.M.; software, M.M.; validation, A.G., S.T. and M.M.; formal analysis, M.M.; investigation, A.G.; resources, S.T.; data curation, A.G. and M.M.; writing—original draft preparation, A.G.; writing—review and editing, M.M. and S.T.; visualization, M.M.; supervision, S.T.; project administration, A.G. All authors have read and agreed to the published version of the manuscript.

Funding: This research received no external funding.

Institutional Review Board Statement: The study was conducted in accordance with the Declaration of Helsinki, and approved by the Institutional Review Board of the University of Bologna (protocol code 25027).

Informed Consent Statement: Informed consent was obtained from all parents of subjects involved in the study.

Data Availability Statement: Data available on request due to restrictions eg privacy or ethical.

Conflicts of Interest: The authors declare no conflict of interest.

References

1. Chamari, K.; Ahmaidi, S.; Blum, J.; Hue, O.; Temfemo, A.; Hertogh, C.; Mercier, B.; Préfaut, C.; Mercier, J. Venous Blood Lactate Increase after Vertical Jumping in Volleyball Athletes. *Eur. J. Appl. Physiol.* **2001**, *85*, 191–194. [CrossRef]
2. Gabbett, T.; Georgieff, B. Physiological and Anthropometric Characteristics of Australian Junior National, State, and Novice Volleyball Players. *J. Strength Cond. Res.* **2007**, *21*, 902–908. [CrossRef] [PubMed]
3. Mendes, F.G.; Lima, A.B.; Christofoletti, M.; Quinaud, R.T.; Collet, C.; Gonçalves, C.E.; Carvalho, H.M. Multidimensional Characteristics of Young Brazilian Volleyball Players: A Bayesian Multilevel Analysis. *PLoS ONE* **2021**, *16*, e0250953. [CrossRef] [PubMed]

4. Fields, J.B.; Metoyer, C.J.; Casey, J.C.; Esco, M.R.; Jagim, A.R.; Jones, M.T. Comparison of Body Composition Variables Across a Large Sample of National Collegiate Athletic Association Women Athletes From 6 Competitive Sports. *J. Strength Cond. Res.* **2018**, *32*, 2452–2457. [CrossRef] [PubMed]
5. Gaurav, V.; Singh, M.; Singh, S. Anthropometric Characteristics, Somatotyping and Body Composition of Volleyball and Basketball Players. *J. Phy. Edu. Sports Man* **2010**, *1*, 28–32.
6. Zhao, K.; Hohmann, A.; Chang, Y.; Zhang, B.; Pion, J.; Gao, B. Physiological, Anthropometric, and Motor Characteristics of Elite Chinese Youth Athletes From Six Different Sports. *Front. Physiol.* **2019**, *10*, 405. [CrossRef]
7. Rubajczyk, K.; Rokita, A. The Relative Age Effect and Talent Identification Factors in Youth Volleyball in Poland. *Front. Psychol.* **2020**, *11*, 1445. [CrossRef]
8. Tsoukos, A.; Drikos, S.; Brown, L.E.; Sotiropoulos, K.; Veligekas, P.; Bogdanis, G.C. Anthropometric and Motor Performance Variables Are Decisive Factors for The Selection of Junior National Female Volleyball Players. *J. Hum. Kinet.* **2019**, *67*, 163–173. [CrossRef]
9. Tsoukos, A.; Drikos, S.; Brown, L.E.; Sotiropoulos, K.; Veligekas, P.; Bogdanis, G.C. Upper and Lower Body Power Are Strong Predictors for Selection of Male Junior National Volleyball Team Players. *J. Strength Cond. Res.* **2019**, *33*, 2760–2767. [CrossRef]
10. Carvalho, A.; Roriz, P.; Duarte, D. Comparison of Morphological Profiles and Performance Variables between Female Volleyball Players of the First and Second Division in Portugal. *J. Hum. Kinet.* **2020**, *71*, 109–117. [CrossRef]
11. Papadopoulou, S.D.; Papadopoulou, S.K.; Rosemann, T.; Knechtle, B.; Nikolaidis, P.T. Relative Age Effect on Youth Female Volleyball Players: A Pilot Study on Its Prevalence and Relationship With Anthropometric and Physiological Characteristics. *Front. Psychol.* **2019**, *10*, 2737. [CrossRef] [PubMed]
12. Malina, R.M.; Cumming, S.P.; Kontos, A.P.; Eisenmann, J.C.; Ribeiro, B.; Aroso, J. Maturity-Associated Variation in Sport-Specific Skills of Youth Soccer Players Aged 13–15 Years. *J. Sports Sci.* **2005**, *23*, 515–522. [CrossRef] [PubMed]
13. Campa, F.; Silva, A.M.; Iannuzzi, V.; Mascherini, G.; Benedetti, L.; Toselli, S. The Role of Somatic Maturation on Bioimpedance Patterns and Body Composition in Male Elite Youth Soccer Players. *Int. J. Environ. Res. Public Health* **2019**, *16*, 4711. [CrossRef] [PubMed]
14. Toselli, S.; Marini, E.; Maietta Latessa, P.; Benedetti, L.; Campa, F. Maturity Related Differences in Body Composition Assessed by Classic and Specific Bioimpedance Vector Analysis among Male Elite Youth Soccer Players. *Int. J. Environ. Res. Public Health* **2020**, *17*, 729. [CrossRef]
15. Živković, M.; Stojiljković, N.; Trajković, N.; Stojanović, N.; Đošić, A.; Antić, V.; Stanković, N. Speed, Change of Direction Speed, and Lower Body Power in Young Athletes and Nonathletes According to Maturity Stage. *Children* **2022**, *9*, 242. [CrossRef]
16. Toselli, S.; Mauro, M.; Grigoletto, A.; Cataldi, S.; Benedetti, L.; Nanni, G.; Di Miceli, R.; Aiello, P.; Gallamini, D.; Fischetti, F.; et al. Maturation Selection Biases and Relative Age Effect in Italian Soccer Players of Different Levels. *Biology* **2022**, *11*, 1559. [CrossRef]
17. Barazetti, L.K.; Varoni, P.R.; Campos, F.d.S.; Demarchi, M.; Baumann, L.; Teixeira, A.S.; Nunes, R.F.H.; Flores, L.J.F. Comparison of Maturation and Physical Performance in Basketball Athletes of Different Playing Positions. *Rev. Bras. De Cineantropometria Desempenho Hum.* **2019**, *21*, e60248. [CrossRef]
18. Romero-García, D.; Vaquero-Cristóbal, R.; Albaladejo-Saura, M.; Esparza-Ros, F.; Martínez-Sanz, J.M. Influence of Biological Maturation Status on Kinanthropometric Characteristics, Physical Fitness and Diet in Adolescent Male Handball Players. *Appl. Sci.* **2023**, *13*, 3012. [CrossRef]
19. Te Wierike, S.C.M.; Elferink-Gemser, M.T.; Tromp, E.J.Y.; Vaeyens, R.; Visscher, C. Role of Maturity Timing in Selection Procedures and in the Specialisation of Playing Positions in Youth Basketball. *J. Sports Sci.* **2015**, *33*, 337–345. [CrossRef]
20. Albaladejo-Saura, M.; Vaquero-Cristóbal, R.; García-Roca, J.A.; Esparza-Ros, F. Influence of Biological Maturation Status on Selected Anthropometric and Physical Fitness Variables in Adolescent Male Volleyball Players. *PeerJ* **2022**, *10*, e13216. [CrossRef]
21. Lohman, T.; Roache, A.; Martorell, R. Anthropometric Standardization Reference Manual. *J. Am. Diet. Assoc.* **1988**, *89*, 872–874. [CrossRef]
22. Slaughter, M.H.; Lohman, T.G.; Boileau, R.A.; Horswill, C.A.; Stillman, R.J.; Van Loan, M.D.; Bemben, D.A. Skinfold Equations for Estimation of Body Fatness in Children and Youth. *Hum. Biol.* **1988**, *60*, 709–723. [PubMed]
23. Frisancho, A.R. *Anthropometric Standards: An Interactive Nutritional Reference of Body Size and Body Composition for Children and Adults*; University of Michigan Press: Ann Arbor, MI, USA, 2008; ISBN 978-0-472-11591-4.
24. Mirwald, R.L.; Baxter-Jones, A.D.G.; Bailey, D.A.; Beunen, G.P. An Assessment of Maturity from Anthropometric Measurements. *Med. Sci. Sports Exerc.* **2002**, *34*, 689–694. [CrossRef]
25. Drenowatz, C.; Wartha, O.; Klenk, J.; Brandstetter, S.; Wabitsch, M.; Steinacker, J. Differences in Health Behavior, Physical Fitness, and Cardiovascular Risk in Early, Average, and Late Mature Children. *Pediatr. Exerc. Sci.* **2013**, *25*, 69–83. [CrossRef]
26. Piccoli, A.; Rossi, B.; Pillon, L.; Bucciante, G. A New Method for Monitoring Body Fluid Variation by Bioimpedance Analysis: The RXc Graph. *Kidney. Intl.* **1994**, *46*, 534–539. [CrossRef] [PubMed]
27. Micheli, M.L.; Pagani, L.; Marella, M.; Gulisano, M.; Piccoli, A.; Angelini, F.; Burtscher, M.; Gatterer, H. Bioimpedance and Impedance Vector Patterns as Predictors of League Level in Male Soccer Players. *Int. J. Sports Physiol. Perform.* **2014**, *9*, 532–539. [CrossRef]
28. Campa, F.; Toselli, S.; Mazzilli, M.; Gobbo, L.A.; Coratella, G. Assessment of Body Composition in Athletes: A Narrative Review of Available Methods with Special Reference to Quantitative and Qualitative Bioimpedance Analysis. *Nutrients* **2021**, *13*, 1620. [CrossRef] [PubMed]

29. Barners, C.; Archer, B.; Hogg, B.; Busch, M.; Bradley, P. The Evolution of Physical and Tech-nical Performance Parameters in the English Premier League. *Int. J. Sports Med.* **2014**, *35*, 1095–1100. [CrossRef]
30. Pion, J.; Segers, V.; Fransen, J.; Debuyck, G.; Deprez, D.; Haerens, L.; Vaeyens, R.; Philippaerts, R.; Lenoir, M. Generic Anthropometric and Performance Characteristics among Elite Adolescent Boys in Nine Different Sports. *Eur. J. Sport Sci.* **2015**, *15*, 357–366. [CrossRef]
31. Parr, J.; Winwood, K.; Hodson-Tole, E.; Deconinck, F.J.A.; Hill, J.P.; Teunissen, J.W.; Cumming, S.P. The Main and Interactive Effects of Biological Maturity and Relative Age on Physical Performance in Elite Youth Soccer Players. *J. Sports Med.* **2020**, *2020*, e1957636. [CrossRef]
32. Peña-González, I.; Fernández-Fernández, J.; Moya-Ramón, M.; Cervelló, E. Relative Age Effect, Biological Maturation, and Coaches' Efficacy Expectations in Young Male Soccer Players. *Res. Quart. Exer. Sport* **2018**, *89*, 373–379. [CrossRef] [PubMed]
33. Johnson, A.; Farooq, A.; Whiteley, R. Skeletal Maturation Status Is More Strongly Associated with Academy Selection than Birth Quarter. *Sci. Med. Footb.* **2017**, *1*, 157–163. [CrossRef]
34. Radnor, J.M.; Staines, J.; Bevan, J.; Cumming, S.P.; Kelly, A.L.; Lloyd, R.S.; Oliver, J.L. Maturity Has a Greater Association than Relative Age with Physical Performance in English Male Academy Soccer Players. *Sports* **2021**, *9*, 171. [CrossRef] [PubMed]
35. Toselli, S.; Campa, F. Anthropometry and Functional Movement Patterns in Elite Male Volleyball Players of Different Competitive Levels. *J. Strength Cond. Res.* **2018**, *32*, 2601. [CrossRef]
36. Pocek, S.; Milosevic, Z.; Lakicevic, N.; Pantelic-Babic, K.; Imbronjev, M.; Thomas, E.; Bianco, A.; Drid, P. Anthropometric Characteristics and Vertical Jump Abilities by Player Position and Performance Level of Junior Female Volleyball Players. *Int. J. Environ. Res. Public Health* **2021**, *18*, 8377. [CrossRef]
37. Bernal-Orozco, M.F.; Posada-Falomir, M.; Quiñónez-Gastélum, C.M.; Plascencia-Aguilera, L.P.; Arana-Nuño, J.R.; Badillo-Camacho, N.; Márquez-Sandoval, F.; Holway, F.E.; Vizmanos-Lamotte, B. Anthropometric and Body Composition Profile of Young Professional Soccer Players. *J. Strength Cond. Res.* **2020**, *34*, 1911–1923. [CrossRef]
38. Toselli, S.; Campa, F.; Maietta Latessa, P.; Greco, G.; Loi, A.; Grigoletto, A.; Zaccagni, L. Differences in Maturity and Anthropometric and Morphological Characteristics among Young Male Basketball and Soccer Players and Non-Players. *Int. J. Environ. Res. Public Health* **2021**, *18*, 3902. [CrossRef]
39. Deprez, D.; Coutts, A.J.; Fransen, J.; Deconinck, F.; Lenoir, M.; Vaeyens, R.; Philippaerts, R. Relative Age, Biological Maturation and Anaerobic Characteristics in Elite Youth Soccer Players. *Int. J. Sports Med.* **2013**, *34*, 897–903. [CrossRef]
40. Müller, L.; Gonaus, C.; Perner, C.; Müller, E.; Raschner, C. Maturity Status Influences the Relative Age Effect in National Top Level Youth Alpine Ski Racing and Soccer. *PLoS ONE* **2017**, *12*, e0181810. [CrossRef]

Journal of
Functional Morphology and Kinesiology

MDPI

Article

How Do Football Playing Positions Differ in Body Composition? A First Insight into White Italian Serie A and Serie B Players

Tindaro Bongiovanni [1,2], Alessio Rossi [3,4,*], Federico Genovesi [5], Giulia Martera [6], Giuseppe Puleo [2], Carmine Orlandi [7], Mirco Spedicato [8], F. Marcello Iaia [9], Riccardo Del Vescovo [10,11], Stefano Gallo [10], Roberto Cannataro [12], Patrizio Ripari [13], Matteo Levi Micheli [14], Stefania Cataldi [15] and Athos Trecroci [9]

1 Department of Biomedical and Neuromotor Sciences, University of Bologna, 40126 Bologna, Italy; tindaro.bongiovanni2@unibo.it
2 Department of Performance, Palermo Football Club, 90146 Palermo, Italy; g.puleo@palermofc.com
3 Department of Computer Science, University of Pisa, 56126 Pisa, Italy
4 National Research Council (CNR), Institute of Information Science and Technologies (ISTI), 56124 Pisa, Italy
5 Medical Department, Manchester City Football Club, Manchester M11 3FF, UK; federico.genovesi@mancity.com
6 Department of Performance Nutrition, Spezia Calcio, 19123 La Spezia, Italy
7 Department of Sport Science, Tor Vergata University of Roma, 00133 Roma, Italy; carmine.orlandi@uniroma2.it
8 Department of Nutrition, U.S. Lecce Football Club, 73100 Lecce, Italy; info@mircospedicato.it
9 Department of Biomedical Science for Health, University of Milan, 20133 Milan, Italy; marcello.iaia@unimi.it (F.M.I.); athos.trecroci@unimi.it (A.T.)
10 Department of Performance, Hellas Verona Football Club, 37135 Verona, Italy; delvescovoriccardo@gmail.com (R.D.V.); stefanogallonutrizionista@gmail.com (S.G.)
11 Villa Stuart Clinic, FIFA Medical Center of Excellence, 00186 Rome, Italy
12 Department of Pharmacy, Health and Nutritional Sciences, University of Calabria, 87036 Rende, Italy; r.cannataro@gmail.com
13 Department of Technological Medicine, University of Chieti-Pescara, 66100 Pescara, Italy; patrizio.ripari@unich.it
14 Department of Experimental and Clinical Medicine, University of Florence, 50100 Florence, Italy; matteo.levimicheli@unifi.it
15 Department of Translational Biomedicine and Neuroscience (DiBraiN), University of Study of Bari, 70126 Bari, Italy; stefania.cataldi@uniba.it
* Correspondence: alessio.rossi@di.unipi.it

Citation: Bongiovanni, T.; Rossi, A.; Genovesi, F.; Martera, G.; Puleo, G.; Orlandi, C.; Spedicato, M.; Iaia, F.M.; Del Vescovo, R.; Gallo, S.; et al. How Do Football Playing Positions Differ in Body Composition? A First Insight into White Italian Serie A and Serie B Players. *J. Funct. Morphol. Kinesiol.* **2023**, *8*, 80. https://doi.org/10.3390/jfmk8020080

Academic Editor: Peter Hofmann

Received: 18 May 2023
Revised: 6 June 2023
Accepted: 9 June 2023
Published: 15 June 2023

Abstract: The present study aimed to investigate how playing positions differ in specific body composition variables in professional soccer players with respect to specific field zones and tactical lines. Five hundred and six Serie A and B professional soccer players were included in the study and analyzed according to their playing positions: goalkeepers (GKs), central backs (CBs), fullbacks (FBs), central midfielders (MIDs), wide midfielders (WMs), attacking midfielders (AMs), second strikers (SSs), external strikers (ESs), and central forwards (CFs), as well as their field zones (central and external) and tactical lines (defensive, middle, and offensive). Anthropometrics (stature and body mass) of each player were recorded. Then, body composition was obtained by means of bioelectric impedance analysis (BIA). GKs and CFs were the tallest and heaviest players, with no differences from each other. Likewise, GKs and CFs, along with CBs, were apparently more muscular (for both upper and lower limbs) and fatter at the same time compared with the other roles. Overall, players of the defensive line (CBs and FBs), along with those playing in central field zones (CBs, MIDs, AMs, SSs, and CFs), were significantly ($p < 0.05$) superior in almost all anthropometric and body composition variables than those of middle and offensive line and external zones, respectively.

Keywords: anthropometry; soccer; morphology; bioelectrical impedance analysis

1. Introduction

Soccer is an intermittent team sport requiring players with well-developed physical, psychological, tactical and technical skills [1]. From a physiological perspective, soccer's demands are complex and vary depending on different factors such as players' performance level for both teammates and opponents, the style of play adopted by the two contending teams, and positional roles that imply specific demands [2–4]. For example, the goalkeepers (GKs) cover approximately 50% less total distance and <10% of the distance at high-intensity speed (>19.8 km/h) than outfield players [5,6], also including very brief explosive movements [7] in their locomotive match demands. Central midfielders (MIDs) cover more total and high-intensity running distances than center backs (CBs), while wide midfielders (WMs) sprint over greater distances than defensive linemen [8]. Further, both full backs (FBs) and MIDs exhibit a higher number of ball possessions compared to other positions [9] that would further differentiate their physical and technical performance on the pitch. Research demonstrates that MIDs and FBs display the highest VO2 max and show the greatest physical capacities by means of exhaustive intermittent running tests [10].

Based on the aforementioned match activity profiles, it stands to reason that players' anthropometry and body composition profiles may be differently characterized as a function of their playing position [4]. A previous study showed that GKs and central forwards (CFs) were taller, heavier, and fatter with respect to MIDs [4]. Similarly, Anderson et al. (2019) [7] underreported higher skinfold thicknesses, as a proxy marker of body fat, in GKs compared with outfield players. However, Mala et al. (2017) [11] did not find any differences among playing positions in body fat. However, they observed a significantly higher lean body mass in GKs compared to defensive (FBs, CBs), middle (WMs and MIDs), and offensive (CFs) linemen. Other authors found that professional GKs were leaner than FBs and MIDs [12]. The fact that GKs are leaner than some outfield players might be the result of regularly engaging in additional resistance training to cope with the increasing demands of modern soccer [7]. Indeed, modern soccer requires GKs to execute fast and explosive actions such as changing directions, jumping, and diving [7], while continuously shifting their center of gravity within a larger operating area that is closer to outfield players [11].

Thus, retrieving specific data on the estimated body composition becomes relevant in a real-world setting, as this could provide practitioners with a deep insight into their athletes' potential while tracking training-related effects. However, limited data are available to describe physical differences linked to playing position. Moreover, scant evidence also exists on how players belonging to different tactical lines (defensive, middle, and offensive) and field zones (central and external) differ in body composition.

Therefore, the aim of this study was to investigate how playing positions differ in specific body composition variables at an individual level. Secondly, this study aimed to evaluate potential differences in the same selected body composition variables by field lines and zones.

2. Materials and Methods

2.1. Subject

A total of 506 elite white soccer players (age = 25.72 ± 4.02 years, height = 183.72 ± 5.86 cm, body mass = 79.91 ± 6.31 kg) competing in professional Italian soccer teams (Serie A and Serie B) voluntarily took part in this study. Players were separated into nine playing positions according to the role typically attributed by their coaching staff (n = 57 goalkeepers—GK, n = 82 central backs—CB, n = 73 fullbacks—FB, n = 43 central midfielders—MID, n = 66 wide midfielders—WM, n = 42 attacking midfielders—AM, n = 37 s strikers—SS, n = 52 external strikers—ES, and n = 54 central forwards—CF) in accordance with the zone of the pitch they used to play. All the participants signed their informed consent before taking part in the experiment (Ethics committee, University of Milan, approval code: 32/16 of 16 November 2016), which complies with the principles of the Declaration of Helsinki.

2.2. Data Acquisition

2.2.1. Procedure

This quantitative study involved the participation of 12 elite soccer clubs, and the assessment was made for each team during the in-season period (in October). Players' body compositions were recorded in the morning (from 8.30 a.m. to 9.30 a.m.) following a 12 h food and fluid fast. All participants were also asked to abstain from drinking caffeinated and alcoholic beverages within 24 h before testing. Likewise, the participants were asked to avoid vigorous exercise within 24 h before assessing, as in previous studies [13].

2.2.2. Body Composition

Body mass and height (or stature) were measured to the nearest 0.1 kg and 0.1 cm, respectively, via a portable stadiometer (Seca 213, Hamburg, Germany) and a flat scale (Seca 877, Hamburg, Germany) while barefoot and wearing a bathing suit.

Bioelectrical impedance analysis (BIA) was performed using a phase-sensitive bioelectrical analyzer (BIA 101 BIVA PRO, Akern, Florence, Italy). The device emits an alternating sinusoidal electric current of 250 μA at an operating monofrequency of 50 kHz (±0.1%). The device was calibrated using the standard control circuit supplied by the manufacturer that has a known impedance. Participants were positioned supine with a leg opening of 45° with respect to the midline of the body, and with the upper limbs positioned 30° away from the trunk. After cleaning the skin with alcohol pads, four adhesive electrodes (Biatrodes Akern Srl, Florence, Italy) were placed on the backs of the hands and another four electrodes on the ankles of the corresponding feet, keeping 5 cm between each electrode [14]. The proximal hand electrode was positioned between the radial and ulnar styloid processes, directly superficial to the distal radioulnar joint. The distal hand electrode was positioned in the center of the third, proximal phalanx. The proximal foot electrode was placed directly between the medial and lateral malleoli at the ankle. The distal foot electrode was placed immediately proximal to the second and third metatarsophalangeal joints [15]. Resistance (Rz), reactance (Xc), and phase angle (PhA) raw data were obtained. R is the opposition to the flow of an injected alternating current, at any current frequency, through intra and extracellular ionic solutions, while Xc represents the dielectric or capacitive component of cell membranes, organelles, and tissue interfaces [16]. From the raw BIA variables, estimates of appendicular arm lean soft tissue (ALST) and leg lean soft tissue (LLST) were obtained as previously [15]. Fat-free mass (FFM) was estimated using the athlete-specific equation of Matias et al. [17] and, consequently, fat mass (FM) was derived by subtracting the body mass minus the fat-free mass in kilograms.

As regards PhA, it has been suggested as a biomarker of cellular health and cell membrane integrity and descriptive of the intracellular (ICW)–extracellular (ECW) water ratio [15].

In addition, estimates of total body water (TBW) and ECW were obtained using equations (Equations (1) and (2)) specific for athletes by Matias et al. [17], where sex is a binary value where 0 and 1 refer to female and male, respectively.

$$\text{TBW (L)} = 0.286 + 0.195 \times \text{stature2}/\text{Rz} + 0.385 \times \text{body mass} + 5.086 \times \text{sex} \quad (1)$$

$$\text{ECW (L)}: 1.579 + 0.055 \times \text{stature2}/\text{Rz} + 0.127 \times \text{body mass} + 0.006 + \text{stature2}/\text{Xc} + 0.932 \times \text{sex} \quad (2)$$

ICW was then calculated by subtracting ECW from TBW.

2.3. Statistical Analysis

One-way analysis of variance (ANOVA) was performed in order to detect statistical differences among playing positions, field lines (defensive, middle, and offensive), and zones (central or external position) for each selected variable. The normality of data distribution assumption was assessed by Shapiro–Wilks' normality test. Additionally, Tukey' post hoc pairwise comparison analysis was performed when ANOVA showed statistical significance. All the analyses were performed in the Python 3.8 programming language. The statistical significance was set at 0.05 (5%).

3. Results

Table 1 shows the descriptive statistics of all the playing positions. Several statistically significant differences among playing positions were detected. From a descriptive point of view, GKs were the tallest and heaviest players, also exhibiting the highest values in TBW, ECW, ICW, FFM, FM, ALST, and LLST. GKs also presented the lowest PhA values along with AMs, while MIDs had the highest. ESs were the lightest players, also exhibiting the lowest values in TBW, ECW, ICW, FFM, ALST, and LLST. FBs were the leanest players (Figure 1a). The post hoc outputs linked to statistical significance are included in the Supplementary Materials for height (Table S1), weight (Table S2), PhA (Table S3), TBW (Table S4), ECW (Table S5), ICW (Table S6), FFM (Table S7), FM (Table S8), ALST (Table S9), and LLST (Table S10). Specifically, the post hoc analyses revealed that GKs were significantly different ($p < 0.01$) in stature from CBs, MIDs, WMs, AMs, SSs, and ESs. CBs were also significantly different ($p < 0.01$) in stature from FBs, MIDs, AMs, SSs, and ESs. FBs were also significantly different ($p < 0.01$) from CFs. MIDs were also significantly different ($p < 0.01$) in stature from WMs and ESs, and CFs. WMs were also significantly different ($p < 0.01$) in stature from SSs, ESs, and CFs. AMs were also significantly different ($p < 0.01$) in stature from SSs and CFs. Moreover, ESs were also significantly different ($p < 0.01$) in stature from CFs.

Table 1. Descriptive statistics expressed as mean (± standard deviation) and statistical analysis. ANOVA statistical significance between playing position: * p-value < 0.001.

Features	GK	CB	FB	MID	WM	AM	SS	ES	CF	ALL
Height	189.15	187.96	181.61	179.87	183.49	181.80	177.49	179.34	187.74	183.72
(cm) *	(3.50)	(3.51)	(4.03)	(4.81)	(4.58)	(4.78)	(5.08)	(5.42)	(4.73)	(5.86)
Body mass	85.89	84.04	77.48	76.96	78.54	77.98	75.92	73.83	84.73	79.91
(kg) *	(4.66)	(4.11)	(4.31)	(5.03)	(5.58)	(5.32)	(4.40)	(5.07)	(5.54)	(6.31)
PhA	7.83	7.96	8.18	8.30	8.00	7.83	8.25	8.20	8.07	8.06
(°) *	(0.60)	(0.65)	(0.58)	(0.78)	(0.55)	(0.61)	(0.72)	(0.37)	(0.64)	(0.63)
TBW	53.85	52.88	49.42	48.93	49.79	49.38	48.15	46.88	53.24	50.54
(L) *	(2.73)	(2.41)	(2.56)	(2.83)	(3.27)	(2.67)	(2.22)	(3.08)	(3.03)	(3.59)
ECW	21.23	20.81	19.44	19.18	19.62	19.52	18.87	18.38	20.89	19.87
(L) *	(1.13)	(0.97)	(1.03)	(1.17)	(1.31)	(1.06)	(0.77)	(1.22)	(1.10)	(1.43)
ICW	32.62	32.07	29.99	29.75	30.17	29.87	29.28	28.50	32.35	30.66
(L) *	(1.66)	(1.51)	(1.56)	(1.73)	(1.99)	(1.66)	(1.49)	(1.88)	(1.96)	(2.20)
FFM	74.14	72.73	67.73	66.96	68.22	67.60	65.78	63.90	73.25	69.3
(kg) *	(4.06)	(3.63)	(3.82)	(4.22)	(4.83)	(3.86)	(3.22)	(4.61)	(4.47)	(5.29)
FM	11.74	11.31	9.75	9.99	10.32	10.38	10.13	9.92	11.48	10.60
(kg) *	(2.08)	(2.28)	(1.80)	(2.51)	(1.62)	(2.00)	(1.76)	(2.24)	(2.52)	(2.21)
FM	13.65	13.42	12.57	12.93	13.12	13.23	13.29	13.41	13.49	13.22
(%)	(2.18)	(2.51)	(2.05)	(2.83)	(1.71)	(1.92)	(1.79)	(2.75)	(2.55)	(2.29)
ALST	7.51	7.35	6.72	6.61	6.75	6.61	6.39	6.21	7.43	6.90
(kg) *	(0.58)	(0.57)	(0.55)	(0.60)	(0.64)	(0.48)	(0.49)	(0.66)	(0.67)	(0.73)
LLST	22.12	21.66	20.05	19.78	20.19	19.97	19.37	18.74	21.83	20.54
(kg) *	(1.37)	(1.24)	(1.29)	(1.43)	(1.61)	(1.25)	(1.05)	(1.57)	(1.49)	(1.76)

Note: PhA = phase angle, TBW = total body water, ECW = extracellular water, ICW = intracellular water, FFM = fat-free mass, FM = fat mass, ALST = arm lean soft tissue, LLST = leg lean soft tissue, GK = goalkeeper, CB = central back, FB = fullback, MID = central midfielder, WM = wide midfielder, AM = attacking midfielder, SS = second striker, ES = external strikers, CF = central forward.

As regards body mass, GKs was significantly different ($p < 0.01$) in body mass from MIDs, WMs, AMs, SSs, and ESs. CBs were significantly different ($p < 0.01$) in body mass from FBs, MIDs, WMs, AMs, SSs, and ESs. FBs, MIDs, WMs, and AMs were also significantly different ($p < 0.01$) in body mass from ESs and CFs. ESs were also significantly different ($p < 0.01$) in body mass from CFs.

For a better visual inspection of each field position, the post hoc analyses of the selected variables (PhA, ECW, ICW, FFM, FM, ALST, and LLST) are represented in Figure 2 by pitches in the form of tactical systems.

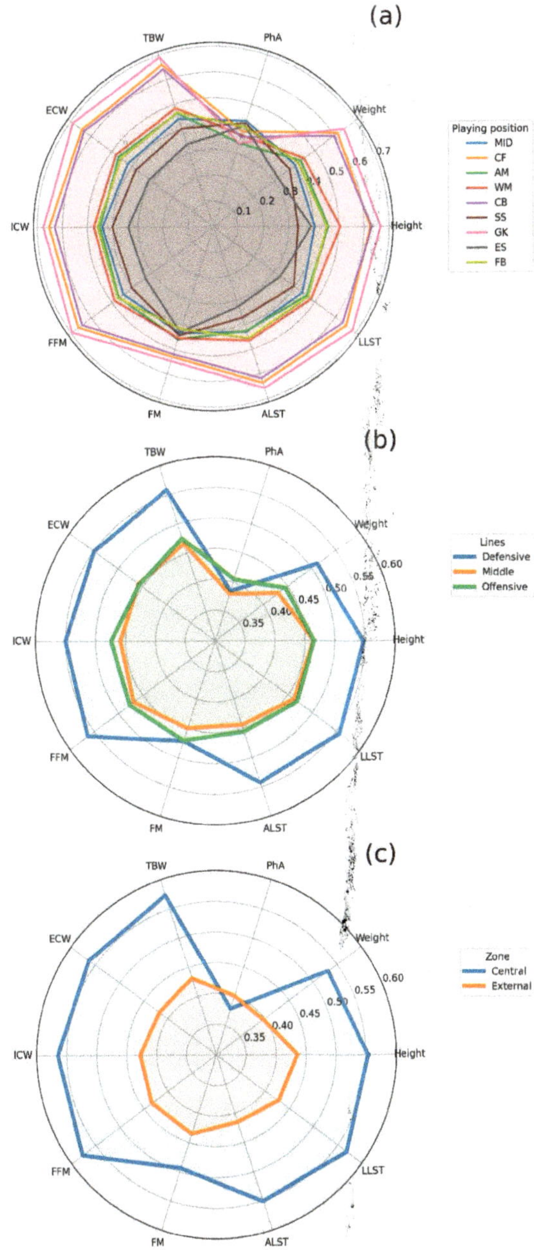

Figure 1. Radar chart with the normalized variables per playing position. (**a**) refers to playing position, (**b**) shows the playing lines, and (**c**) is linked to the pitch zone. Note: PhA = phase angle, TBW = total body water, ECW = extracellular water, ICW = intracellular water, FFM = fat-free mass, FM = fat mass, ALST = arm lean soft tissue, LLST = leg lean soft tissue, GK = goalkeeper, CB = central back, FB = fullback, MID = central midfielder, WM = wide midfielder, AM = attacking midfielder, SS = second striker, ES = external striker, CF = central forward. The features were normalized by min-max standard scaler on the entire dataset. The maximum value refers to 1, while the minimal one to 0.

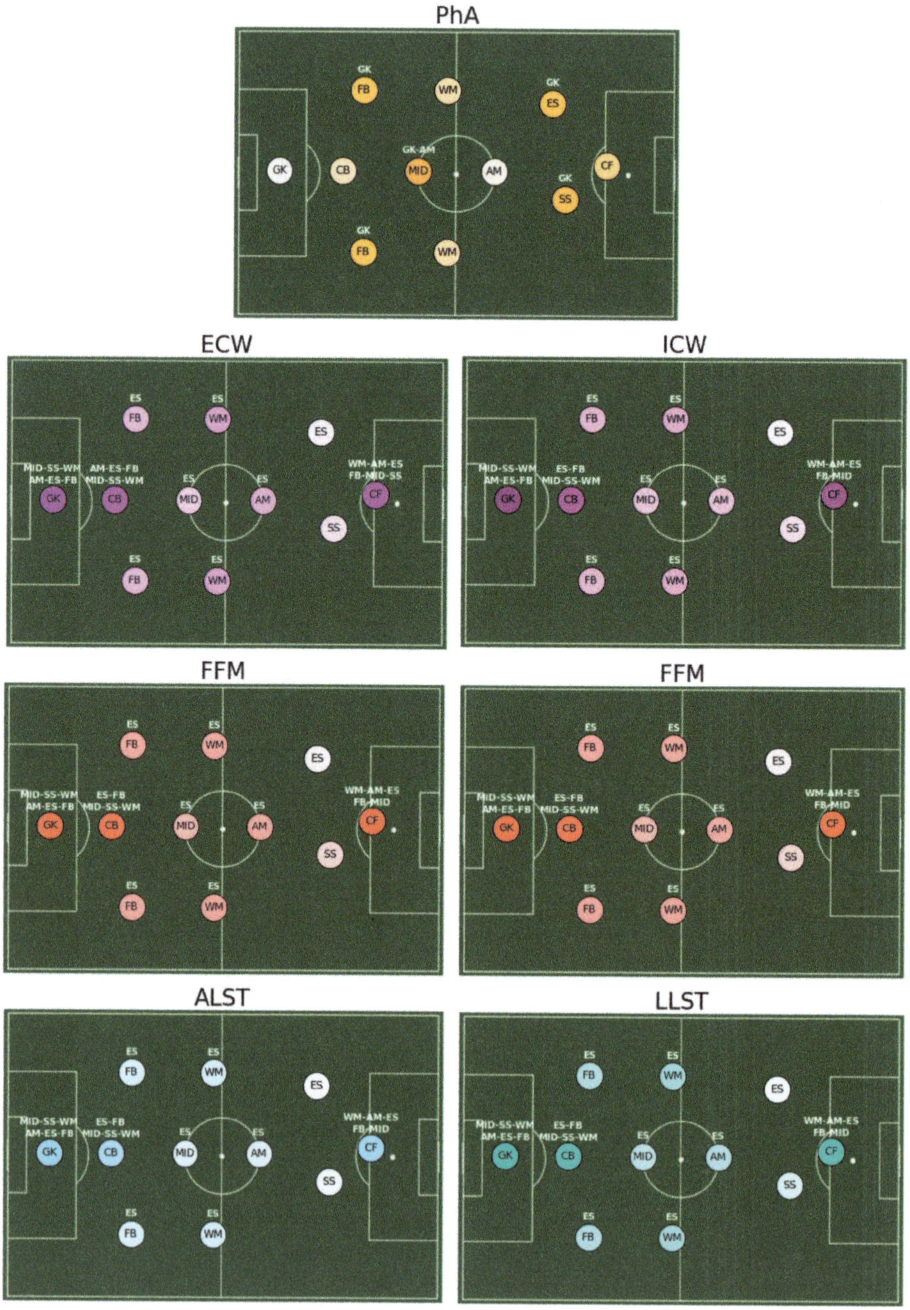

Figure 2. Differences between players' playing positions for PhA (phase angle), ECW (extracellular water), ICW (intracellular water), FFM (fat-free mass), FM (fat mass), ALST (arm lean soft tissue), LLST (leg lean soft tissue). Values increase with darker colors. GK = goalkeeper, CB = central back, FB = fullback, MID = central midfielder, WM = wide midfielder, AM = attacking midfielder, SS = second striker, ES = external strikers, CF = central forward. The darker the color of the dots is, the higher the values of the specific playing position is.

Tables 2 and 3 report the descriptive statistics of the players belonging to specific field lines (defensive, middle, and offensive) and zones (central and external). Except for PhA and fat mass (FM), players of the defensive line were significantly ($p < 0.05$) superior in all variables compared with middle and offensive linemen. Likewise, players of the central zone of the pitch (CBs, MIDs, SSs, and CFs) were superior ($p < 0.05$) in all variables than external players except for PhA.

Table 2. Descriptive statistics expressed as mean (standard deviation) and statistical analysis regarding the tactical lines. Statistical ($p < 0.05$) difference: ^{a} and ^{b} difference from middle and offensive.

Features	Defensive	Middle	Offensive
Height (cm) ^{a,b}	184.97 (4.92)	181.99 (4.91)	182.03 (6.77)
Body mass (kg) ^{a,b}	80.95 (5.33)	77.93 (5.36)	78.49 (7.08)
PhA (°)	8.06 (0.63)	8.04 (0.66)	8.16 (0.59)
TBW (L) ^{a,b}	51.25 (3.02)	49.43 (2.99)	49.61 (4.05)
ECW (L) ^{a,b}	20.16 (1.21)	19.47 (1.21)	19.45 (1.56)
ICW (L) ^{a,b}	31.09 (1.85)	29.97 (1.83)	30.16 (2.51)
FFM (Kg) ^{a,b}	70.38 (4.47)	67.69 (4.41)	67.92 (5.97)
FM (kg)	10.57 (2.20)	10.24 (2.00)	10.57 (2.34)
ALST (Kg) ^{a,b}	7.05 (0.64)	6.67 (0.59)	6.72 (0.83)
LLST (Kg) ^{a,b}	20.9 (1.50)	20.01 (1.46)	20.07 (1.99)

Note: PhA = phase angle, TBW = total body water, ECW = extracellular water, ICW = intracellular water, FFM = fat-free mass, FM = fat mass, ALST = arm lean soft tissue, LLST = leg lean soft tissue.

Table 3. Descriptive statistics expressed as mean (standard deviation) and statistical analysis regarding field zones.

Features	Central	External
Height (cm) *	185.16 (5.55)	180.97 (5.14)
Body mass (kg) *	81.68 (5.92)	76.70 (5.18)
PhA (°)	8.03 (0.68)	8.14 (0.56)
TBW (L) *	51.54 (3.29)	48.74 (3.06)
ECW (L) *	20.27 (1.28)	19.16 (1.23)
ICW (L) *	31.27 (2.05)	29.59 (1.87)
FFM (Kg) *	70.76 (4.85)	66.68 (4.54)
FM (kg) *	10.92 (2.40)	10.02 (1.86)
ALST (Kg) *	7.08 (0.69)	6.56 (0.63)
LLST (Kg) *	21.02 (1.62)	19.68 (1.53)

* Statistical ($p < 0.05$) difference. Note: PhA = phase angle, TBW = total body water, ECW = extracellular water, ICW = intracellular water, FFM = fat-free mass, FM = fat mass, ALST = arm lean soft tissue, LLST = leg lean soft tissue.

4. Discussion

The main findings of this study revealed that, along with anthropometry, different body composition profiles are identified by playing position in professional soccer players. From the current analysis, it emerged that GKs and CFs were the tallest and heaviest players, with no differences from each other. Specifically, GKs possess their own distinctive anthropometric and body composition characteristics in terms of ECW, ICW, FFM, FM, ALST, and LLST, especially compared to FB, MID, AM, WM, SS and ES. These characteristics are also largely shared by CFs.

GKs and CFs exhibited the highest values in both ALST and LLST along with FFM, while SS and ES presented the lowest. ALST and LLST are derived measures of skeletal muscle, identifying the largest non-adipose tissue component of an individual's body composition (Quinterio et al., 2009) [18]. Compared with outfield players, GKs regularly engage in additional resistance training for maintenance and growth of muscle mass [7], which would justify the higher ALST and LLST values. In turn, aside from performing the most high to very high intensity activity, CFs undergo the most contact situations, imposing pushing and pulling activities for both the upper and lower body [19]. It is likely that their specific need to be physically prepared would lead them to emphasize additional strength-related training compared with other field-based positions. This result supports the consistent link between the appendicular lean soft tissue of both the upper and lower body [20] in obtaining informative data on regional muscular mass.

If, on the one hand, GKs seem to exhibit much greater muscle mass in both upper and lower limbs, on the other hand, they are fatter [21,22] than other outfield players (e.g., FB, MID, ES) along with CBs and CFs. To the best extent of the authors' knowledge, this represents a novelty within the literature that should be investigated in depth. Similarly, Mala et al. (2017) [11] reported the highest values for FFM and FM in under-19 elite GKs, even though significant differences were observed only for FFM. Routinely, the weekly training loads accumulated by the outfield players are greater than GKs to influence their energy expenditure [7], and consequently, their percentage of fat. Separate discussion for CBs and CFs, whose FM levels might depend on other factors (e.g., specific duties on the pitch). For instance, extra mass, albeit inactive as fat tissue, may be an advantage in hand-to-hand actions commonly experienced by both CFs and CBs. Indeed, CFs often have to hold the ball and shield it while dueling with defensive linemen (e.g., CB) that seek to win the ball. Conversely, FBs were the leanest players, supporting their dynamically demanding role on the pitch.

ECW and ICW data represent additional sources of information to control for potential body composition changes closely linked to players' playing position and their on-field performance [23]. Enhanced cellular hydration (i.e., ICW increases) may be indicative of increased glycogen synthesis (because of the highly osmotic features of glycogen) that would promote anabolism via cellular swelling [24,25]. At this point, players might benefit from this condition from a muscular function point of view. In fact, ICW was previously observed as one of the best predictors for jumping height performance in male professional soccer players [23]. According to the present findings, between-role differences of both ECW and ICW collectively matched those of FFM, especially for GKs, CBs, and CFs, who reported the highest values. This result seems to reflect the anabolic adjustment via cellular swelling capable of stimulating pathways that could increase protein synthesis. As a consequence, muscular players would also exhibit high ICW and ECW, which is grounded in earlier associations of body water with upper-body strength levels in individual [26,27] and team sport athletes [28].

PhA was highest for MIDs compared with AMs and GKs, who had the lowest values. An athlete with a higher PhA value has a greater muscle mass and a higher cellular integrity [29], putting him/her at a greater advantage during explosive action [20]. However, results of ALST and LLST by GKs appear not supporting this. Of note, it is worth noting that PhA is also considered a prognostic marker of cell health due to its positive effect on physical activity [30]. The process through which physical activity acts on PhA appears to entail a variety of mechanisms, which manifest in a better integrity and functionality of the cell membrane, changes in intracellular composition, and enhanced tissue capacity [31]. If transferred into the real-world setting, it might be assumed that PhA can discriminate between players' physical activity profiles. In keeping, a moderate association between PhA and short-term maximal intensity efforts in soccer players [32] was found. For instance, this would reflect the match demand activities of MIDs versus GKs. Unfortunately, at present, this remains speculative due to the lack of evidence. Further research will have to establish whether the role of match-based physical activities linked to specific playing position is explained by PhA outcomes. This information would be relevant for the coaching staff when arranging ad hoc monitoring processes over the season.

An interesting side finding of this study was that players of middle and offensive lines presented different body composition profiles from defensive linemen, who were higher in stature, body mass, and indirect measures of muscle mass (e.g., ALST, LLST, FFM, ECW, ICW). It should be noted that the defensive line consists of FBs and CBs, who presented anthropometric profiles at odds. Although FBs were the leanest, the anthropometric and body composition characteristics of CBs made a substantial upward contribution in the differentiation against middle (e.g., MID) and offensive linemen (e.g., CF). Yet, although CFs present similar characteristics, ESs' data made a substantial downward contribution that provided outcomes for offensive linemen comparable with middle linemen. Moreover, outfield players competing within the central zones (e.g., CB, MID, AM, and CF) were taller, heavier, fatter, and more muscled than those of the external zones (i.e., FB, WM, ES, and SS). A likely explanation may be attributed to the fact that players in the central zones (in and outside the box or along the midfield) of the pitch perform within a crowded area in which collision, hand-to-hand duels, and tackles are on the agenda during a match. Altogether, these actions require specific anthropometric and body composition profiles that can be easily identifiable by the current results.

This study is not devoid of limitations. Potential factors that could influence body composition profiles, such as dietary habits, individual training regimens, or injury history, were not controlled. Future research should account for these additional factors to provide a more comprehensive understanding of the current findings. Furthermore, BIA equations are typically developed and validated on specific populations, often with limited diversity in terms of age, sex, ethnicity, and body composition characteristics. Thus, our results are exclusive to white players. This would introduce a potential ethnic bias and restricts the generalizability of our findings to individuals from other ethnic backgrounds.

5. Conclusions

This study disclosed different anthropometric and body composition profiles among playing positions in professional soccer players. In particular, the present findings showed that GKs and CFs were the tallest and heaviest players, with no differences from each other. Additionally, GKs and CFs, along with CBs, showed greater body muscularity and fatness at the same time, as opposed to the other roles. Of note, playing in the central zone of the pitch makes ball possession difficult due to the high density of players and the numerous hand-to-hand contacts. This supports the current side findings, in which players competing in the central zones (CB, MID, AM, SS, and CF) of the pitch and in the defensive line (CB and FB) presented the highest stature and body mass as well as the highest measures of muscle mass (e.g., ALST and LLST) and body fat (FM), increasing their efficacy during duels. Taken together, these findings may be of relevance for designing position-specific training programs that would help, for example, GKs and CFs to exploit their high level of muscle mass by focusing on additional strength- and power-based stimuli.

Supplementary Materials: The following supporting information can be downloaded at: https://www.mdpi.com/article/10.3390/jfmk8020080/s1.

Author Contributions: Conceptualization, T.B., A.R. and A.T.; methodology, T.B., F.G., G.M., G.P., C.O., M.S., F.M.I., R.D.V., S.G., R.C., P.R., M.L.M. and S.C.; formal analysis, T.B. and A.R.; data curation, T.B.; writing—original draft preparation, T.B., A.R. and A.T.; writing—review and editing, F.G., G.M., G.P., C.O., M.S., F.M.I., S.G., R.C., P.R., M.L.M. and S.C.; visualization, A.R.; supervision, F.M.I. and T.B. All authors have read and agreed to the published version of the manuscript.

Funding: This work is supported by the European Community's H2020 Program under the Funding Scheme H2020-INFRAIA-2019-1 Research Infrastructures Grant Agreement 871042, www.sobigdata.eu, SoBigData++: European Integrated Infrastructure for Social Mining and Big Data Analytics. The funders had no role in study design, data collection and analysis, decision to publish, or preparation of the manuscript.

Institutional Review Board Statement: The study was conducted in accordance with the Declaration of Helsinki, and approved by the Ethic committee, University of Milan, approval code: 32/16 of 16 November 2016.

Informed Consent Statement: Informed consent was obtained from all subjects involved in the study.

Data Availability Statement: All the relevant data are provided in the text and Supplementary Materials.

Conflicts of Interest: The authors declare no conflict of interest.

References

1. Stølen, T.; Chamari, K.; Castagna, C.; Wisløff, U. Physiology of Soccer: An Update. *Sports Med.* **2005**, *35*, 501–536. [CrossRef]
2. Formenti, D.; Rossi, A.; Bongiovanni, T.; Campa, F.; Cavaggioni, L.; Alberti, G.; Longo, S.; Trecroci, A. Effects of Non-Sport-Specific Versus Sport-Specific Training on Physical Performance and Perceptual Response in Young Football Players. *Int. J. Environ. Res. Public Health* **2021**, *18*, 1962. [CrossRef]
3. Gil, S.M.; Gil, J.; Ruiz, F.; Irazusta, A.; Irazusta, J. Physiological and Anthropometric Characteristics of Young Soccer Players According to Their Playing Position: Relevance for the Selection Process. *J. Strength Cond. Res.* **2007**, *21*, 438–445. [CrossRef]
4. Sutton, L.; Scott, M.; Wallace, J.; Reilly, T. Body Composition of English Premier League Soccer Players: Influence of Playing Position, International Status, and Ethnicity. *J. Sports Sci.* **2009**, *27*, 1019–1026. [CrossRef]
5. Bradley, P.S.; Di Mascio, M.; Peart, D.; Olsen, P.; Sheldon, B. High-Intensity Activity Profiles of Elite Soccer Players at Different Performance Levels. *J. Strength Cond. Res.* **2010**, *24*, 2343–2351. [CrossRef] [PubMed]
6. Di Salvo, V.; Benito, P.J.; Calderón, F.J.; Di Salvo, M.; Pigozzi, F. Activity Profile of Elite Goalkeepers during Football Match-Play. *J. Sports Med. Phys. Fit.* **2008**, *48*, 443–446.
7. Anderson, L.; Close, G.L.; Morgans, R.; Hambly, C.; Speakman, J.R.; Drust, B.; Morton, J.P. Assessment of Energy Expenditure of a Professional Goalkeeper From the English Premier League Using the Doubly Labeled Water Method. *Int. J. Sports Physiol. Perform.* **2019**, *14*, 681–684. [CrossRef]
8. Di Salvo, V.; Gregson, W.; Atkinson, G.; Tordoff, P.; Drust, B. Analysis of High Intensity Activity in Premier League Soccer. *Int. J. Sports Med.* **2009**, *30*, 205–212. [CrossRef]
9. Bush, M.D.; Archer, D.T.; Hogg, R.; Bradley, P.S. Factors Influencing Physical and Technical Variability in the English Premier League. *Int. J. Sports Physiol. Perform.* **2015**, *10*, 865–872. [CrossRef] [PubMed]
10. Bush, M.; Barnes, C.; Archer, D.T.; Hogg, B.; Bradley, P.S. Evolution of Match Performance Parameters for Various Playing Positions in the English Premier League. *Hum. Mov. Sci.* **2015**, *39*, 1–11. [CrossRef] [PubMed]
11. Mala, L.; Maly, T.; Zahalka, F. Body Composition Differences in Elite Young Soccer Players Based on Playing Position. *Anthropologist* **2017**, *27*, 17–22. [CrossRef]
12. Slimani, M.; Znazen, H.; Hammami, A.; Bragazzi, N.L. Comparison of Body Fat Percentage of Male Soccer Players of Different Competitive Levels, Playing Positions and Age Groups: A Meta-Analysis. *J. Sports Med. Phys. Fit.* **2018**, *58*, 857–866. [CrossRef]
13. Campa, F.; Bongiovanni, T.; Trecroci, A.; Rossi, A.; Greco, G.; Pasta, G.; Coratella, G. Effects of the COVID-19 Lockdown on Body Composition and Bioelectrical Phase Angle in Serie A Soccer Players: A Comparison of Two Consecutive Seasons. *Biology* **2021**, *10*, 1175. [CrossRef] [PubMed]
14. Campa, F.; Bongiovanni, T.; Matias, C.N.; Genovesi, F.; Trecroci, A.; Rossi, A.; Iaia, F.M.; Alberti, G.; Pasta, G.; Toselli, S. A New Strategy to Integrate Heath–Carter Somatotype Assessment with Bioelectrical Impedance Analysis in Elite Soccer Players. *Sports* **2020**, *8*, 142. [CrossRef] [PubMed]
15. Bongiovanni, T.; Rossi, A.; Trecroci, A.; Martera, G.; Iaia, F.M.; Alberti, G.; Pasta, G.; Lacome, M. Regional Bioelectrical Phase Angle Is More Informative than Whole-Body Phase Angle for Monitoring Neuromuscular Performance: A Pilot Study in Elite Young Soccer Players. *Sports* **2022**, *10*, 66. [CrossRef] [PubMed]
16. Bongiovanni, T.; Mascherini, G.; Genovesi, F.; Pasta, G.; Iaia, F.M.; Trecroci, A.; Ventimiglia, M.; Alberti, G.; Campa, F. Bioimpedance Vector References Need to Be Period-Specific for Assessing Body Composition and Cellular Health in Elite Soccer Players: A Brief Report. *J. Funct. Morphol. Kinesiol.* **2020**, *5*, 73. [CrossRef]
17. Matias, C.N.; Campa, F.; Santos, D.A.; Lukaski, H.; Sardinha, L.B.; Silva, A.M. Fat-Free Mass Bioelectrical Impedance Analysis Predictive Equation for Athletes Using a 4-Compartment Model. *Int. J. Sports Med.* **2021**, *42*, 27–32. [CrossRef]

18. Quintero, A.J.; Wright, V.J.; Fu, F.H.; Huard, J. Stem Cells for the Treatment of Skeletal Muscle Injury. *Clin. Sports Med.* **2009**, *28*, 1–11. [CrossRef] [PubMed]
19. Bloomfield, J.; Polman, R.; O'Donoghue, P. Physical Demands of Different Positions in FA Premier League Soccer. *J. Sports Sci. Med.* **2007**, *6*, 63–70.
20. Bongiovanni, T.; Trecroci, A.; Rossi, A.; Iaia, F.M.; Pasta, G.; Campa, F. Association between Change in Regional Phase Angle and Jump Performance: A Pilot Study in Serie A Soccer Players. *Eur. J. Investig. Health Psychol. Educ.* **2021**, *11*, 860–865. [CrossRef]
21. Gil, S.; Ruiz, F.; Irazusta, A.; Gil, J.; Irazusta, J. Selection of Young Soccer Players in Terms of Anthropometric and Physiological Factors. *J. Sports Med. Phys. Fit.* **2007**, *47*, 25–32.
22. Sporis, G.; Jukic, I.; Ostojic, S.M.; Milanovic, D. Fitness Profiling in Soccer: Physical and Physiologic Characteristics of Elite Players. *J. Strength Cond. Res.* **2009**, *23*, 1947–1953. [CrossRef] [PubMed]
23. Bongiovanni, T.; Tinsley, G.; Martera, G.; Orlandi, C.; Genovesi, F.; Puleo, G.; Rossi, A.; Trecroci, A. Regional Lean Soft Tissue and Intracellular Water Are Associated with Changes in Lower-Body Neuromuscular Performance: A Pilot Study in Elite Soccer Players. *Eur. J. Investig. Health Psychol. Educ.* **2022**, *12*, 882–892. [CrossRef] [PubMed]
24. Häussinger, D.; Roth, E.; Lang, F.; Gerok, W. Cellular Hydration State: An Important Determinant of Protein Catabolism in Health and Disease. *Lancet* **1993**, *341*, 1330–1332. [CrossRef] [PubMed]
25. Lang, F.; Busch, G.L.; Ritter, M.; Völkl, H.; Waldegger, S.; Gulbins, E.; Häussinger, D. Functional Significance of Cell Volume Regulatory Mechanisms. *Physiol. Rev.* **1998**, *78*, 247–306. [CrossRef] [PubMed]
26. Silva, A.M.; Fields, D.A.; Heymsfield, S.B.; Sardinha, L.B. Body Composition and Power Changes in Elite Judo Athletes. *Int. J. Sports Med.* **2010**, *31*, 737–741. [CrossRef]
27. Silva, A.M.; Fields, D.A.; Heymsfield, S.B.; Sardinha, L.B. Relationship between Changes in Total-Body Water and Fluid Distribution with Maximal Forearm Strength in Elite Judo Athletes. *J. Strength Cond. Res.* **2011**, *25*, 2488–2495. [CrossRef]
28. Silva, A.M.; Matias, C.N.; Santos, D.A.; Rocha, P.M.; Minderico, C.S.; Sardinha, L.B. Increases in Intracellular Water Explain Strength and Power Improvements over a Season. *Int. J. Sports Med.* **2014**, *35*, 1101–1105. [CrossRef]
29. Lukaski, H.C.; Piccoli, A. Bioelectrical Impedance Vector Analysis for Assessment of Hydration in Physiological States and Clinical Conditions. In *Handbook of Anthropometry: Physical Measures of Human Form in Health and Disease*; Preedy, V.R., Ed.; Springer: New York, NY, USA, 2012; pp. 287–305, ISBN 978-1-4419-1788-1.
30. Mundstock, E.; Amaral, M.A.; Baptista, R.R.; Sarria, E.E.; Dos Santos, R.R.G.; Filho, A.D.; Rodrigues, C.A.S.; Forte, G.C.; Castro, L.; Padoin, A.V.; et al. Association between Phase Angle from Bioelectrical Impedance Analysis and Level of Physical Activity: Systematic Review and Meta-Analysis. *Clin. Nutr.* **2019**, *38*, 1504–1510. [CrossRef] [PubMed]
31. Barbosa-Silva, M.C.G.; Barros, A.J. Bioelectric impedance and individual characteristics as prognostic factors for post-operative complications. *Clin. Nutr.* **2005**, *24*, 830–838. [CrossRef]
32. Nabuco, H.C.G.; Silva, A.M.; Sardinha, L.B.; Rodrigues, F.B.; Tomeleri, C.M.; Ravagnani, F.C.P.; Cyrino, E.S.; Ravagnani, C.F.C. Phase Angle Is Moderately Associated with Short-Term Maximal Intensity Efforts in Soccer Players. *Int. J. Sports Med.* **2019**, *40*, 739–743. [CrossRef]

Journal of
Functional Morphology and Kinesiology

MDPI

Article

Evaluation of the Effectiveness of a Nordic Walking and a Resistance Indoor Training Program: Anthropometric, Body Composition, and Functional Parameters in the Middle-Aged Population

Alessia Grigoletto [1], Mario Mauro [2,*] and Stefania Toselli [2,*]

[1] Department of Biomedical and Neuromotor Sciences, University of Bologna, Via Selmi 3, 40126 Bologna, Italy; alessia.grigoletto2@unibo.it
[2] Department for Life Quality Studies, University of Bologna, 47921 Rimini, Italy
* Correspondence: mario.mauro4@unibo.it (M.M.); stefania.toselli@unibo.it (S.T.)

Abstract: Sedentary behaviors are increasing in the population, so strategies for the increment of physical activity levels are needed. The use of green space seems to be a valid support to be more active. The present study aimed to compare the effectiveness of a period of outdoor training (Nordic walking (NW)) with indoor resistance training (GYM) in a nonclinical population based on anthropometric characteristics, body composition, and functional parameters. This study was conducted on 102 participants (77 middle-aged people performed NW and 25 performed indoor training). Participants were measured twice: at baseline and after three months. Anthropometric measurements (weight, BMI, skinfolds, perimeters), body composition, bioelectrical impedance, vectorial analysis (BIA and BIVA), and physical tests were carried out. A two-way repeated measures analysis of variance (ANOVA) was performed to evaluate the effect of the treatments, groups, and sexes. There were several intervention effects linked to a decrease in fat parameters (such as skinfolds, fat mass, and percentage of fat mass). Considering the type of intervention, NW showed a higher increase in muscle mass and a higher decrease in fat parameters than the GYM group. In conclusion, the two types of training could represent a good way to remain active and prevent sedentary behaviors.

Keywords: anthropometric characteristics; body composition; indoor training; Nordic walking; outdoor training; physical activity; physical test

Citation: Grigoletto, A.; Mauro, M.; Toselli, S. Evaluation of the Effectiveness of a Nordic Walking and a Resistance Indoor Training Program: Anthropometric, Body Composition, and Functional Parameters in the Middle-Aged Population. *J. Funct. Morphol. Kinesiol.* **2023**, *8*, 79. https://doi.org/10.3390/jfmk8020079

Academic Editors: Olivier Hue and Abdul Rashid Aziz

Received: 13 April 2023
Revised: 13 May 2023
Accepted: 13 June 2023
Published: 15 June 2023

1. Introduction

Physical inactivity is one of the most relevant sedentary behaviors, which causes massive effects on the public health global economy [1–3]. Participation in regular physical activity (PA) can significantly reduce the risk of developing cardiovascular disease, stroke, sarcopenic obesity, cancers, and diabetes, and improve mental health outcomes, such as depression and anxiety [4,5]. In addition, participation in PA is useful for maintaining and slowing physiological age predicated on the decline of the musculoskeletal system [6,7]. While the importance of PA is well-established, a significant proportion of the adult population remains inactive [8]. In Italy, despite the evidence, only 31% of adults declared to have a physically active job [9]. Di Bonaventura et al. (2018) reported that 12.89% of Italian people were obese (9.49% were obese class I, 2.28% were obese class II, and 1.12% were obese class III) [10]. Several factors influence participation in PA, and greater attention has recently focused on the role of the environment in promoting PA [11,12]. Green space seems to be an optimal environment for exercise, due to the safety, accessibility, and attractiveness of these places [13]. Several observational studies have searched to establish whether a relationship between green space and PA exists [11]. However, studies in this area are still lacking and are far from conclusive [14]. A systematic review demonstrated the paucity of high-quality evidence in the studies carried out so far and the necessity for further research in this area [12]. Thus, presently, it is not possible to establish if PA carried out in green spaces is more effective than indoor PA in producing physical, physiological, and motor changes in participants.

To achieve this purpose, the analysis of body composition can provide useful information since it is an indicator of health, nutritional status, and functional capacity [15]. In the last years, the analysis of body composition by bioelectrical impedance analysis (BIA) has become one of the most used methods, due to its easy use, precision, and accuracy [16–18]. By employing the bioimpedance-based predictive equation, it is possible to estimate body composition parameters, such as fat mass, muscle mass, and body water, and monitor their change [19]. By the qualitative approach, it is also possible to estimate body composition through the raw bioimpedance parameters (resistance (R) and reactance (Xc)) as a point on the R–Xc graph, in which length and slope are considered. The vector slope indicates the extracellular/intracellular (ECW/ICW) ratio and the integrity of the cell membrane [19,20]. In addition, some studies have shown how the phase angle (PhA), which is an indicator of health status, can be influenced and modulated by exercise [21–23]. An inverse relationship between PhA and inflammatory biomarkers [21] and a positive association with cellular health has been reported [22,23].

Body composition improvements are important aspects to take into account when we try to identify what could be the best type of activity for the middle-aged population. Performing PA in green urban spaces has several important benefits, but usually, it is performed with lower intensity than indoor PA. For this reason, we decided to compare indoor and outdoor PA performed with the same intensity to better understand if one could have a greater impact on anthropometric and body composition characteristics.

To our knowledge, no studies compare the effectiveness of indoor and outdoor PA on body composition and physical parameters in Italy. Nordic walking (NW) is an easy type of PA that is usually proposed for the clinical population and the elderly, but that also shows several potential benefits for nonclinical populations [24]. Resistance training is a kind of PA that can maintain good health conditions and reverse the adverse effects of ageing on cellular integrity and function. Both these kinds of PA are usually suggested for the middle-aged population to remain active. For this reason, the present study aimed to evaluate the efficacy of a period of three months of training outdoors (in particular, NW) and in GYM (resistance training) environments on a healthy middle-aged population.

2. Materials and Methods

2.1. Study Design and Participants

This is an intervention study design that comprehended 3 months of PA (NW as outdoor PA and resistance training as indoor PA) and two measurements (at baseline and after the training program). Recruitment occurred thanks to two sports society: "Nordic Walking Italy", specifically their headquarters in Venice, and "Arca", based in Mirano (VE). The two sports societies made announcements to recruit people to participate in their normal activities, and they also explained the possibility of participating in the present study. To increase participation and adherence in the study, each adult could select the NW or GYM activity. Nordic Walking Italy conducts activities throughout the province of Venice, in city parks, along the banks, and always in the open air. They manage different walking groups in Mestre, Marghera, Spinea, and Martellago. Conversely, Arca is based in Mirano (VE) and conducts activities in the school gym of the municipality. The exclusion criteria were (a) have a chronic disabling disease, being bedridden, institutionalized, or hospitalized, (b) not being independently mobile, i.e., not requiring human assistance or the aid of devices such as crutches, walkers, etc., and (c) having amputations, pacemakers, or the presence of a chronic metabolic disease.

Before starting the participants' enrollment, the sample size estimation for the repeated measures ANOVA F test for between–within groups with a Greenhouse–Geisser correction was assessed. The study parameters included were as follows: $\alpha = 0.05$, $1 - \beta = 0.80$, number of groups = 2, number of repeated measures = 2, between–within variance explained = 0.05, correlation = 0.25, and error variance = 2; the estimated sample size was 120. After a preliminary explanation of the study protocol, a total of 135 participants were enrolled in the study. Fifteen participants did not meet the inclusion criteria and were excluded before the protocol began (Figure 1). Three adults who chose NW and fifteen people who preferred GYM activities did not complete the period of training, so they were excluded from the study. Therefore, the sample was finally composed of 102 participants who performed both the measurements (before and after the training period). NW participants numbered 77, and the GYM group was composed of 25 people. All participants signed an informed consent to participate in the study. The study was approved by the Bioethics Committee of the University of Bologna (prot. N. 022254).

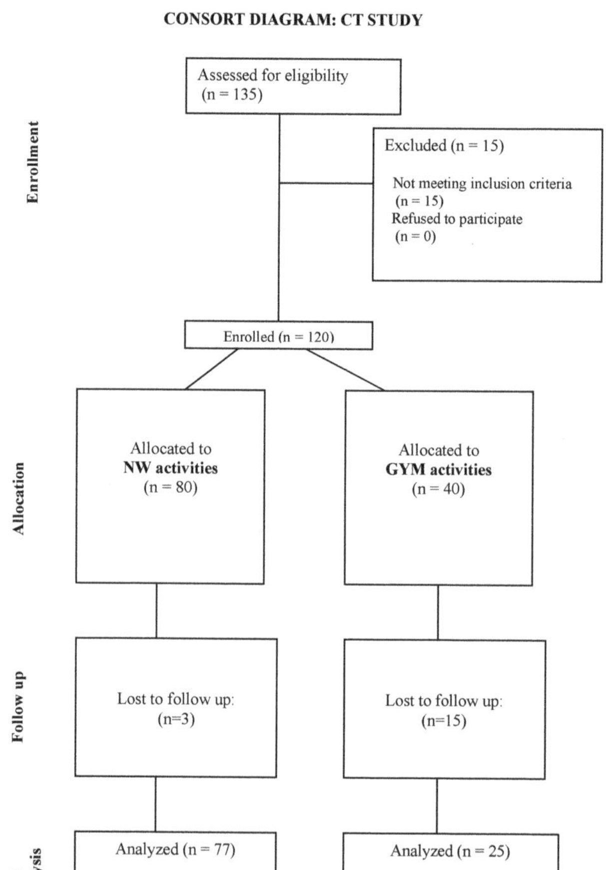

Figure 1. Participant flowchart.

2.2. Intervention Training Programs

Participants were engaged in two training sessions of about 60 min each, two times a week. Every training session was composed of 10 min of warm-up, 45 min of the main part, and 5 min of stretching exercise. For the NW training, three instructors followed the groups in different parks, proposing the same kind of training to the different groups, with the same kind of intensity. For the GYM training, the same instructors followed the group and proposed several resistance exercises. For both the NW and GYM groups, instructors proposed 15 min of upper limb exercises and 10 min of core and stability exercises. In the NW training, both upper limb and core exercises were performed with body weight resistance, during walking (upper limb) or in a lying position (core). The upper limb exercises were side and front risers, rows, intra and extra rotations for the shoulders, and military presses. The core exercises included different versions of planks, crunches, and sit ups. Each exercise was repeated for 45 s, with a 15-s rest, two times. For the remaining 20 min of the main part, the NW group performed walking exercises at various speeds and inclinations, while the GYM group performed lower-limb resistance exercises, such as squats, glute bridges, rear and side lunges, and deadlifts with one or two legs. Each exercise was repeated for 45 s, with a 15-s rest, two times. All the resistance exercises were executed with elastic bands of different resistances represented by colors (red, yellow, green, blue, and black).

To control the training intensity, instructors taught the participants to use the rating of perceived exertion scale (RPE, CR-10). Instructors collected participants' RPE before, during, and at the end of the training. The intensity level was set from 5 to up to 8 on the RPE scale. RPE before exercises was detected to ensure that each participant was able to perform the training with no risk. During exercise, RPE was used to induce desired stimuli; when a participant perceived an exertion lower than 5, instructors encouraged them to increase the exercise intensity (speed, inclination, or band), whereas if it was higher than 8, the participant was directed to slow down. Thirty minutes after the end of a training session, RPE was recorded to calculate the training load (TL = RPE $\times$ minutes of training) [25].

2.3. Anthropometric Characteristics

Participants' anthropometric measures were recorded twice: at the baseline and after the three months of training. Height was recorded with a standing stadiometer (GPM, Steckborn, Switzerland), while a calibrated electronic scale (Seca, Basel, Switzerland) was used to measure the body mass. Body mass index (BMI) was calculated as the ratio of body weight to height squared (kg/m^2), and the WHO cutoff was used to estimate the weight status of the subjects: a BMI value less than 18.5 was classified as underweight, from 18.5 to 24.9 was considered normal weight, from 25 to 29.9 was overweight, and more than 30 was classified as obese [26]. In addition, circumference (relaxed and contracted arm, waist, hip, and calf) and skinfold (biceps, triceps, subscapular, suprailiac, supraspinale, lateral, and medial calf) measurements were carried out. Circumferences were taken using a nonstretchable tape measure (GPM, Steckborn Switzerland), and skinfolds were measured with a skinfold caliper (Lange, Beta Technology, Cambridge, MD, USA). The total upper arm and calf area, upper arm and calf muscle area, and upper arm and calf area were calculated [27]. Body density was calculated using the Durnin et al. equations, and then body composition parameters were estimated using Siri's converting equation [24,28]. All the anthropometric measurements were carried out by the same operator, specifically trained according to a standardized protocol [29–31].

2.4. Body Composition

The impedance measurements were performed with a bioimpedance analyzer (BIA 101 Anniversary, Akern, Florence, Italy) at a frequency of 50 kHz. The accuracy of the BIA instrument was validated before each test session, following the manufacturer's instructions. The participants were assessed in the supine position with legs abducted 45° compared to the median line of the body and arms abducted 30° from the trunk. After cleansing the skin with alcohol, two electrodes were placed five centimeters apart from each other on the right hand and two on the right foot. Participants were instructed to abstain from food and liquids for at least four hours before the test, to urinate about 30 min before the measures, to not consume alcoholic beverages for at least 48 h, and to avoid the use of diuretics at least seven days before each assessment. Vector length was calculated as (adjusted R2 + adjusted Xc2) 0.5 and PhA as the arctangent of (Xc/R) × (180°/π). Bioimpedance vector analysis was carried out using the BIVA method, normalizing the R and Xc parameters for height (h) in meters. Bioelectrical-specific values for women were used as a reference to build the tolerance ellipses on the R–Xc graph [32]. R, Xc, and PhA were plotted in the BIVA as a vector within a specific tolerance ellipse (specific profile for sex and age); this allowed the evaluation of soft tissue through patterns based on percentiles of their electrical characteristics [33]. A BIVA vector that falls in the 50% tolerance ellipse represents a normal tissue impedance, while a vector in the 75% tolerance ellipse displays an abnormal tissue impedance. BIVA outcomes could be analyzed through the vector direction to the y and x-axis. Horizontal displacement means changes in soft tissue mass (less soft tissue to the right pole and more soft tissue to the left pole); vertical displacements show changes in the hydration of the tissue (hyperhydration in the short vectors and dehydration in the long vectors) [33].

2.5. Physical Test

Three physical tests were performed by all participants. To avoid any confounding effect of time of day [34], all test sessions were performed in the morning, both at the baseline and after three months.

To evaluate the strength of the hands, a dynamometer (Takei Scientific Instrument Co., Niigata City, Japan) was used both for the right and left handgrip. Participants were in a sitting position at a 90-degree flexion of their elbow and performed three trials with a 1 min rest period between each test. The highest value of all three measurements was used for analysis.

A chair-stand test (squat test) was executed to assess the strength and endurance of the lower limbs. Every test was preceded by an explanation and demonstration of the test. People were allowed one practice trial before the actual measurements. The same standard chair without armrests was used for all the participants. Participants were instructed to sit in the middle of the chair, back straight, feet approximately shoulder-width apart, and placed on the floor at an angle slightly back from the knees, with one foot slightly in front of the other to help maintain balance when standing. The instructions to participants were to stand up and sit down again as many times as possible for 30 s. Participants were encouraged to continue to sit and stand throughout the test. The number of repetitions was recorded, and it represented the unit for this measure [35].

The 6-Minute Walking Test is a simple test to measure exercise capacity [36]. It was explained that the participants should have to walk for six minutes, and they were instructed to follow their gait and to slow down or stop if they became fatigued, but to resume once able. Each time the subject passed the starting position a lap was recorded. Using an even-toned encouraging phrase, the time remaining in the test was reported to the participants at one-minute intervals. The timer was not stopped if the participants needed to rest. Once the six minutes concluded, the participants were instructed to stop and remain stationary while the endpoint was marked. Once marked, the total distance walked was calculated in meters [37].

2.6. Statistical Analysis

The analysis was performed with Stata software for Windows 10, version 17 (publisher: StataCorp, 2021. Stata Statistical Software: Release 17. College Station, TX, USA, StataCorp LP). Descriptive analyses were performed, and each result was reported as the variable mean ± standard deviation (SD) at two different times (baseline and after three months of PA). To check the normal distribution of the variables, a Shapiro–Wilk test was carried out. A transformation function (natural logarithm) was applied to reduce curve skewness if variable data did not distribute as a Gaussian curve. A two-way repeated measures analysis of variance (ANOVA) was computed to compare groups, considering treatment, time, and sex effects. To meet the GLM sphericity assumption, a Greenhouse–Geisser correction was then applied. A Hotelling's test was performed to observe eventual differences in the BIVA representation.

Statistical significance was set at $p < 0.05$.

Finally, the statistical power achieved was calculated with the sample size = 102, number of groups = 2, number of repeated measures = 2, between–within variance explained = 0.05, error variance = 1.5, and correlation = 0.2: $1 - \beta = 0.823$.

3. Results

3.1. Training Load of the Participants

Table 1 reports the TL of the participants in the two different training programs.

Table 1. TL of the participants in the two different training programs.

Week	Day	NW (Mean ± SD)	GYM (Mean ± SD)	F	p
Week 1	Day 1	395.36 ± 58.09	402.50 ± 57.28	0.02	0.052
	Day 2	387.86 ± 51.12	397.50 ± 55.42	0.25	0.085
Week 2	Day 1	390.00 ± 67.69	382.50 ± 55.42	0.56	0.753
	Day 2	371.79 ± 56.54	397.50 ± 58.18	1.46	0.652
Week 3	Day 1	381.43 ± 50.43	367.40 ± 36.74	4.46	0.123
	Day 2	397.50 ± 63.25	405.00 ± 56.65	0.05	0.257
Week 4	Day 1	395.36 ± 63.47	395.00 ± 63.59	1.26	0.951
	Day 2	394.29 ± 64.58	397.50 ± 60.81	1.36	0.746
Week 5	Day 1	401.79 ± 57.12	382.30 ± 55.42	2.65	0.563
	Day 2	397.50 ± 56.70	397.20 ± 57.36	0.08	0.452
Week 6	Day 1	380.36 ± 51.52	397.80 ± 60.81	3.20	0.874
	Day 2	401.79 ± 57.12	405.00 ± 55.66	0.07	0.658
Week 7	Day 1	394.29 ± 64.58	395.00 ± 65.39	5.20	0.887
	Day 2	397.50 ± 65.70	395.30 ± 68.10	3.21	0.632
Week 8	Day 1	380.86 ± 52.51	372.50 ± 43.26	2.03	0.358
	Day 2	409.71 ± 57.12	406.00 ± 56.65	1.02	0.742
Week 9	Day 1	380.36 ± 25.16	382.50 ± 55.42	4.25	0.896
	Day 2	407.91 ± 67.50	390.00 ± 30.65	0.02	0.554
Week 10	Day 1	397.50 ± 66.50	405.50 ± 56.58	0.04	0.665
	Day 2	394.27 ± 64.58	397.56 ± 55.42	0.10	0.578
Week 11	Day 1	380.36 ± 51.52	382.50 ± 55.58	3.89	0.832
	Day 2	397.00 ± 57.60	395.63 ± 63.59	4.02	0.752
Week 12	Day 1	401.79 ± 57.12	395.00 ± 59.63	0.66	0.348
	Day 2	394.29 ± 64.58	397.50 ± 60.81	0.59	0.658

There were no significant differences between the TL of the two training programs.

3.2. Baseline Characteristics of the Participants

The largest sample was comprised of females (70, 69.3%) with a mean age of 56.96 ± 6.64 years. Men who participated in the study (31, 36.7%) were older than women (61.30 ± 8.37 years).

Table 2 reports the characteristics of the sample divided by the kind of training performed (NW or GYM activity).

Table 2. Anthropometric characteristics, body composition, and physical test values for groups.

Var	♀ (n = 70) GYM (n = 14) Pre Mean (SD)	♀ GYM (n = 14) Post Mean (SD)	♀ NW (n = 56) Pre Mean (SD)	♀ NW (n = 56) Post Mean (SD)	♂ (n = 31) GYM (n = 10) Pre Mean (SD)	♂ GYM (n = 10) Post Mean (SD)	♂ NW (n = 21) Pre Mean (SD)	♂ NW (n = 21) Post Mean (SD)	ANOVA Comparisons Intervention Effect F	Intervention Effect p	Type Effect F	Type Effect p	Sex Effect F	Sex Effect p
Weight, kg	65.65 (11.69)	65.34 (12.05)	59.88 (10.69)	63.41 (14.00)	84.58 (8.99)	83.86 (7.53)	78.40 (7.06)	76.20 (7.80)	0.01	0.937	4.14	0.045 *	0.06	0.799
BMI, kg/m^2	24.01 (3.81)	23.80 (3.89)	22.54 (3.57)	23.96 (5.63)	27.19 (3.02)	26.97 (2.81)	24.99 (1.66)	24.29 (1.98)	0.02	0.881	2.61	0.109	1.42	0.236
Triceps SK, mm	20.55 (3.43)	19.29 (3.85)	16.07 (3.87)	16.36 (3.86)	16.81 (4.86)	15.90 (4.31)	9.80 (5.33)	11.60 (3.34)	2.53	0.115	31.24	<0.001 *	1.59	0.211
Biceps SK, mm	12.57 (4.62)	11.25 (4.40)	14.64 (5.30)	13.29 (3.75)	10.81 (3.09)	10.62 (4.09)	10.00 (3.86)	9.70 (3.33)	6.82	0.01 *	1.1	0.296	1.02	0.315
Subscapular SK, mm	17.00 (6.54)	14.55 (4.66)	15.00 (3.09)	15.79 (3.26)	20.9 (4.65)	17.14 (4.52)	15.30 (3.43)	16.70 (2.75)	17.62	<0.001 *	1.68	0.198	0.02	0.876
Supraspinal SK, mm	19.05 (6.40)	18.32 (5.34)	18.71 (4.89)	18.64 (4.99)	22.81 (4.88)	22.00 (4.51)	21.30 (4.16)	20.50 (4.09)	2.3	0.133	0.25	0.621	2.3	0.133
Suprailiac SK, mm	18.43 (6.07)	16.89 (5.98)	18.86 (5.32)	17.5 (4.72)	21.57 (5.86)	19.52 (6.78)	20.60 (5.10)	18.50 (4.67)	12.15	<0.001 *	0	0.966	0.64	0.427
Arm relaxed circ, cm	28.38 (3.55)	28.96 (3.42)	25.70 (3.13)	26.08 (3.08)	30.08 (1.97)	30.13 (3.48)	28.83 (2.21)	29.23 (2.03)	4.78	0.031 *	8.79	<0.01 *	0.14	0.712
Arm stretched circ, cm	29.44 (3.42)	29.54 (3.40)	26.23 (3.14)	26.60 (3.12)	32.09 (2.42)	31.87 (2.46)	30.26 (2.11)	28.65 (7.01)	0.16	0.689	15	<0.001 *	0	0.973
Waist circ, cm	79.66 (11.58)	78.48 (12.17)	80.49 (8.27)	78.79 (6.98)	96.56 (9.53)	95.14 (9.42)	95.69 (6.07)	94.85 (4.65)	4.09	0.046 *	0	0.953	1.04	0.309
Hip circ, cm	101.94 (8.69)	100.72 (8.78)	98.53 (7.28)	97.45 (6.17)	104.68 (4.52)	104.46 (4.44)	100.69 (5.29)	99.84 (4.15)	9.37	<0.01 *	4.68	0.033 *	0	0.981
Medial calf SK, mm	17.63 (3.44)	16.58 (6.00)	17.88 (7.24)	15.43 (5.17)	12.57 (4.32)	12.68 (7.00)	11.30 (2.87)	12.00 (1.05)	2.2	0.141	0.41	0.522	0.56	0.458
Lateral calf SK, mm	17.54 (3.61)	16.76 (6.10)	13.64 (4.65)	13.57 (3.99)	12.57 (4.32)	12.68 (7.00)	9.50 (2.27)	10.00 (2.11)	0.47	0.493	11.71	<0.001 *	3.01	0.086
Calf circ, cm	36.58 (2.62)	35.60 (5.08)	31.43 (7.10)	34.14 (3.41)	38.15 (3.02)	37.10 (6.40)	36.75 (1.92)	36.92 (1.76)	0.48	0.488	8.18	<0.01 *	0.04	0.84
Resistance, Ω	523.15 (73.63)	510.87 (66.39)	579.56 (78.25)	555.60 (82.39)	488.03 (52.69)	473.74 (74.65)	452.00 (38.43)	442.72 (41.92)	2.48	0.119	1.91	0.171	0.1	0.756
Reactance, Ω	56.67 (6.33)	55.73 (9.00)	60.46 (11.93)	52.96 (6.99)	52.52 (9.98)	57.11 (8.97)	57.37 (8.52)	57.23 (10.23)	0.84	0.361	0.44	0.511	9.25	<0.01 *
Phase angle, °	6.28 (0.94)	7.03 (1.50)	5.82 (0.53)	5.51 (0.59)	6.21 (1.28)	7.49 (1.23)	7.27 (0.88)	7.44 (1.12)	12.42	<0.001 *	2.5	0.118	8.76	<0.01 *
HGS right, kg	25.77 (5.98)	26.05 (5.75)	22.79 (4.61)	23.93 (4.48)	42.60 (10.13)	42.05 (9.72)	40.20 (7.94)	40.20 (7.64)	0.17	0.682	2.47	0.119	3.48	0.065
HGS left, kg	25.30 (4.9)	25.43 (5.65)	23.64 (4.38)	24.00 (4.24)	41.90 (8.54)	41.29 (8.61)	38.00 (6.7)	38.70 (6.58)	0.02	0.893	2.65	0.106	1.54	0.217
Squat, n	15.73 (3.77)	17.41 (3.69)	14.36 (2.76)	18.50 (3.92)	14.33 (3.80)	17.52 (3.63)	22.00 (6.73)	24.10 (5.53)	28.49	<0.001 *	9.29	<0.01 *	0.24	0.625
Walk, meters	541.07 (70.07)	578.82 (66.21)	460.61 (50.77)	481.61 (63.52)	534.74 (93.65)	564.02 (66.45)	592.00 (48.76)	644.00 (82.13)	28.06	<0.001 *	3.28	0.073	0.24	0.628
%F, %	36.33 (3.89)	34.95 (3.99)	36.03 (2.91)	35.76 (2.46)	31.13 (3.43)	29.47 (3.62)	27.25 (3.15)	27.49 (2.86)	18.15	<0.001 *	1.36	0.246	2.46	0.119
FM, kg	24.15 (6.35)	23.15 (6.38)	21.72 (4.95)	22.87 (6.21)	26.42 (4.62)	24.78 (4.23)	21.49 (3.99)	21.05 (3.90)	4.96	0.028 *	3.7	0.057	0.38	0.537
FFM, kg	41.50 (5.90)	42.19 (6.24)	38.16 (6.08)	40.54 (7.96)	58.16 (5.77)	59.08 (5.28)	56.91 (4.03)	55.15 (4.73)	3.33	0.071	3.67	0.059	1.16	0.285
TUA, cm^2	65.10 (16.67)	67.67 (16.21)	60.84 (25.88)	70.22 (12.95)	72.32 (9.21)	73.19 (16.12)	89.60 (11.02)	89.40 (9.25)	5.64	0.019 *	2.62	0.109	0.62	0.433
UMA, cm^2	38.99 (11.35)	42.79 (11.04)	21.52 (6.50)	23.41 (8.05)	49.36 (8.81)	51.65 (10.62)	18.19 (3.97)	19.35 (2.66)	16.07	<0.001 *	107.61	<0.001 *	0.66	0.419
UFA, cm^2	26.11 (6.72)	24.88 (7.60)	18.59 (4.65)	19.22 (4.81)	22.96 (6.47)	21.53 (8.27)	13.30 (7.27)	15.82 (4.65)	0.9	0.344	25.06	<0.001 *	0.87	0.352
TCA, cm^2	107.06 (15.48)	105.18 (18.13)	82.36 (30.20)	93.63 (18.79)	116.55 (18.43)	112.66 (28.97)	107.79 (10.97)	108.75 (10.10)	0.01	0.918	11.46	0.001 *	0.06	0.809
CMA, cm^2	74.92 (11.76)	71.72 (21.91)	60.84 (25.88)	70.22 (12.95)	90.07 (14.19)	89.10 (26.13)	89.60 (11.02)	89.40 (9.25)	0.13	0.721	1.78	0.185	0.59	0.444
CFA, cm^2	32.14 (6.01)	27.72 (9.51)	21.52 (6.50)	23.41 (8.05)	26.49 (8.22)	23.56 (7.63)	18.19 (3.97)	19.35 (2.66)	8.98	<0.01 *	23.56	<0.001 *	1.62	0.207

Notes: SD, standard deviation; F, Snedecor–Fisher test value; *p*, *p*-value; BMI, body mass index; SK, skinfold thickness; circ, circumference; HGS, hand grip strength; %F, percentage of fat mass; Fm, fat mass; FFM, fat-free mass; TUA, total upper area; UMA, upper muscle area; UFA, upper fat area; TCA, total calf area; CMA, calf mass area; CFA, calf fat area; ♀, female; ♂, male; *, statistically significant.

3.3. Effects of Three Months of Training

Table 2 shows several significant differences induced by the intervention, by the two types of training, and by sex.

Regarding the effects of the interventions, the biceps, subscapular, and suprailiac skinfolds showed a significant decrease. At the same time, waist circumference, %F, FM, and CFA presented a significant decrease. Conversely, arm-relaxed circumference, phase angle, number of squats, TUA, and UMA showed a significant increase after the period of training.

Considering the comparison of the two intervention groups, people who practiced NW had a greater decrease in weight, triceps and lateral calf skinfolds, hip circumference, UFA, and CFA. On the contrary, the value of the arm-relaxed circumference showed a significant increase in the NW group in comparison with the GYM group.

The calf circumference, number of squats, and TCA presented a reverse trend. People in the GYM group showed a significant increase in these variables.

Considering the differences linked to sex, men had significantly higher value for the phase angles and a significantly lower value for reactance than women.

3.4. Effects of NW and GYM Training on BIVA

Figure 2 shows the BIVA ellipses of the NW and GYM groups at baseline and follow-up: no significant changes appeared between the two groups ($p = 1.1$ in the pre-analysis and $p = 0.6$ in the post-analysis).

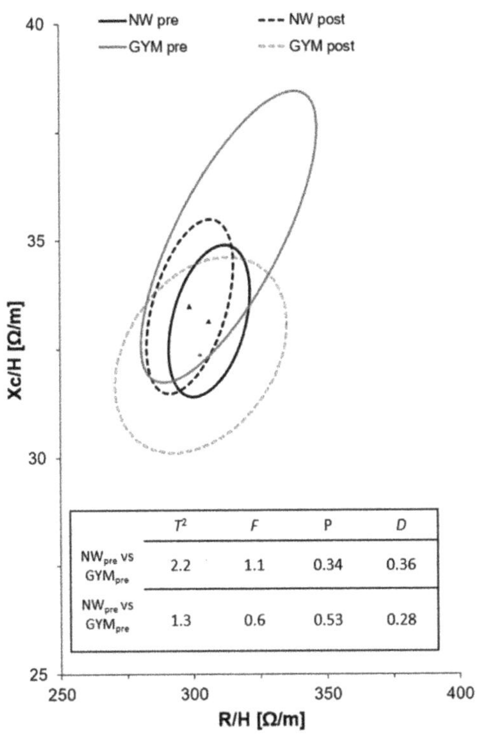

Figure 2. R/H-Xc/H and paired graphs for the multivariate changes in classic resistance and reactance in the GYM and NW groups. Mean vector displacements with 95%, confidence ellipses, and results of the Hotelling's T^2 test are shown. Note: triangles represent NW mean points and dots represent GYM mean points.

Figure 3 shows a significant difference in the impedance value in the GYM group. In particular, the reactance had a significant decrease. The reactance is a measure of cellularity integrity, and the decrease could be a symptom of inflammation. The NW group shows a reduction of resistance and an increase in reactance, but these results are not significant.

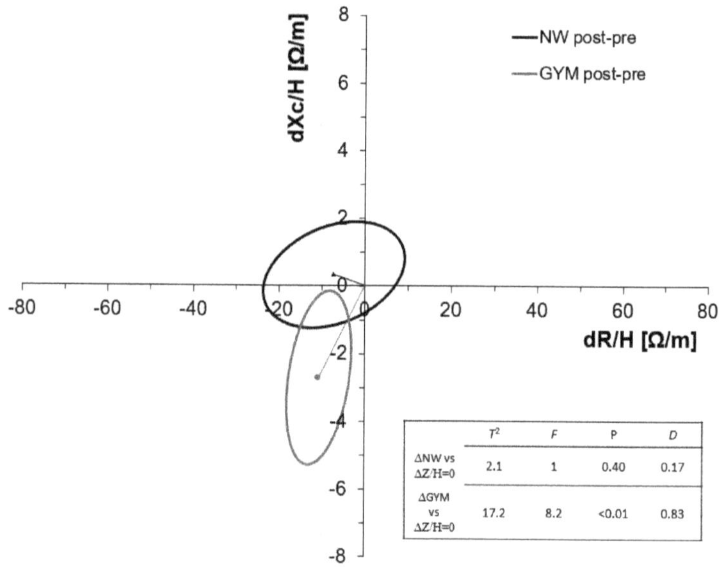

	T^2	F	P	D
ΔNW vs ΔZ/H=0	2.1	1	0.40	0.17
ΔGYM vs ΔZ/H=0	17.2	8.2	<0.01	0.83

Figure 3. Paired BIVA graph on impedance delta among the NW and GYM groups. Note: triangles represent NW mean points and dots represent GYM mean points.

4. Discussion

The present study aimed to evaluate the effectiveness of a period of three months of outdoor (NW) and GYM (resistance) training in healthy middle-aged people. To our knowledge, there are no studies that consider the comparison between the two types of training (NW and GYM) on body composition and physical motor characteristics. NW has gained popularity worldwide as a health-promoting activity [38]. NW could be considered a total-body version of walking, with greater body muscle activity due to the use of poles and potentially enhanced physical fitness benefits [39,40]. NW has several important benefits for the population, such as resting blood pressure and heart rate, increasing exercise capacity, quality of life, and maximal oxygen consumption [41]. Resistance training is one of the most used types of PA, and in addition, it has the potential to help people maintain a good health condition and reverse the adverse effects of ageing on cellular integrity and function [42]. In fact, authors reported improvements in physical performance, movement control, walking speed, and functional independence, which may assist the prevention and management of several chronic diseases [43]. In addition, resistance training improved cardiovascular health and increases bone mineral density [44]. Although the two types of PA could potentially have positive effects after a period of training, further research is needed to reveal the optimal dose–response relationship [45].

In the present study, considering the whole sample, the three months of NW and GYM training showed positive effects: in both activities, a significant decrease in FM and %F and a significant increase in the squat test were observed. This represents a positive aspect, which could be linked to an increase in the strength of the lower body and to an increase in the capacity of resistance. This is partially in contrast with a previous study about NW which assumed that the use of poles, used as a support, reduced the training effect on lower extremities [46]. Having more strength and resistance could drive people to continue PA for a longer period and thus be more active [31]. The previous study also showed a significant increase in handgrip strength, in contrast with the results of the present study [46,47]. Maybe the period of three months was too short to observe a significant change in upper-body muscle strength. Both the intervention groups showed an increase in PhA. The increase in this parameter is generally associated with an increase in strength (in this case, of the lower body) and an alteration in cellular membrane integrity or body fluid, or a combination of both [48]. This aspect is important because muscle strength is recognized as a good predictor of adverse health outcomes [49]. This result indicates the promotion of additional positive effects on cellularity cell size and integrity in the cell membrane. The PhA changes highlighted are in line with the results of previous studies [50]. Several studies have considered PhA and its relationship with health status, and it is an important factor to prevent the ageing process [48]. The BIVA changes may be due to changes in nutritional habits during the intervention period, an aspect that has not been monitored and could have caused disparity changes in R and Xc, as reported in previous studies [49]. The present results partially contrast with a previous study, which found significant improvement in BIVA and fat parameters after a resistance training period [50]. This could also be linked to the period of training; Fukuda et al. (2016) found a significant increase in BIVA parameters after a period of six months of resistance training [50]. So, probably, three months of training is too short to observe significant changes in BIVA parameters.

In addition, the whole sample of NW showed a significant decrease in other parameters, such as hip circumference. Regarding the comparison between the two groups, the NW group seemed to have more positive effects. NW had a greater decrease in several parameters connected to body fat (triceps skinfold, UFA, and CFA).

A previous study compared the effects of conventional walking, NW, and resistance training in older adults [51]. The results showed that walking improves cardiorespiratory fitness, resistance exercise improves muscle strength, and NW is a combination of the two types of activities and provides improvement to both components [51]. Performing NW takes less time than performing the same amount of walking with additional resistance training sessions. Experimental research suggested that performing the activity in nature has additional benefits in comparison to performing it in an indoor environment [51], and in addition, exposure to nature could provide restoration from stress and mental fatigue [52]. A greater long-term adherence to exercise participation was shown in outdoor PA by some studies than in GYM exercise interventions [49–52]. The present study has some limitations that should be addressed. The period of training of three months could be considered relatively short. It could be interesting to extend the period of training to six months, or a year, to determine if the results could be different. In addition, the sample size was limited; it could be interesting for future research to include more participants. Furthermore, participants were not asked for information about diet and alimentary behavior. So, for future research, it will be an important aspect to consider.

5. Conclusions

The present study aimed to evaluate the benefits of a period of NW and indoor resistance training in the general middle-aged population to understand the effectiveness of the two types of PA. Both NW and indoor training have positive effects on the participants. NW is usually proposed for specific kinds of populations or the rehabilitation of chronic disease, although it seems to have several potential benefits also for the general population. However, the popularity of this sport is increasing, and it would be important to encourage its practice in the population to promote a decrease in sedentary behavior.

Author Contributions: Conceptualization, A.G. and S.T.; methodology, S.T.; software, M.M.; validation, A.G., S.T., and M.M.; formal analysis, A.G.; investigation, M.M.; resources, A.G.; data curation, S.T.; writing—original draft preparation, A.G.; writing—review and editing, M.M. and S.T.; visualization, M.M.; supervision, S.T.; project administration, A.G. All authors have read and agreed to the published version of the manuscript.

Funding: This research received no external funding.

Institutional Review Board Statement: The study was conducted in accordance with the Declaration of Helsinki and approved by the Bioethics Committee of the University of Bologna (protocol code 022254 of 9 October 2020).

Informed Consent Statement: Informed consent was obtained from all subjects involved in the study.

Data Availability Statement: Data are available on request from the first author.

Conflicts of Interest: The authors declare no conflict of interest.

References

1. Braza, M.; Shoemaker, W.; Seeley, A. Neighborhood Design and Rates of Walking and Biking to Elementary School in 34 California Communities. *Am. J. Health Promot.* **2004**, *19*, 128–136. [CrossRef]
2. Frank, L.D.; Pivo, G. Impacts of Mixed Use and Density on Utilization of Three Modes of Travel: Single-Occupant Vehicle, Transit, and Walking. *Transp. Res. Rec.* **1994**, *1466*, 44–52.
3. Rodríguez, D.A.; Joo, J. The Relationship between Non-Motorized Mode Choice and the Local Physical Environment. Transportation Research Part D: Transport and Environment. *Transp. Res. Part D Transp. Environ.* **2004**, *9*, 151–173. [CrossRef]
4. Lindsey, G.; Han, Y.; Wilson, J.; Yang, J. Neighborhood Correlates of Urban Trail Use. *J. Phys. Act. Health* **2006**, *3*, S139–S157. [CrossRef] [PubMed]
5. Zamboni, M.; Mazzali, G.; Fantin, F.; Rossi, A.; Di Francesco, V. Sarcopenic Obesity: A New Category of Obesity in the Elderly. *Nutr. Metab. Cardiovasc. Dis.* **2008**, *18*, 388–395. [CrossRef] [PubMed]
6. World Health Organization 2020 Guidelines on Physical Activity and Sedentary Behaviour—PMC. Available online: https://www.ncbi.nlm.nih.gov/pmc/articles/PMC7719906/ (accessed on 2 May 2022).
7. Tomlinson, D.J.; Erskine, R.M.; Morse, C.I.; Winwood, K.; Onambélé-Pearson, G. The Impact of Obesity on Skeletal Muscle Strength and Structure through Adolescence to Old Age. *Biogerontology* **2016**, *17*, 467–483. [CrossRef]
8. World Health Organization, Regional Office for Europe. ITALY Physical Activity Factsheet. 6. Available online: https://ec.europa.eu/assets/eac/sport/library/factsheets/italy-factsheet_en.pdf (accessed on 5 January 2022).
9. Hallal, P.C.; Andersen, L.B.; Bull, F.C.; Guthold, R.; Haskell, W.; Ekelund, U. Lancet Physical Activity Series Working Group Global Physical Activity Levels: Surveillance Progress, Pitfalls, and Prospects. *Lancet* **2012**, *380*, 247–257. [CrossRef]
10. DiBonaventura, M.; Nicolucci, A.; Meincke, H.; Le Lay, A.; Fournier, J. Obesity in Germany and Italy: Prevalence, Comorbidities, and Associations with Patient Outcomes. *Clinicoecon Outcomes Res.* **2018**, *10*, 457–475. [CrossRef]
11. Mytton, O.T.; Townsend, N.; Rutter, H.; Foster, C. Green Space and Physical Activity: An Observational Study Using Health Survey for England Data. *Health Place* **2012**, *18*, 1034–1041. [CrossRef]
12. Wang, H.; Dai, X.; Wu, J.; Wu, X.; Nie, X. Influence of Urban Green Open Space on Residents' Physical Activity in China. *BMC Public Health* **2019**, *19*, 1093. [CrossRef]
13. Toselli, S.; Bragonzoni, L.; Dallolio, L.; Alessia, G.; Masini, A.; Marini, S.; Barone, G.; Pinelli, E.; Zinno, R.; Mauro, M.; et al. The Effects of Park Based Interventions on Health: The Italian Project "Moving Parks". *Int. J. Environ. Res. Public Health* **2022**, *19*, 2130. [CrossRef]
14. Lachowycz, K.; Jones, A.P. Greenspace and Obesity: A Systematic Review of the Evidence. *Obes. Rev.* **2011**, *12*, e183–e189. [CrossRef]
15. Lukaski, H.C.; Vega Diaz, N.; Talluri, A.; Nescolarde, L. Classification of Hydration in Clinical Conditions: Indirect and Direct Approaches Using Bioimpedance. *Nutrients* **2019**, *11*, 809. [CrossRef]
16. Ackland, T.R.; Lohman, T.G.; Sundgot-Borgen, J.; Maughan, R.J.; Meyer, N.L.; Stewart, A.D.; Müller, W. Current Status of Body Composition Assessment in Sport. *Sports Med.* **2012**, *42*, 227–249. [CrossRef]
17. Gatterer, H.; Schenk, K.; Burtscher, M. Assessment of Human Body Composition Methods and Limitations. In *Body Composition*; CRC Press: Boca Raton, FL, USA, 2017; ISBN 978-1-351-26000-8.
18. Campa, F.; Matias, C.; Gatterer, H.; Toselli, S.; Koury, J.C.; Andreoli, A.; Melchiorri, G.; Sardinha, L.B.; Silva, A.M. Classic Bioelectrical Impedance Vector Reference Values for Assessing Body Composition in Male and Female Athletes. *Int. J. Environ. Res. Public Health* **2019**, *16*, 5066. [CrossRef]
19. Marini, E.; Campa, F.; Buffa, R.; Stagi, S.; Matias, C.N.; Toselli, S.; Sardinha, L.B.; Silva, A.M. Phase Angle and Bioelectrical Impedance Vector Analysis in the Evaluation of Body Composition in Athletes. *Clin. Nutr.* **2020**, *39*, 447–454. [CrossRef] [PubMed]
20. Tomeleri, C.M.; Ribeiro, A.S.; Cavaglieri, C.R.; Deminice, R.; Schoenfeld, B.J.; Schiavoni, D.; Dos Santos, L.; de Souza, M.F.; Antunes, M.; Venturini, D.; et al. Correlations between Resistance Training-Induced Changes on Phase Angle and Biochemical Markers in Older Women. *Scand. J. Med. Sci. Sports* **2018**, *28*, 2173–2182. [CrossRef] [PubMed]
21. Souza, M.F.; Tomeleri, C.M.; Ribeiro, A.S.; Schoenfeld, B.J.; Silva, A.M.; Sardinha, L.B.; Cyrino, E.S. Effect of Resistance Training on Phase Angle in Older Women: A Randomized Controlled Trial. *Scand. J. Med. Sci. Sport* **2017**, *27*, 1308–1316. [CrossRef] [PubMed]
22. Grigoletto, A.; Mauro, M.; Oppio, A.; Greco, G.; Fischetti, F.; Cataldi, S.; Toselli, S. Effects of Nordic Walking Training on Anthropometric, Body Composition and Functional Parameters in the Middle-Aged Population. *Int. J. Environ. Res. Public Health* **2022**, *19*, 7433. [CrossRef] [PubMed]

23. Obesity and Overweight. Available online: https://www.who.int/news-room/fact-sheets/detail/obesity-and-overweight (accessed on 20 January 2022).
24. Lohman, T.; Roache, A.; Martorell, R. Anthropometric Standardization Reference Manual. *Med. Sci. Sports Exerc.* **1992**, *24*, 952. [CrossRef]
25. Haddad, M.; Stylianides, G.; Djaoui, L.; Dellal, A.; Chamari, K. Session-RPE Method for Training Load Monitoring: Validity, Ecological Usefulness, and Influencing Factors. *Front. Neurosci.* **2017**, *11*, 612. [CrossRef]
26. Durnin, J.V.; Womersley, J. Body Fat Assessed from Total Body Density and Its Estimation from Skinfold Thickness: Measurements on 481 Men and Women Aged from 16 to 72 Years. *Br. J. Nutr.* **1974**, *32*, 77–97. [CrossRef]
27. Siri, W.E. *Body Composition from Fluid Spaces and Density: Analysis of Methods*; University of California: Berkeley, CA, USA, 1956.
28. Sergi, G.; Bussolotto, M.; Perini, P.; Calliari, I.; Giantin, V.; Ceccon, A.; Scanferla, F.; Bressan, M.; Moschini, G.; Enzi, G. Accuracy of Bioelectrical Impedance Analysis in Estimation of Extracellular Space in Healthy Subjects and in Fluid Retention States. *Ann. Nutr. Metab.* **1994**, *38*, 158–165. [CrossRef] [PubMed]
29. Piccoli, A.; Rossi, B.; Pillon, L.; Bucciante, G. A New Method for Monitoring Body Fluid Variation by Bioimpedance Analysis: The RXc Graph. *Kidney Int.* **1994**, *46*, 534–539. [CrossRef] [PubMed]
30. Lukaski, H.C.; Piccoli, A. Bioelectrical Impedance Vector Analysis for Assessment of Hydration in Physiological States and Clinical Conditions. In *Handbook of Anthropometry: Physical Measures of Human Form in Health and Disease*; Preedy, V.R., Ed.; Springer: New York, NY, USA, 2012; pp. 287–305. ISBN 978-1-4419-1788-1.
31. Chtourou, H.; Engel, F.A.; Fakhfakh, H.; Fakhfakh, H.; Hammouda, O.; Ammar, A.; Trabelsi, K.; Souissi, N.; Sperlich, B. Diurnal Variation of Short-Term Repetitive Maximal Performance and Psychological Variables in Elite Judo Athletes. *Front. Physiol.* **2018**, *9*, 1499. [CrossRef] [PubMed]
32. Rikli, R.E.; Jones, C.J. *Senior Fitness Test Manual*; Human Kinetics: Champaign, IL, USA, 2013; ISBN 978-1-4504-1118-9.
33. Karanth, M.S.; Awad, N.T. Six Minute Walk Test: A Tool for Predicting Mortality in Chronic Pulmonary Diseases. *J. Clin. Diagn. Res.* **2017**, *11*, OC34–OC38. [CrossRef]
34. Nolen-Doerr, E.; Crick, K.; Saha, C.; de Groot, M.; Pillay, Y.; Shubrook, J.H.; Donley, D.; Hornsby, W.G. Six-Minute Walk Test as a Predictive Measure of Exercise Capacity in Adults with Type 2 Diabetes. *Cardiopulm. Phys. Ther. J.* **2018**, *29*, 124–129. [CrossRef]
35. Shim, J.; Kwon, H.; Kim, H.; Kim, B.; Jung, J. Comparison of the Effects of Walking with and without Nordic Pole on Upper Extremity and Lower Extremity Muscle Activation. *J. Phys. Ther. Sci.* **2013**, *25*, 1553. [CrossRef]
36. van den Bosch, M.; Ode Sang, Å. Urban Natural Environments as Nature-Based Solutions for Improved Public Health—A Systematic Review of Reviews. *Environ. Res.* **2017**, *158*, 373–384. [CrossRef]
37. Figard-Fabre, H.; Fabre, N.; Leonardi, A.; Schena, F. Physiological and Perceptual Responses to Nordic Walking in Obese Middle-Aged Women in Comparison with the Normal Walk. *Eur. J. Appl. Physiol.* **2010**, *108*, 1141–1151. [CrossRef]
38. Rodgers, C.D.; VanHeest, J.L.; Schachter, C.L. Energy Expenditure during Submaximal Walking with Exerstriders. *Med. Sci. Sports Exerc.* **1995**, *27*, 607–611. [CrossRef] [PubMed]
39. dos Santos, L.; Ribeiro, A.S.; Gobbo, L.A.; Nunes, J.P.; Cunha, P.M.; Campa, F.; Toselli, S.; Schoenfeld, B.J.; Sardinha, L.B.; Cyrino, E.S. Effects of Resistance Training with Different Pyramid Systems on Bioimpedance Vector Patterns, Body Composition, and Cellular Health in Older Women: A Randomized Controlled Trial. *Sustainability* **2020**, *12*, 6658. [CrossRef]
40. Westcott, W.L. Resistance Training Is Medicine: Effects of Strength Training on Health. *Curr. Sports Med. Rep.* **2012**, *11*, 209–216. [CrossRef]
41. Fragala, M.S.; Cadore, E.L.; Dorgo, S.; Izquierdo, M.; Kraemer, W.J.; Peterson, M.D.; Ryan, E.D. Resistance Training for Older Adults: Position Statement From the National Strength and Conditioning Association. *J. Strength. Cond. Res.* **2019**, *33*, 2019–2052. [CrossRef] [PubMed]
42. Kukkonen-Harjula, K.; Hiilloskorpi, H.; Mänttäri, A.; Pasanen, M.; Parkkari, J.; Suni, J.; Fogelholm, M.; Laukkanen, R. Self-Guided Brisk Walking Training with or without Poles: A Randomized-Controlled Trial in Middle-Aged Women. *Scand. J. Med. Sci. Sport.* **2007**, *17*, 316–323. [CrossRef] [PubMed]
43. Toselli, S.; Badicu, G.; Bragonzoni, L.; Spiga, F.; Mazzuca, P.; Campa, F. Comparison of the Effect of Different Resistance Training Frequencies on Phase Angle and Handgrip Strength in Obese Women: A Randomized Controlled Trial. *Int. J. Environ. Res. Public. Health* **2020**, *17*, 1163. [CrossRef] [PubMed]
44. Barrea, L.; Muscogiuri, G.; Laudisio, D.; Di Somma, C.; Salzano, C.; Pugliese, G.; de Alteriis, G.; Colao, A.; Savastano, S. Phase Angle: A Possible Biomarker to Quantify Inflammation in Subjects with Obesity and 25(OH)D Deficiency. *Nutrients* **2019**, *11*, 1747. [CrossRef]
45. Cruz-Jentoft, A.J.; Bahat, G.; Bauer, J.; Boirie, Y.; Bruyère, O.; Cederholm, T.; Cooper, C.; Landi, F.; Rolland, Y.; Sayer, A.A.; et al. Sarcopenia: Revised European Consensus on Definition and Diagnosis. *Age Ageing* **2019**, *48*, 16–31. [CrossRef]
46. Ribeiro, A.S.; Schoenfeld, B.J.; Dos Santos, L.; Nunes, J.P.; Tomeleri, C.M.; Cunha, P.M.; Sardinha, L.B.; Cyrino, E.S. Resistance Training Improves a Cellular Health Parameter in Obese Older Women: A Randomized Controlled Trial. *J. Strength. Cond. Res.* **2020**, *34*, 2996–3002. [CrossRef]
47. Fukuda, D.H.; Stout, J.R.; Moon, J.R.; Smith-Ryan, A.E.; Kendall, K.L.; Hoffman, J.R. Effects of Resistance Training on Classic and Specific Bioelectrical Impedance Vector Analysis in Elderly Women. *Exp. Gerontol.* **2016**, *74*, 9–12. [CrossRef]
48. Takeshima, N.; Rogers, N.L.; Rogers, M.E.; Islam, M.M.; Koizumi, D.; Lee, S. Functional Fitness Gain Varies in Older Adults Depending on Exercise Mode. *Med. Sci. Sport. Exerc.* **2007**, *39*, 2036–2043. [CrossRef] [PubMed]

49. Bojorquez, I.; Ojeda-Revah, L. Urban Public Parks and Mental Health in Adult Women: Mediating and Moderating Factors. *Int. J. Soc. Psychiatry* **2018**, *64*, 637–646. [CrossRef] [PubMed]
50. Church, T.S.; Earnest, C.P.; Morss, G.M. Field Testing of Physiological Responses Associated with Nordic Walking. *Res. Q. Exerc. Sport* **2002**, *73*, 296–300. [CrossRef] [PubMed]
51. van den Bosch, M. Natural Environments, Health, and Well-Being. Available online: https://oxfordre.com/environmentalscience/view/10.1093/acrefore/9780199389414.001.0001/acrefore-9780199389414-e-333 (accessed on 13 July 2022).
52. Newton, J. *Wellbeing and the Natural Environment: A Brief Overview of the Evidence*; University of Bath: Bath, UK, 2007.

Journal of
Functional Morphology and Kinesiology

MDPI

Article

Comparing the Effects of Multicomponent and Concurrent Exercise Protocols on Muscle Strength in Older Adults

Filipe Rodrigues [1,2,*], Miguel Jacinto [1,2], Raul Antunes [1,2,3], Diogo Monteiro [1,2,4], Diogo Mendes [1,2], Rui Matos [1,2] and Nuno Amaro [1,2]

1 ESECS—Polytechnic of Leiria, 2411-901 Leiria, Portugal; miguel.s.jacinto@ipleiria.pt (M.J.); raul.antunes@ipleiria.pt (R.A.); diogo.monteiro@ipleiria.pt (D.M.); diogo.l.mendes@ipleiria.pt (D.M.); rui.matos@ipleiria.pt (R.M.); nuno.amaro@ipleiria.pt (N.A.)
2 Life Quality Research Center, 2040-413 Rio Maior, Portugal
3 Center for Innovative Care and Health Technology, 2410-541 Leiria, Portugal
4 Research Center in Sport Sciences, Health Sciences and Human Development, 5001-801 Vila Real, Portugal
* Correspondence: filipe.rodrigues@ipleiria.pt

Abstract: This study aimed to compare the effects of a multicomponent exercise program and a concurrent exercise program on muscle strength in community-dwelling elderly subjects. Participants (n = 35; male = 17; female = 18; Mage = 69.17, SD = 5.01 years) were screened and included in the study. Among them, 19 individuals were assigned to the multicomponent group, while 16 were assigned to the concurrent group. The results of the repeated-measures ANOVA revealed significant main effects for the group factor ($F(1,15) = 66.59$, $p < 0.001$, $\eta^2 = 0.81$) and the group*time factor ($F(1,15) = 16.95$, $p < 0.001$, $\eta^2 = 0.53$) for the 30-second chair test. Furthermore, significant main effects were observed only for the group factor ($F(1,15) = 19.28$, $p < 0.001$, $\eta^2 = 0.56$) for the 30-second arm curl. Regarding the Timed Up and Go test, significant main effects were found for the group factor ($F(1,15) = 35.56$, $p < 0.001$, $\eta^2 = 0.70$) and the group*time factor ($F(1,15) = 11.68$, $p < 0.001$, $\eta^2 = 0.43$). Lastly, significant main effects were observed for the group*time factor ($F(1,15) = 5.19$, $p = 0.038$, $\eta^2 = 0.25$) for handgrip strength. The multicomponent exercise group displayed a greater mean increase compared to the concurrent exercise group. While both the multicomponent and the concurrent exercise programs were effective in improving muscle strength in community-dwelling older adults, the multicomponent exercise group exhibited superior outcomes compared to the concurrent exercise group across the physical fitness measures. These findings suggest that a multicomponent exercise program may be more beneficial for enhancing muscle strength in this population.

Keywords: healthy aging; fall risk; sarcopenia; exercise program

check for updates

Citation: Rodrigues, F.; Jacinto, M.; Antunes, R.; Monteiro, D.; Mendes, D.; Matos, R.; Amaro, N. Comparing the Effects of Multicomponent and Concurrent Exercise Protocols on Muscle Strength in Older Adults. *J. Funct. Morphol. Kinesiol.* **2024**, *9*, 3. https://doi.org/10.3390/jfmk9010003

Academic Editor: Gianpiero Greco

Received: 2 November 2023
Revised: 23 November 2023
Accepted: 29 November 2023
Published: 20 December 2023

1. Introduction

The aging population and the promotion of healthy aging have become significant concerns in modern society. With an increasing number of older adults living independently in community settings, it is crucial to identify effective strategies to maintain their physical function and overall wellbeing. Exercise interventions have shown great potential for improving various aspects of health in older adults, particularly muscle strength, which plays a critical role in maintaining independence and quality of life [1]. Implementing targeted exercise programs for this population can lead to substantial benefits in terms of maintaining physical function and preventing age-related decline [2,3].

Community exercise programs play a crucial role in promoting physical activity among community-dwelling older adults. Community exercise programs offer numerous benefits for older adults. First, they provide access to structured physical activity opportunities that are tailored to the needs and abilities of older adults [3,4]. Secondly, these programs typically offer a variety of exercise modalities, allowing participants to choose activities that suit their preferences and interests. Furthermore, community exercise programs foster a sense of belonging and social interaction among older adults [5]. Community exercise programs also offer a level of supervision and guidance from trained professionals, ensuring safe and effective exercise practices [4]. This is particularly important for older adults who may have specific health considerations or limitations. By promoting physical activity among older adults, these programs help reduce the burden of chronic diseases, enhance functional capacity, and potentially decrease healthcare costs [6]. Two prominent approaches in exercise programming for the elderly are multicomponent exercise programs and concurrent exercise programs.

In the realm of exercise programming for the elderly, two prominent paradigms emerge: multicomponent and concurrent exercise programs. The former artfully integrate a variety of exercises—from resistance training to aerobic activities, balance exercises, and flexibility training—aiming to holistically enhance overall health and functional ability [4,7]. In juxtaposition, concurrent exercise programs seamlessly merge aerobic and resistance training within a singular session, with a pronounced focus on amplifying cardiovascular fitness and muscle strength. The significance of muscle strength in the elderly is undeniable, governing their capacity to perform daily tasks, maintain balance, and prevent debilitating falls. Age-associated declines in this strength not only impede routine activities but also escalate the likelihood of falls and the onset of frailty [8]. Nevertheless, when fortified through resistance training, especially when combined with other forms of exercise, these declines can be effectively counteracted, revitalizing debilitated muscles. Both approaches have demonstrated their efficacy in augmenting muscle strength among the elderly; however, their distinct methodologies yield varied results. Multicomponent programs, rich in exercise diversity, promise potentially comprehensive enhancements in overall physical fitness [4,9], whereas concurrent programs, harmonizing cardiovascular and strength training, might edge towards pronounced gains in cardiovascular health and muscle strength [10,11]. The choice between these programs should consider the individual's specific needs to maximize benefits and support the preservation of muscle strength and overall physical health in the elderly.

While ample evidence underscores the positive impact of exercise on muscle strength in the elderly, a gap exists in comparative studies between multicomponent and concurrent exercise interventions. While previous research has delved into the benefits of one type vis-à-vis a control group, direct comparisons between these two predominant exercise modalities remain sparse. Furthermore, many of the existing exercise protocols emerge from laboratory settings, potentially limiting their applicability to the more dynamic and variable community context. Understanding the relative efficacy of multicomponent versus concurrent exercise programs in the real-world community setting is paramount for sculpting evidence-based exercise guidelines for the elderly [9,12]. Considering this, our study endeavors to juxtapose the effects of multicomponent and concurrent exercise programs on muscle strength among community-dwelling elderly subjects.

We aim to investigate the impact of two exercise programs on muscle strength, and to compare their respective outcomes in the elderly. We hypothesize that both multicomponent and concurrent exercise programs will exert a positive influence on enhancing muscle mass. Furthermore, we postulate that the concurrent exercise program will induce a more substantial increase compared to the multicomponent exercise program, given its inclusion of a more extensive strength training component in the exercise protocol.

2. Materials and Methods

2.1. Participants

The following eligibility criteria were established for this study based on the objectives and safety considerations: Participants had to be at least 60 years old, capable of standing and walking with or without assistance, not involved in any exercise program, and living in the community. Individuals with a history of chronic neuromuscular, cardiovascular, or metabolic issues that could pose a risk during classes or evaluations were excluded from participation for safety reasons. Moreover, participants were required to be available for all three sessions per week of the physical exercise program and the evaluation periods. Exclusion criteria included participating in less than 75% of the sessions or being absent for more than 5 consecutive sessions. Throughout the study, the participants were advised to maintain their regular physical activity routines, such as engaging in gardening or household activities. The intervention lasted for 20 weeks, with an additional 2 weeks—1 for the pre-intervention assessment and 1 for the post-intervention assessment. The pre- and post-intervention evaluations were conducted by two experienced exercise physiologists, under the supervision of a senior researcher. All of the participants underwent a familiarization session during the pre-intervention assessments. The exercise physiologists provided detailed explanations of all of the tests, and the participants had the opportunity to practice each test without being evaluated for the study. To ensure reliability, intra-observer consistency was examined using the intraclass correlation. The coefficient of 0.88 was derived from the overall mean across all tests for both the multicomponent and concurrent groups. This underscores the reliability of our measurements and provides confidence in the robustness of the data. Any existing health groups or issues related to the intervention were managed in accordance with standard medical practices and documented as adverse events.

In determining the appropriate sample size for our study, an a priori power analysis was conducted using G*Power 3.2. Given the parameters of F tests with repeated-measures ANOVA, and factoring in a within–between interaction, we set an effect size f of 0.25, an alpha error probability of 0.05, and sought a power of 0.95. Additionally, the study design accounted for two groups and two measurements, with a correlation among repeated measures set at 0.8 and a non-sphericity correction epsilon of 1. This analysis recommended a minimum sample size of 24 participants. To account for potential attrition or unforeseen challenges during the study, an additional 10% was factored into our recruitment target, bringing the total to 27 participants.

2.2. Procedures

Participants were recruited from the pre-existing community program known as the "60+ Program", an established educational program for the elderly that incorporates regular physical exercise sessions. Individuals who voluntarily signed up for the 60+ Program expressed their interest in participating in various activities, including research studies. This ensured that the present research was conducted within the framework of the existing educational program tailored for the elderly population. Our recruitment strategies encompassed a variety of channels, including social media platforms, internet advertisements, and the official webpage of the 60+ Program. Detailed information regarding the study, its objectives, and the specific eligibility criteria was disseminated through these avenues. Following an expression of interest, potential participants underwent a screening process to assess their eligibility based on specific criteria, such as being aged 60 years or above and active participation in the 60+ Program. Eligible individuals were provided with comprehensive information about the study procedures, potential risks and benefits, and their rights as research participants. Written informed consent was obtained from all of the participants before their inclusion in the study. To ensure a balanced distribution of participants across the study groups, the allocation of individuals was performed a priori based on their preferences regarding training hour sessions. The participants were not aware in advance of the specific type of training that they would undergo, i.e., multicomponent or concurrent. While gender and age might have naturally varied within these groups due to training hour preferences, our primary objective was to maintain consistency in the allocation process and uphold the blinding to the training type.

The research procedures adhered to the ethical guidelines and principles outlined in the Declaration of Helsinki [13]. The study protocol received approval from the Life Quality Research Center (EA06.2022.CIEQV), guaranteeing the protection of the participants' rights, privacy, and confidentiality throughout the study. The participants were assured of the voluntary nature of their participation and were given the freedom to withdraw from the study at any time without facing any negative consequences.

2.3. Intervention

The exercise interventions in this study adhered to the principles of FITT-VP [14], which encompass frequency, intensity, time, type, volume, and progression. The intervention comprised three weekly morning sessions designed in accordance with the FITT principles and overseen by a highly experienced exercise physiologist specialized in adult and senior exercise prescription. The exercise physiologist provided personalized adaptations, encouragement, and closely monitored exercise intensity using validated measures like the talk test and the Borg scale. Furthermore, after each component, and at the conclusion of each training session, the exercise physiologist distributed these measurement tools to all of the participants. The participants were encouraged to exert themselves according to their individual capabilities. Throughout the intervention period, close monitoring was in place for adherence to the exercise program, progression, and the identification of any adverse events, including incidents such as falls. Exercise sessions were scheduled on weekday mornings, following a one-day-on, one-day-off pattern. The participants took part in three exercise sessions each week, with each session lasting 45–60 min. The intensity of these exercise sessions varied, spanning from low to high levels, and was tailored to each individual's fitness level. One group followed a multicomponent exercise program, incorporating resistance training, aerobic activities, balance exercises, and flexibility training [4]. The other group participated in a concurrent training program, combining aerobic exercise with resistance training during the same session [11].

The multicomponent program encompassed resistance, cardiorespiratory, balance, agility, and flexibility training. The variety was ensured through three distinct sessions. The exercise sessions began with warm-ups lasting between 5 and 10 min, which included slow walking, dynamic stretching exercises, and dual-task activities. Activities to improve cardiorespiratory fitness, lasting 10–15 min each, were established. These activities encompassed walking, jogging, aerodance, and dance exercises as means to promote cardiorespiratory function. As the name implies, walking entailed moving forward by taking steps on the tips of one's toes, on heels, and incorporating a knee-raising stride around a predefined path. Jogging, similarly, took place on a predetermined route, with the participants instructed to enhance their hip and knee flexion as they increased their pace. The aerodance routines involved rhythmic exercises synchronized to the music's beat. Likewise, dance exercises were performed in pairs in accordance with the tempo of the music. A pair of workouts, each spanning a minimum of 10 min, was selected for this purpose. The cardiorespiratory training sessions initially fell within the range of 6 to 7 on the perceived exertion scale, signifying a moderate level of intensity. Subsequently, over the course of 16 weeks, they advanced to achieve a moderate-to-vigorous intensity, as indicated by scores of 7 and 8 on the Borg scale and/or moderate-to-vigorous intensity on the talk test (i.e., heavy breathing, difficulty talking). The resistance training component lasted between 10 and 15 min. Resistance exercises were conducted utilizing various equipment, including bodyweight, ankle weights, rubber bands, and dumbbells. During the circuit, the participants engaged in a range of one to three sets of these resistance exercises. The inter-set rest periods within the circuit varied from 40 to 60 seconds. The chosen exercises specifically targeted essential muscle groups, including those responsible for knee flexion/extension, shoulder abduction/adduction, elbow flexion/extension, pectoral muscles, and back muscles. Each session consisted of four distinct exercises, each aimed at engaging different key muscle groups. In each session, the participants completed chair squats, seated arm abduction and adduction, arm curls, and shoulder shrugs using dumbbells. In another session, the exercises included seated single-leg extension and flexion with ankle weights, arm flexion and extension with dumbbells, and peck deck exercises with rubber bands. During the third session, the participants engaged in standing calf raises, arm curls with a shoulder press, and seated rows using dumbbells. The training intensity transitioned from a light-to-moderate level (4–5 points on the Borg Scale) to a moderate intensity (5–7 points on the Borg Scale) after eight weeks from the commencement of the exercise program, and then to moderate-to-vigorous intensity (7–8 points on the Borg Scale). This adjustment aimed to optimize adaptation and the effectiveness of the workout. The participants initially started with a single set of 8 repetitions and progressively increased to two sets, with each set consisting of 12–15 repetitions. It is worth noting that all of the participants were capable of counting, and if a participant could complete 12 repetitions with minimal effort, the exercise physiologist would encourage an additional 3 repetitions. Balance training, involving static and dynamic elements, was conducted for a duration of 5–10 min, employing wooden sticks, softballs, and balloons. This training encompassed activities such as throwing and/or catching softballs, as well as engaging in single-leg static and dynamic exercises with bats and balloons to enhance balance and agility. To ensure safety during these exercises, the exercise physiologists maintained a safe distance of 2 meters between the participants. Intensity advancement occurred by motivating the participants to either perform exercises at a swifter pace or sustain static movements for extended durations. Consequently, the intensity transitioned from being categorized as light-to-moderate initially (3–5 points on the Borg Scale) to reaching a moderate level (5–7 points on the Borg Scale). It was regulated so as to not exceed moderate intensity, given that the participants had already been involved in moderate-to-vigorous activities during the cardiorespiratory and resistance training segments. Concluding each session, the participants engaged in stretching and flexibility exercises. Every session wrapped up with a 5-min cooldown period focusing on stretching, with an emphasis on maintaining a 1:1 ratio between active and passive stretching. In other words, each stretch was held for 10 seconds, followed by a 10-second pause before moving on to the next exercise or limb. The flexibility routines were customized to address the specific muscles used in the exercises. For example, when the participants performed chair squats, their stretching exercises were focused on the glutes, hamstrings, and quadriceps.

The concurrent program combined elements of both aerobic and resistance training. The exercise sessions commenced with warm-up routines that extended for 5 to 10 min. These warm-ups encompassed activities such as leisurely walking, dynamic stretching exercises, and exercises involving multitasking. Afterwards, for the cardiorespiratory component, much like the multicomponent exercise program, the participants performed activities such as walking, jogging, and aerobic dance exercises. Notably, the cardiorespiratory aspect of this program extended for about 20 min, which was longer in comparison to the multicomponent exercise program. Initially, the cardiorespiratory training sessions were rated at a perceived exertion scale level of 6 to 7, reflecting a moderate level of intensity. However, over the course of 16 weeks, these sessions progressed to attain a moderate-to-vigorous level of intensity, as evidenced by scores of 7 and 8 on the Borg scale and/or the experience of a moderate-to-vigorous level of intensity according to the talk test (i.e., characterized by heavy breathing and difficulty talking). The resistance training sessions, spanning 15–20 min in duration, incorporated identical exercises to those in the multicomponent program. The participants in the concurrent training intervention executed the very same exercises as their counterparts in the multicomponent intervention. However, the distinguishing factor was that in the concurrent training intervention, the participants began with a single set of 8 repetitions and subsequently advanced to three sets, which was one set more than the multicomponent intervention participants. With the inclusion of this additional set for each exercise, the training volume exceeded that of the multicomponent intervention. The training intensity shifted from an initial light-to-moderate level (as indicated by 4–5 points on the Borg Scale) to a moderate intensity (ranging from 5–7 points on the Borg Scale) after eight weeks from the start of the exercise program. Subsequently, it progressed to a moderate-to-vigorous intensity (7–8 points on the Borg Scale). At the end of each session, the participants participated in stretching and flexibility exercises. A 5-min cooldown phase concluded every session, with a strong focus on stretching and a particular emphasis on sustaining a 1:1 balance between active and passive stretching. To clarify, this entailed holding each stretch for 10 seconds, followed by a 10-second pause before proceeding to the next exercise or limb. Flexibility exercises were tailored to the muscles that were engaged in the activities. For instance, if the participants carried out chair squats, they incorporated stretching exercises targeting the glutes, hamstrings, and quadriceps.

2.4. Outcomes

The following outcome measures were assessed in all subjects: the 30-second chair stand test, the 30-second arm curl test, the Timed Up and Go (TUG) test, and the handgrip strength test. These measures were selected to evaluate various aspects of physical function and muscle strength in community-dwelling older adults. The 30-second chair stand test assesses lower body strength and functional mobility. The participants were instructed to stand up from a seated position and sit back down as many times as possible within 30 seconds. This test is widely used in assessing lower extremity muscle strength and has demonstrated good validity and reliability in older adults [15]. The 30-second arm curl test evaluates upper body strength and endurance. In this test, the participants were instructed to complete as many bicep curls as they could within a 30-second timeframe using a designated weight (female = 2.5 kg; male = 3.5 kg). The participants used their dominant arm and maintained proper form throughout the test to ensure accurate results. This assessment provides insight into the muscle strength of the upper extremities and has been validated as both a reliable and accurate measure for older adults [15]. The TUG test assesses the time taken by a participant to stand up from a chair, walk 8 feet (2.44 m), turn around, return, and sit back down. The TUG test is widely used as a functional assessment tool in older adults and has demonstrated good reliability [15,16]. Handgrip strength is a widely used measure of overall muscle strength and a predictor of functional performance in older adults. The CAMRY EH101 Electronic Hand Dynamometer (Zhongshan Camry Electronic Co. Ltd., Zhongshan, China) was employed to measure handgrip strength. The participants were instructed to exert maximum effort while seated on a chair with back support and fixed armrests, ensuring that their feet were flat on the floor and their forearms rested on the chair's arms. The investigator applied a motivational stimulus to encourage the participant to exert their maximum grip effort. Two values were taken in the dominant hand, and the highest value was used for analysis. This test involved the participants squeezing a dynamometer with maximum force using their dominant hand. Handgrip strength has shown strong associations with various health outcomes and is considered to be a valid and reliable measure of muscle strength [17].

2.5. Statistical Analyses

Descriptive statistics, including means and standard deviations, were calculated for all variables under investigation. The normality of the data was assessed using the Shapiro–Wilk test for sample sizes less than 50, while homoscedasticity was examined using Levene's test. To explore differences between dependent variables, a within–between–within ANOVA 2×2 design (2 groups $\times$ 2 time points) was performed using SPSS version 27. The significance level for rejecting the null hypothesis was set at 5% for all statistical tests. Sphericity assumptions were evaluated using Mauchly's test, and in cases where this assumption was violated, the Greenhouse–Geisser adjusted values and degrees of freedom were reported, which are indicated by the presence of decimal degrees of freedom. Post hoc tests with Bonferroni adjustments were conducted following the repeated-measures analyses to examine pairwise comparisons. The effect size, η_p^2, was calculated, and the reference values for interpretation were as follows: "small" effect = 0.01, "medium" effect = 0.06, and "large" effect = 0.14. All statistical analyses were performed using IBM SPSS Statistics version 27.

Attendance was evaluated in every session by the exercise physiologist before commencing the exercise session. Data from participants were included in the analyses if the participant attended 75% or more of the sessions.

3. Results

A flowchart illustrating the allocation of participants in this study is presented in Figure 1. Initially, all potential participants (n = 35; male = 17; female = 18; Mage = 69.17, SD = 5.01 years) underwent screening and were subsequently included in the study. Among them, 19 individuals (male = 9; female = 10; Mage = 70.05, SD = 4.88 years) were assigned to the multicomponent group, while 16 individuals (male = 8; female = 8; Mage = 68.13, SD = 5.12 years) were assigned to the concurrent group. Two participants from the multicomponent group withdrew from the program due to personal reasons, resulting in a final count of n = 17 for the multicomponent group. In contrast, all 16 participants in the concurrent group successfully completed the program. However, two participants from the concurrent group did not participate in the post-protocol measurements, leading to a final count of n = 14 for the concurrent group. To address missing data, the expectation-maximization method was employed for imputation, enabling the estimation of missing values based on available data for a more comprehensive analysis. Comparative analysis between the raw data and imputed data revealed no significant differences ($p < 0.05$). Thus, the reported results are related to the raw data for transparency.

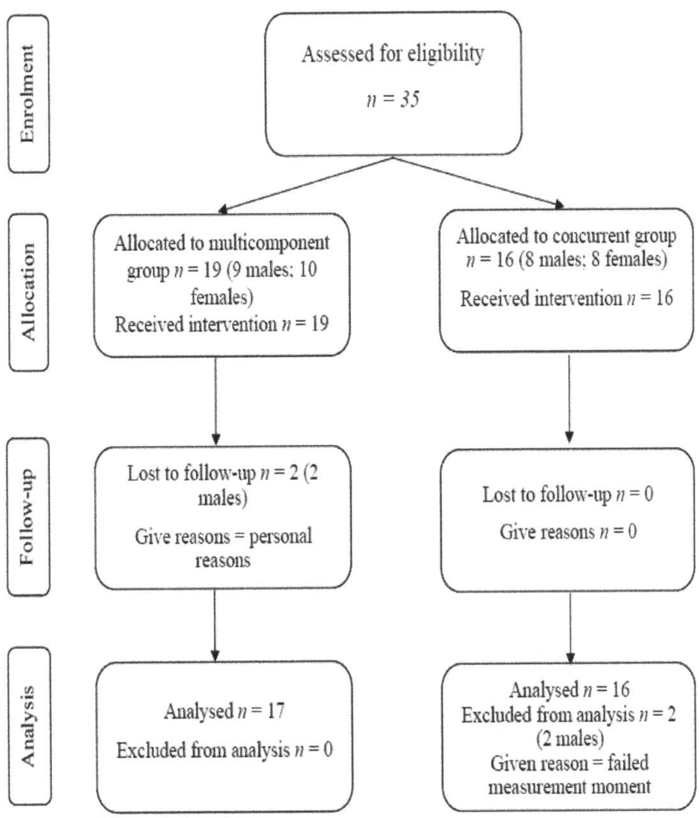

Figure 1. Flowchart of the participants.

Table 1 displays the means and standard deviations for the pre (T0) and post (T1) measurements of the outcome variables: 30-second chair stand, 30-second arm curl, Timed Up and Go, and handgrip strength. For the 30-second chair stand, the repeated-measures ANOVA revealed significant main effects for the group factor (Table 2). The multicomponent group exhibited an increase of 21.75%, increasing from an average of 14.15 to

17.22 repetitions, while the concurrent group showed an increase of 7.37%, rising from 15.58 to 16.73 repetitions from pre- to post-intervention. In the case of the 30-second arm curl, significant main effects were observed solely for the group factor. The multicomponent group demonstrated a significant increase of 23.54%, progressing from an average of 19.84 to 24.53 repetitions, whereas the concurrent group experienced an increase of 4.07%, going from 22.37 to 23.28 repetitions between T0 and T1. Regarding the Timed Up and Go test, the repeated-measures ANOVA results unveiled significant main effects for both the group factor and the group*time factor. The multicomponent group displayed a decrease in time of 2.04%, reducing from 4.89 seconds to 4.79 seconds. Conversely, the concurrent group exhibited an improvement of 9.45%, decreasing from 5.08 seconds to 4.60 seconds from pre- to post-measurement. Lastly, for handgrip strength, significant main effects were observed for the group*time factor. The multicomponent group demonstrated a modest rise of 5.98% in strength, increasing from 30.95 kg to 32.80 kg. In contrast, the concurrent group experienced a minor decline of 0.67%, decreasing from 31.12 kg to 30.91 kg between the two timepoints.

Table 1. Descriptive statistics.

Variables	Units	Multicomponent Group				Concurrent Group			
		M_{T0}	SD_{T0}	M_{T1}	SD_{T1}	M_{T0}	SD_{T0}	M_{T1}	SD_{T1}
30 s chair stand	Repetitions	14.15	5.03	17.22	5.37	15.58	4.52	16.73	4.66
30 s arm curl	Repetitions	19.84	6.39	24.53	5.73	22.37	2.63	23.28	7.33
Timed Up and Go test	Seconds	4.89	0.64	4.79	0.89	5.08	0.46	4.60	0.46
Handgrip strength	Kilograms	30.95	9.39	32.80	10.35	31.12	6.84	30.91	6.88

Notes: M = mean; SD = standard deviation; T0 = pre-intervention; T1 = post-intervention.

Table 2. Repeated measurements comparison.

Variables	Mean Square	F	df1	df2	p	η^2_p	Pairwise Comparisons
30 s chair stand							
Time	2.503	0.170	1	15	0.686	0.011	ns
Group	81.732	66.596	1	15	$\leq$0.001	0.816	$1 \neq 2$
Time*group	77.931	16.953	1	15	$\leq$0.001	0.531	$1 \neq 2$
30 s arm curl							
Time	51.01	1.31	1	15	0.269	0.081	ns
Group	435.11	19.28	1	15	$\leq$0.001	0.562	$1 \neq 2$
Time*group	10.84	0.181	1	15	0.677	0.012	ns
Timed Up and Go test							
Time	0.209	0.593	1	15	0.453	0.038	ns
Group	1.45	35.561	1	15	$\leq$0.001	0.703	$1 \neq 2$
Time*group	2.14	11.687	1	15	0.004	0.438	$1 \neq 2$
Handgrip strength							
Time	1.683	0.027	1	15	0.871	0.002	ns
Group	17.621	2.62	1	15	0.126	0.149	ns
Time*group	101.635	5.19	1	15	0.038	0.257	$1 \neq 2$

Notes: F = F test; df1 and df2 = degrees of freedom; p = significance level; η^2_p = partial eta squared; ns = not significant.

An attendance rate of 87% was observed for participants in the multicomponent exercise group, while the concurrent exercise group reported an 84% attendance rate. Regarding falls and fall-related injuries, the exercise physiologists observed two falls during the intervention period, neither resulting in injuries that hindered continued participation. The participants reported no falls outside of the structured fitness program. Notably, no emergencies or hospitalizations were recorded throughout the study period.

4. Discussion

The primary objective of our study was to contrast the effects of a multicomponent exercise regimen against those of a concurrent exercise program on muscle strength in community-dwelling older adults. Our results, underpinned by the repeated-measures ANOVA, unveiled significant main effects for both the group and the group*time factors, particularly evident in the 30-second chair test and the Timed Up and Go test. For the 30-second arm curl, the group difference stood out as the sole significant main effect, whereas, for handgrip strength, the interaction of group and time was the distinguishing factor. Worthy of mention is the distinct variance in the exercise stimuli between the two groups, a foundational tenet of our study design. This variance was not an oversight but a deliberate intention, designed to tease apart the nuanced impacts and benefits of a multifaceted training strategy versus a combined one. Such intentional differences in training protocols are akin to contrasting an experimental group with a control group, emphasizing the distinctive nature of the training methodologies that we examined.

Our findings highlight that the multicomponent group consistently demonstrated a more pronounced mean improvement across the physical fitness metrics in comparison to the concurrent exercise group. This is consistent with prior research conducted among both physically inactive older women [16] and their active counterparts aged 50–75 years [9,17]. These studies echo our observation of the superior advantages offered by multicomponent exercise programs. Theoretical constructs advocate that integrating diverse exercise modalities, each targeting unique facets of fitness, fosters amplified gains in muscle strength [9]. This is attributed to the collective benefits derived from melding resistance training with balance exercises and aerobic activities. The foundation of this method is rooted in the perception that varied exercise modalities stimulate an array of muscle groups and physiological systems, leading to holistic enhancements in both strength and functional capacity [1]. The predominant main effects detected for the multicomponent group in our research reaffirm the positive influence of this approach on muscle strength across diverse metrics.

Diving deeper into the muscular dynamics, the mechanisms underpinning muscle resistance and strength offer valuable insights into the differential outcomes observed between the two exercise regimes. The multicomponent program, with its blend of resistance, aerobic, and balance exercises, arguably imposes a heightened challenge on the musculature. This demand potentially triggers adaptive responses that bolster the muscle's force-generation capacity [4]. In juxtaposition, concurrent training, although beneficial for cardiovascular health, might encounter obstacles in fully realizing muscle resistance and strength gains. The merged demands of resistance and aerobic exercises in a single session can, at times, create antagonistic muscular adaptations [10,11]. Such interference can potentially curtail muscle hypertrophy and strength development relative to a dedicated resistance training regimen.

Our study was deliberately designed with a pronounced emphasis on strength measures, as evident from the similar duration dedicated to strength training across both the multicomponent and concurrent exercise interventions. This emphasis was underpinned by the understanding that strength outcomes, particularly in the context of our targeted demographic, have considerable implications for overall physical performance, injury prevention, and functional capacity [2,3,18,19]. However, a discerning examination of the two interventions reveals notable differences in the cardiorespiratory components. While both interventions involved walking, jogging, and aerobic dance exercises, the multicomponent exercise intervention allocated 10 to 15 min to these activities, in contrast to the 20 min dedicated to them in the concurrent exercise program. This heightened aerobic exposure in the concurrent program could potentially introduce confounding factors when analyzing strength outcomes, given the known interference effects of concurrent training on strength adaptations. Moreover, the multicomponent intervention introduced unique components of agility and balance, lasting 5 to 10 min. Agility and balance exercises, although often underestimated, play a pivotal role in neuromuscular performance and strength outcomes.

They challenge the musculature in dynamic and often unpredictable patterns, necessitating rapid force production and intricate neuromuscular coordination. Such activities engage a broad spectrum of muscle groups, from core stabilizers to peripheral muscles, potentially augmenting strength adaptations [18,20]. Moreover, the balance component, leveraging props like wooden sticks, softballs, and balloons, further emphasized proprioceptive acuity and muscle activation in stabilizing movements. In contrast, the concurrent program, by its inherent design, sought to amalgamate aerobic and strength training more integrally. While this approach has its merits, particularly for enhancing overall physical fitness, it might induce an interference effect where the pronounced aerobic component could attenuate maximal strength gains [1–3].

Both interventions, although distinct in their aerobic and agility/balance elements, consistently upheld fundamental principles such as progressive overload, session diversification for ongoing engagement, and dedicated warm-up and cooldown phases. These shared tenets highlight the significance of these principles in exercise programming, regardless of the specific objectives. While the multicomponent exercise program demonstrated superior outcomes, the substantial enhancements in muscle strength observed from the pre- to post-intervention in the concurrent training group should not be overlooked. As documented in previous studies, the concurrent exercise program, blending resistance and aerobic training, has evidenced favorable impacts on muscle strength [11]. The notable gains seen in the concurrent group resonate with this existing literature [11,20,21]. Even though the improvement of effect sizes were comparatively subdued in the concurrent group versus the multicomponent group, it is crucial to acknowledge that concurrent training also holds the potential for bolstering muscle strength in older adults living in the community. When tailoring exercise regimens for this demographic, individual inclinations and practicality must be weighed [22,23]. Some may perceive the concurrent program as more pleasurable or more manageable, factors that can foster greater long-term commitment and participation. Hence, while the outcomes might render the multicomponent program more effective, the concurrent training remains a commendable alternative for enhancing muscle strength among older adults.

Upon closer analysis of the handgrip strength results, we observed a nuanced interaction between time and group, with a statistically significant time*group interaction effect. This interaction suggests that the two groups had divergent trajectories in handgrip strength across the duration of the study. The absence of significant main effects for time and group on handgrip strength, combined with the notable interaction, suggests that the two exercise protocols had different impacts on handgrip strength over time. One could infer that the multicomponent group's intervention was more effective in improving handgrip strength compared to the concurrent group, which slightly regressed. However, it is essential to consider the potential implications of our chosen dynamometer system on these outcomes [24]. The instrument's design and its demand on the participants, especially older adults, could have influenced their genuine capacity or willingness to exert maximum force. As such, the observed non-significant change in the concurrent group may not wholly reflect the actual potential changes in handgrip strength due to the exercise intervention. We recommend that future research endeavors consider employing more user-friendly and intuitive dynamometers, especially when working with older adult populations, to better capture true grip strength without confounding influences [20]. While our study did not explicitly gauge the comfort levels or solicit feedback from the older adults regarding the user-friendliness of the dynamometer, it is pertinent to acknowledge the broader body of evidence highlighting the importance of instrument comfort in accurate measurements. Various studies and expert feedback have intimated that the design and ergonomics of certain dynamometers might not be ideal for older populations, potentially influencing their ability or willingness to exert maximum force [25,26]. This is especially salient when considering the hand anatomy, potential arthritic conditions, and muscle strength in elderly participants. Discomfort or perceived difficulty in using the tool might inadvertently result in lower grip strength measurements. Therefore, in line with these considerations and our observed results, we advocate for future studies to prioritize the use of more ergonomic and comfortable dynamometers, ensuring that the data acquired genuinely represent the strength capacities of older adults without the interference of external factors [19,25,26].

Limitations and Agenda for Future Research

Our study primarily emphasized strength measures and, as such, did not include comprehensive assessments of aerobic fitness, potentially overlooking the intertwined effects of strength and aerobic training on overall physical performance. Future studies should consider incorporating both strength and aerobic fitness evaluations to provide a more holistic understanding of training effects, especially when examining protocols that blend different exercise modalities. Our study is subject to several limitations that should be acknowledged. Firstly, the a priori allocation of participants to the multicomponent and concurrent exercise groups may have introduced selection bias and potential confounding factors. A randomized allocation would have enhanced the internal validity of the study by minimizing such biases. Secondly, the small sample size in our study restricts the generalizability of the findings. With a limited number of participants, the statistical power to detect smaller effects is diminished, and the precision of our estimates may be compromised. A larger sample size would have provided more robust results and improved the external validity of the study. Another limitation is the absence of follow-up measures. Without long-term assessments, we are unable to ascertain the durability or sustainability of the observed improvements in muscle strength. Conducting follow-up measurements would have allowed us to evaluate the persistence of the intervention effects and provide insights into the long-term benefits of the exercise programs. The study did not include a control group, which might have provided a clearer benchmark for interpreting the observed differences between the two intervention groups. This omission limits the direct attribution of improvements solely to the interventions. Furthermore, our study focused solely on community-dwelling older adults, which may restrict the generalizability of the findings to other populations, such as institutionalized older adults or those with specific health conditions. Future research should aim to include a more diverse sample to enhance the applicability of the results. Lastly, it is important to acknowledge that our study primarily assessed muscle strength as the outcome measure, while other aspects of physical fitness or functional outcomes were not evaluated. A more comprehensive assessment of various fitness parameters would have provided a more holistic understanding of the effects of the exercise programs.

The practical implications of this study are noteworthy, particularly in the context of community programs for older adults. Implementing multicomponent exercise programs in community settings can offer significant advantages in enhancing muscle strength and promoting overall physical fitness in this population. These programs can be designed to incorporate low-cost materials, making them accessible and affordable for community-based initiatives. By utilizing readily available resources, such as resistance bands or bodyweight exercises, the financial burden associated with implementing exercise programs can be minimized, allowing for broader participation and long-term sustainability. Moreover, community exercise programs provide an excellent platform for social engagement among older adults. By participating in group activities and exercises, older adults can foster social connections, enhance their sense of belonging, and combat social isolation. These social interactions can contribute to overall wellbeing and can have positive effects on mental health, creating a supportive and inclusive environment for the elderly population.

5. Conclusions

The findings from our study suggest that both multicomponent and concurrent exercise programs have merits in terms of muscle strength improvements in older adults. Specifically, the multicomponent exercise program exhibited greater outcomes in some measures of muscle strength compared to the concurrent exercise program. Notably, while we observed enhancements in certain aspects of muscle strength, handgrip strength did not exhibit significant between-group differences, emphasizing the need for a nuanced interpretation of the results. The benefits of regular exercise for older adults are vast. Engagement in structured exercise routines has been consistently linked to a multitude of health benefits, including, but not limited to, enhanced muscle strength, improved balance, increased mobility, and augmented overall functional capacity. By integrating regular exercise into their daily routine, older adults can not only fortify their physical health but also foster a sense of community and social interaction—elements that are critical to their holistic wellbeing.

Community-based multicomponent exercise programs, especially those that utilize accessible and low-cost materials, present a feasible approach to bolstering muscle strength and overall physical fitness in community-dwelling older adults. Beyond the evident physical advantages, these programs serve as catalysts for social interaction, underlining their importance for the broader wellbeing of the elderly. Given these insights, there is an evident need to further promote, support, and refine community exercise initiatives tailored for the older population. Such endeavors will not only directly benefit their physical health but will also positively impact their overall quality of life.

Author Contributions: Conceptualization, F.R.; methodology, D.M. (Diogo Monteiro); software, N.A.; validation R.M.; formal analysis, R.A.; resources, D.M. (Diogo Mendes); writing—original draft preparation, F.R.; writing—review and editing, M.J.; visualization, N.A.; supervision, R.M.; project administration, N.A.; funding acquisition, M.J. All authors have read and agreed to the published version of the manuscript.

Funding: This research was supported by national funds through the Portuguese Foundation for Science and Technology, I.P., under project UID/CED/04748/2020.

Institutional Review Board Statement: This study was conducted in accordance with the Declaration of Helsinki and approved by the Institutional Review Board of the Life Quality Research Center (protocol code EA06.2022.CIEQV, approved on 13 September 2022).

Informed Consent Statement: Informed consent was obtained from all subjects involved in the study. Written informed consent has been obtained from the patients to publish this paper.

Data Availability Statement: The data utilized in this study were obtained under a specific license exclusively for the purposes of this research. The data supporting the findings of this study are not publicly available but can be requested and accessed upon reasonable inquiry, subject to permission from the Life Quality Research Center and the corresponding author.

Acknowledgments: We extend our sincere gratitude to the participants who willingly volunteered and provided their consent to participate in this study.

Conflicts of Interest: The authors declare no conflict of interest.

References

1. Marques, D.L.; Neiva, H.P.; Marinho, D.A.; Marques, M.C. Manipulating the Resistance Training Volume in Middle-Aged and Older Adults: A Systematic Review with Meta-Analysis of the Effects on Muscle Strength and Size, Muscle Quality, and Functional Capacity. *Sports Med.* **2022**, *53*, 503–518. [CrossRef] [PubMed]
2. Di Lorito, C.; Long, A.; Byrne, A.; Harwood, R.H.; Gladman, J.R.F.; Schneider, S.; Logan, P.; Bosco, A.; van der Wardt, V. Exercise Interventions for Older Adults: A Systematic Review of Meta-Analyses. *J. Sport. Health Sci.* **2021**, *10*, 29–47. [CrossRef] [PubMed]
3. Fien, S.; Linton, C.; Mitchell, J.S.; Wadsworth, D.P.; Szabo, H.; Askew, C.D.; Schaumberg, M.A. Characteristics of Community-Based Exercise Programs for Community-Dwelling Older Adults in Rural/Regional Areas: A Scoping Review. *Aging Clin. Exp. Res.* **2022**, *34*, 1511–1528. [CrossRef] [PubMed]
4. Rodrigues, F.; Amaro, N.; Matos, R.; Mendes, D.; Monteiro, D.; Morouço, P. The Impact of an Exercise Intervention Using Low-Cost Equipment on Functional Fitness in the Community-Dwelling Older Adults: A Pilot Study. *Front. Physiol.* **2022**, *13*, 1039131. [CrossRef] [PubMed]
5. Killingback, C.; Tsofliou, F.; Clark, C. Older People's Adherence to Community-Based Group Exercise Programmes: A Multiple-Case Study. *BMC Public Health* **2017**, *17*, 115. [CrossRef] [PubMed]
6. Izquierdo, M.; Merchant, R.A.; Morley, J.E.; Anker, S.D.; Aprahamian, I.; Arai, H.; Aubertin-Leheudre, M.; Bernabei, R.; Cadore, E.L.; Cesari, M.; et al. International Exercise Recommendations in Older Adults (ICFSR): Expert Consensus Guidelines. *J. Nutr. Health Aging* **2021**, *25*, 824–853. [CrossRef] [PubMed]

7. da Silva, N.M.; de França, M.S.; de Almeida, D.K.F.H.; de Lima, E.S.G.; dos Santos, V.H.B.; Souza, J.V.d.A.; Larrad, A.R.; Aloise, D.d.A.; Lima, N.M.F.V. Effects of a Multicomponent Exercise Program on Groups of Community-Dwelling Older Adults with Low Schooling: A Pilot Study. *J. Aging Res.* **2021**, *2021*, 8829332. [CrossRef]
8. Trombetti, A.; Reid, K.F.; Hars, M.; Herrmann, F.R.; Pasha, E.; Phillips, E.M.; Fielding, R.A. Age-Associated Declines in Muscle Mass, Strength, Power, and Physical Performance: Impact on Fear of Falling and Quality of Life. *Osteoporos. Int.* **2016**, *27*, 463–471. [CrossRef]
9. Rodrigues, G.d.S.; Rodrigues, K.P.; de Almeida, M.L.; Sobrinho, A.C.d.S.; Noronha, N.Y.; Benjamim, C.J.R.; da Silva, S.; Rodrigues, J.A.L.; Júnior, C.R.B. Comparing Fourteen Weeks of Multicomponent Training Versus Combined Training in Physically Inactive Older Women: A Randomized Trial. *Int. J. Environ. Res. Public Health* **2023**, *20*, 2699. [CrossRef]
10. Hurst, C.; Weston, K.L.; McLaren, S.J.; Weston, M. The Effects of Same-Session Combined Exercise Training on Cardiorespiratory and Functional Fitness in Older Adults: A Systematic Review and Meta-Analysis. *Aging Clin. Exp. Res.* **2019**, *31*, 1701–1717. [CrossRef]
11. Sousa, N.; Mendes, R.; Abrantes, C.; Sampaio, J.; Oliveira, J. Effectiveness of Combined Exercise Training to Improve Functional Fitness in Older Adults: A Randomized Controlled Trial. *Geriatr. Gerontol. Int.* **2014**, *14*, 892–898. [CrossRef] [PubMed]
12. Rodrigues, K.P.; Prado, L.; de Almeida, M.L.; Yamada, A.K.; Finzeto, L.C.; Bueno Júnior, C.R. Effects of Combined Versus Multicomponent Training in Physically Active Women Aged 50–75 Years. *Res. Q. Exerc. Sport.* **2022**, *93*, 710–717. [CrossRef] [PubMed]
13. World Medical Association. World Medical Association World Medical Association Declaration of Helsinki: Ethical principles for medical research involving human subjects. *JAMA* **2013**, *310*, 2191–2194. [CrossRef] [PubMed]
14. Chodzko-Zajko, W.J.; Proctor, D.N.; Fiatarone Singh, M.A.; Minson, C.T.; Nigg, C.R.; Salem, G.J.; Skinner, J.S. Exercise and Physical Activity for Older Adults. *Med. Sci. Sports Exerc.* **2009**, *41*, 1510. [CrossRef] [PubMed]
15. Rikli, R.E.; Jones, C.J. Development and Validation of Criterion-Referenced Clinically Relevant Fitness Standards for Maintaining Physical Independence in Later Years. *Gerontol.* **2013**, *53*, 255–267. [CrossRef] [PubMed]
16. Rodrigues, F.; Teixeira, J.E.; Forte, P. The Reliability of the Timed Up and Go Test among Portuguese Elderly. *Healthcare* **2023**, *11*, 928. [CrossRef] [PubMed]
17. Jakobsen, L.H.; Rask, I.K.; Kondrup, J. Validation of Handgrip Strength and Endurance as a Measure of Physical Function and Quality of Life in Healthy Subjects and Patients. *Nutrition* **2010**, *26*, 542–550. [CrossRef]
18. Rodrigues, F.; Domingos, C.; Monteiro, D.; Morouço, P. A Review on Aging, Sarcopenia, Falls, and Resistance Training in Community-Dwelling Older Adults. *Int. J. Environ. Res. Public Health* **2022**, *19*, 874. [CrossRef]
19. Baker, B.S.; Miller, K.; Weitzel, K.J.; Duren, D.L.; Gammon, R.; Mills-Gray, S.; Ball, S.D. Resistance Training Reduces Age- and Geography-Related Physical Function Discrepancies in Older Adults. *Gerontol. Geriatr. Med.* **2021**, *7*. [CrossRef]
20. Baker, B.S.; Miller, K.; Weitzel, K.J.; Duren, D.L.; Gammon, R.; Mills-Gray, S.; Ball, S.D. Acute Resistance Training May Have Lasting Benefit to Middle-Aged Adults. *Gerontol. Geriatr. Med.* **2021**, *7*. [CrossRef]
21. Crowe, E.M.; Ball, S.D. Effectiveness of Advanced Stay Strong, Stay Healthy in Community Settings. *Gerontol. Geriatr. Med.* **2015**, *1*. [CrossRef] [PubMed]
22. Ball, S.; Gammon, R.; Kelly, P.J.; Cheng, A.-L.; Chertoff, K.; Kaume, L.; Abreu, E.L.; Brotto, M. Outcomes of Stay Strong, Stay Healthy in Community Settings. *J. Aging Heal.* **2013**, *25*, 1388–1397. [CrossRef] [PubMed]
23. Kim, M.; Shinkai, S. Prevalence of Muscle Weakness Based on Different Diagnostic Criteria in Community-Dwelling Older Adults: A Comparison of Grip Strength Dynamometers. *Geriatr. Gerontol. Int.* **2017**, *17*, 2089–2095. [CrossRef] [PubMed]
24. Huang, L.; Liu, Y.; Lin, T.; Hou, L.; Song, Q.; Ge, N.; Yue, J. Reliability and Validity of Two Hand Dynamometers When Used by Community-Dwelling Adults Aged over 50 Years. *BMC Geriatr.* **2022**, *22*, 580. [CrossRef]
25. Abe, T.; Loenneke, J.P.; Thiebaud, R.S.; Loftin, M. The Bigger the Hand, the Bigger the Difference? Implications for Testing Strength With 2 Popular Handgrip Dynamometers. *J. Sport Rehabil.* **2019**, *28*, 278–282. [CrossRef]
26. Guerra, R.S.; Amaral, T.F.; Sousa, A.S.; Fonseca, I.; Pichel, F.; Restivo, M.T. Comparison of Jamar and Bodygrip Dynamometers for Handgrip Strength Measurement. *J. Strength Cond. Res.* **2017**, *31*, 1931. [CrossRef]

Journal of
Functional Morphology and Kinesiology

MDPI

Article

A Single, Multimodal Exercise Tolerance Test Can Assess Combat Readiness in Army-ROTC Cadets: A Brief Report

Derek A. Crawford [1,2,*], Katie M. Heinrich [2,3,*], Christopher K. Haddock [2], W. S. Carlos Poston [2], R. Sue Day [2], Christopher Kaipust [2], Blake Skola [1,2], Amanda J. Wakeman [1], Eric Kunkel [1], Addison Bell [1], Emily Wilhite [1], Nathanial Young [1], Allison Whitley [1] and Madelyn Fritts [1]

[1] Department of Nutrition, Kinesiology, and Health, University of Central Missouri, Warrensburg, MO 64093, USA; skola@ndri-usa.org (B.S.); wakeman@ucmo.edu (A.J.W.); epk64130@ucmo.edu (E.K.); amb50060@ucmo.edu (A.B.); eew68580@ucmo.edu (E.W.); njy58580@ucmo.edu (N.Y.); anw89880@ucmo.edu (A.W.); mbf51100@ucmo.edu (M.F.)
[2] NDRI-USA, New York, NY 10001, USA; keithhaddock@hopehri.com (C.K.H.); carlosposton@hopehri.com (W.S.C.P.); day.susie@gmail.com (R.S.D.); kaipust@ndri-usa.org (C.K.)
[3] Department of Kinesiology, Kansas State University, Manhattan, KS 66506, USA
* Correspondence: dcrawford@ucmo.edu (D.A.C.); kmhphd@ksu.edu (K.M.H.)

Abstract: The Army Combat Fitness Test (ACFT) is a multi-event assessment battery designed to determine the combat readiness of U.S. Army personnel. However, for Reserve Officers' Training Corps (ROTC) programs the logistical demands of collegiate life make repeated administration of the ACFT challenging. The present study sought to design and evaluate a single, multimodal exercise tolerance test (METT) capable of serving as a time-efficient proxy measure of combat readiness. Methods: Using a formal instrument design process, we constructed the METT to mimic the demands of the ACFT and assessed its reliability, validity, and responsiveness. Results: The METT demonstrates minimal measurement error (i.e., a 2% coefficient of variation), concurrent validity with the ACFT ($R^2 = 0.327$, $F = 10.67$, $p < 0.001$), the ability to classify cadets who may be at-risk for failing the ACFT ($X^2 = 8.16$, $p = 0.017$, sensitivity = 0.878, specificity = 0.667), and appropriate change following a training intervention (5.69 ± 8.9%). Conclusions: The METT has the potential to provide a means to monitor progress, identify areas for improvement, and guide informed decision-making regarding individualization of cadet combat training plans.

Keywords: military; performance; testing

Citation: Crawford, D.A.; Heinrich, K.M.; Haddock, C.K.; Poston, W.S.C.; Day, R.S.; Kaipust, C.; Skola, B.; Wakeman, A.J.; Kunkel, E.; Bell, A.; et al. A Single, Multimodal Exercise Tolerance Test Can Assess Combat Readiness in Army-ROTC Cadets: A Brief Report. *J. Funct. Morphol. Kinesiol.* **2023**, *8*, 152. https://doi.org/10.3390/jfmk8040152

Academic Editor: Helmi Chaabene

Received: 15 September 2023
Revised: 23 October 2023
Accepted: 26 October 2023
Published: 1 November 2023

1. Introduction

The U.S. Army Reserve Officers' Training Corps (ROTC) is the primary preparatory program for college students who wish to pursue a career in the Army [1]. Throughout the program, students are expected to meet specific body composition recommendations and physical fitness standards [1]. With respect to physical fitness, cadets complete the Army Combat Fitness Test (ACFT) as the assessment of record used to determine their combat readiness [2]. The ACFT is composed of six individual physical tests (i.e., a 3-repetition maximum deadlift, a sprint-drag-carry task, hand release push-ups, a plank task, a standing medicine ball throw, and a 2-mile run time to completion) [2]. The ACFT individual component tasks are performed within the same session, with adequate rest in between, resulting in a test battery lasting approximately 70 to 120 min in duration [2]. This time demand, coupled with large cadres (e.g., 100+ cadets) with often differing schedule demands and equipment constraints, presents a logistical challenge when administering the ACFT in collegiate settings.

Fortunately, Army Command only requires the administration of the ACFT once per academic year for ROTC programs. However, while this alleviates logistical challenges, cadets are ultimately judged and potentially assigned supplemental physical training based on their performance during the ACFT. With limited availability to test and re-test cadets using the ACFT, there is a need for a simpler assessment method that may provide more flexibility to those designing and implementing ROTC physical training programs. A time-efficient, comprehensive assessment of cadets' progress during training would allow for more nuanced decisions on exercise programming variables to improve combat readiness and whether additional training is necessary.

Recently, physical work capacity is posited as a unique metric of human fitness that is distinct from traditional measures such as VO_{2MAX}, muscular strength, etc. [3]. Assessment of work capacity necessitates temporally combing multimodal (e.g., many different bio-motor abilities) physical tasks and completing them at a relatively high intensity (i.e., as fast as possible) [4]. Additionally, work capacity assessments can be designed in a way as to be "task-specific", in that, the elements included within the assessment and the time domain assessed determine the utility for predicting performance outcomes of interest. For example, in an athlete population, a work capacity assessment attempting to predict on-field performance would need to include elements and be of a duration that simulate technical skill and bioenergetic demands. With the bio-motor abilities associated with combat readiness already defined (i.e., the ACFT component tasks), it should be feasible to develop a work capacity assessment to predict combat readiness.

Thus, the purpose of the present study was to develop and preliminarily evaluate a multimodal exercise tolerance test (METT) of physical work capacity as it relates to predicting combat readiness using the ACFT as a criterion measure. Such a test would provide ROTC leadership with the ability to effectively monitor cadet progress more efficiently during an academic year. This may potentially result in lower recidivism rates and higher rates of advancement to active service among cadets via better designed and/or tailored physical training programs. We expect to develop a METT capable of predicting, and discriminating, ACFT performance.

2. Materials and Methods

2.1. Participants

Table 1 provides the sex-specific biometric data of the 47 cadets (28% female) who agreed to participate in this study. Participants were required to be an active member of the University's Army ROTC program for at least one semester prior to study commencement. All participants reported no significant disease or health conditions (e.g., diabetes) that may have contraindicated participation in vigorous exercise testing and/or programs. Written informed consent was obtained prior to study participation and all procedures were approved by the University Institutional Review Board for Protection of Human Research Subjects.

Table 1. Sex-specific biometric data.

	Female	Male
n	13	34
Age	20.6 ± 1.0	21.2 ± 2.1
Height (cm)	164.0 ± 6.8	179.0 ± 6.4
Weight (kg)	63.3 ± 9.2	82.8 ± 12.2
FFM (kg)	41.8 ± 4.5	59.1 ± 12.8
BF%	30.5 ± 4.9	23.1 ± 5.2
BMD (g/cm^2)	1.23 ± 0.1	1.35 ± 0.1
Years in ROTC	2.46 ± 0.8	2.62 ± 1.2

2.2. Development of the Multimodal Exercise Tolerance Test (METT)

Over the course of two academic semesters, the authors employed the Instrument Development Process to conceptualize, design, and beta-test a METT to assess work capacity related to combat readiness [5]. This process consisted of (1) concept identification, (2) test construction, (3) reliability, and (4) validity testing. Within the fall academic semester, the author group focused on concept identification (i.e., identifying physical capacities of combat readiness that need to be challenged and underlying bioenergetic demands) and test construction (i.e., exercise/movement task selection, intensity/volume, and duration needs) phases. Using the ACFT components as a framework, the following physical capacities were identified as contributing to combat readiness: *lower and upper extremity strength/power, total body stability/coordination, lower and upper extremity muscular endurance, maximal running speed, change of direction ability,* and *cardiovascular endurance.* Figure 1 outlines the final construction of the METT for assessing combat readiness.

	Task 1	Task 2	Task 3	Task 4	Task 5	Task 6
Round 1	**Sprint / Agility Circuit** (as fast as possible)	**9 repetitions Deadlift**	**15 repetitions Hand Release Push Ups**	**Farmer's Carry** (as fast as possible)	**9 repetitions S-to-Overhead**	**15 repetitions Step Ups**
Round 2	**Sprint / Agility Circuit** (as fast as possible)	**6 repetitions Deadlift**	**12 repetitions Hand Release Push Ups**	**Farmer's Carry** (as fast as possible)	**6 repetitions S-to-Overhead**	**12 repetitions Step Ups**
Round 3	**Sprint / Agility Circuit** (as fast as possible)	**3 repetitions Deadlift**	**9 repetitions Hand Release Push Ups**	**Farmer's Carry** (as fast as possible)	**3 repetitions S-to-Overhead**	**9 repetitions Step Ups**

Figure 1. Outline of Components within the METT for ROTC Cadets. For the spring/agility circuit, cadets sprint forward for 94 feet, right shuffle 15 feet, backpedal 15 feet, left shuffle 15 feet, then reverse the path returning to the start position. For the deadlift task, both sexes use 75% of body mass loaded on a trap bar. This same load is used during the farmer's carry task in which cadets carried the load 94 feet down and 94 feet back to the starting position. For the shoulder-to-overhead task, loads are 50% and 40% of body mass for males and females, respectively, loaded on a standard barbell. For the step-up task, implement heights are 16 and 20 inches for females and males, respectively.

Once the test was constructed, an iterative stimulus (i.e., exercise loads and volume) and design (e.g., logistical constraints of test administration) optimization phase took place. Within this phase, loading intensities for all externally loaded exercises were optimized for maximizing the amount of work (in ft-lbs measured using an optical linear transducer; EliteForm Integrated, EliteForm, Lincoln, NE, USA) that a college-aged individual could complete in the anticipated time domain of the task. For example, for the targeted repetitions for the deadlift task (i.e., 9) were able to be complete in an average of 15 s. Loads (as a percentage of body mass) were systematically increased until work performed in 15 s peaked.

Figure 2 illustrates the recommended setup for administration of the METT. To maximize the ecological validity of the assessment, the distance constraints for the sprint/agility circuit and farmer's carry tasks were set as to allow for two testing "lanes" to fit within a standard size basketball court. This allowed for ROTC administrators to logistically assess multiple cadets at a time within their regular training sessions and facilities.

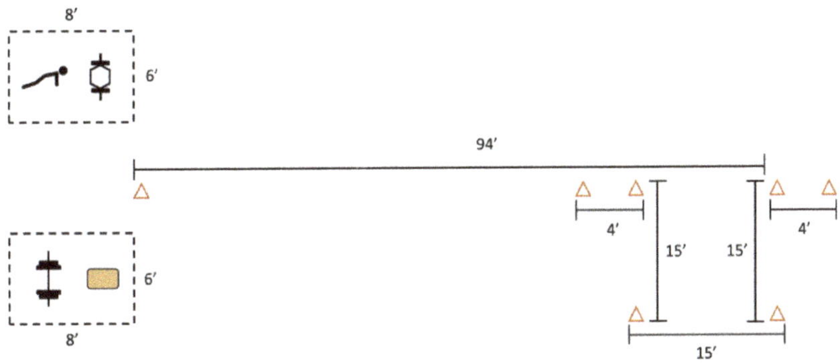

Figure 2. Suggested layout for the METT for ROTC cadets. Orange triangles represent cones, hexagon image represents the trap bar, tan box represents the step-up instrument, dashed lines are to only suggest space allocation(s) for the deadlift, push-up, shoulder-to-overhead, and step-up tasks. Dimensions are reported in feet.

2.3. Physical Testing Procedures

2.3.1. Body Measurements

During a laboratory visit, height was measured to the nearest 0.1 cm using a wall-mounted stadiometer, weight was measured to the nearest 0.1 kg using a medical-grade scale (PS-7700, Befour, Inc., Saukville, WI, USA), and body composition was measured by dual X-ray absorptiometry (DXA; Prodigy iDXA, General Electric, Boston, MA, USA). Cadets were instructed to refrain from exercise and alcohol consumption for a 12-h period immediately preceding their body composition assessment.

2.3.2. Combat Readiness

All participants completed the ACFT in accordance with the procedures outlined in the Army fitness manual [2]. Consisting of the six events noted in the introduction (e.g., hand release pushups, medicine ball throw, etc.), each event is associated with a 100-point score with a maximum of 600 points possible. The event scores were standardized into z-scores and a total score of performance ($ACFT_{TSP}$) was created by calculating the mean of each cadet's z-scores to represent a single measure of combat readiness relative to the cadre. In addition to this continuous variable, a dichotomous variable was created to identify those cadets who either "passed" or who "failed"/were "at-risk" of failing the ACFT following the criteria of scoring below 60 points in any one event or in the 60 s across more than two events, respectively.

2.3.3. METT Procedures

Cadets complete the METT as part of a regularly scheduled training session during the 2nd and 15th week of the academic semester. During the assessment, cadets were observed by a peer who used a stopwatch to record their time to completion for each individual task to the nearest 0.1 s. All task times were added together to reflect total test time. Cadets were provided demonstration of movement standards and allowed to practice movements prior to testing. Cadets completed the METT as fast as possible. Data collection sheets were returned to research staff who checked data accuracy and entered them into a spreadsheet for later analyses.

2.4. Experimental Procedures

All baseline assessments and physical testing procedures were conducted during the first 2 weeks of the Spring 2023 academic semester. Cadets then completed an 11-week High Intensity Functional Training (HIFT) intervention designed to increase general work capacity [6]. The general framework for the periodization and progression of the HIFT intervention were developed by the research team, but specific details regarding exercise selection, scheduling, and delivery location were made by cadre training staff members. Following the completion of an 11-week HIFT intervention, body measurements, the ACFT, and METT tests were completed again over a 2-week period. Only baseline data were used to assess the validity and reliability of the METT while baseline and post-intervention data were used to determine the responsiveness of the test.

2.5. Data Analyses

Descriptive statistics were calculated for all variables across both the baseline and post-intervention. Normality was assessed using the Shapiro–Wilks test. All analyses were performed using the R statistical programming language (v. 4.1) within the Jamovi graphical user interface (v. 2.3) [7,8]. A Pearson's correlation coefficient matrix for all variables was calculated to assess content validity of METT components. The *GAMLj: General analysis for linear models* package was used to construct a model to assess the concurrent validity of the METT for predicting combat readiness [9]. Discriminant validity was assessed using a logistic regression model and the associated cut-off scores for passing or failing the ACFT were estimated using a Receiver Operator Characteristic curve via the *ROCR: Visualizing the performance of scoring classifiers* package [10]. Change scores (% change) for METT time to completion, and descriptive statistics, were calculated to evaluate the measure's responsiveness. An alpha level of 0.05 was used for all inferential analyses.

3. Results

3.1. METT Reliability

During the development process, beta testing procedures within the research team provided estimates of the mean within-subjects (i.e., test-retest) and mean assessment (i.e., intra- and inter-rater) variation in time to completion (in seconds) for the METT. Using these pilot data, within-subjects' coefficient of variation (CV) was observed to be 1.3% of the time to completion. The intra-rater CV was observed to be 0.02% and inter-rater CV was observed to be 0.73% of the time to completion. The authors recommend measurement error intervals for the METT be estimated as the sum of the potential within-subject (i.e., 1.3%) and inter-rater (i.e., 0.73%) CV, equaling an estimated $\pm$ 2.03% measurement error.

3.2. METT Validity

3.2.1. Content Validity

Table 2 presents the correlation matrix between the individual components of the METT (time to completion in seconds) and ACFT assessments (percentile rank). Each individual component of the METT demonstrates a significant, negative correlation with at least one component of the ACFT. Of note, some discrepancies exist between METT components and their hypothesized ACFT counterparts. For example, METT Task 2 (i.e., deadlift repetitions) does not correlate with the three-repetition maximum deadlift load within the ACFT ($p = 0.996$) and METT Task 1 (i.e., sprint/agility drill) does not correlate with the sprint-drag-carry task within the ACFT ($p = 0.109$) as was expected. However, other components of the METT align with their targeted ACFT counterparts as intended. For example, total time to completion and METT Task 4 (i.e., farmer's carry) significantly correlated with the 2-mile run performance and the plank task within the ACFT, respectively. Interestingly, the farmer's carry (METT Task 4) best related to ACFT tasks, being significantly correlated with five out of six components (with the three-repetition maximum deadlift as the outlier).

Table 2. Correlation matrix for METT and ACFT individual components (n = 47).

	M (SD)	3DL	SPT	HRP	PLK	SDC	2-MR
Sprint/Agility Time (s)	28.9 ± 5.2	−0.223	−0.087	−0.108	**−0.478** *	−0.237	**−0.526** *
Deadlift Time (s)	14.5 ± 5.0	0.001	0.048	−0.318 *	−0.401 *	0.029	−0.129
HRP Time (s)	27.3 ± 10.6	−0.288 *	−0.18	**−0.563** *	−0.223	−0.286	−0.373 *
Farmer's Carry Time (s)	34.6 ± 8.2	−0.242	−0.294 *	−0.331 *	**−0.518** *	−0.338 *	**−0.598** *
S-to-Overhead Time (s)	19.6 ± 11.3	−0.126	−0.075	**−0.498** *	−0.371 *	−0.237	−0.284
Step Ups Time (s)	29.5 ± 10.5	−0.142	−0.049	−0.269	−0.164	−0.26	−0.338 *
Total Test Time (s)	447.9 ± 84.6	−0.253	−0.24	**−0.545** *	**−0.473** *	−0.331 *	**−0.481** *

* indicates $p < 0.05$, bold indicates $p < 0.001$; M = mean, SD = standard deviation, 3DL = three-repetition maximum deadlift, SPT = standing power throw, HRP = hand release push-ups, PLK = plank, SDC = sprint-drag-carry, 2-MR = 2-mile run; S-to-Overhead = shoulder to overhead press.

3.2.2. Concurrent Validity

Table 3 provides the parameter estimates for a general linear model for predicting combat readiness (i.e., the composite $ACFT_{TSP}$ variable) using the METT time to completion (scaled to sample z-scores) at the baseline. As expected, there is a significant, negative relationship wherein a 1-standard deviation decrease in the METT time to completion results in a 0.460-standard deviation increase in the AFCT performance.

Table 3. General linear model output for predicting $ACFT_{TSP}$ (n = 47).

Overall Model Test		$R^2 = 0.486$	$F_{(2,44)} = 13.54$	$p < 0.001$
Parameter	**Coefficient**	**SE**	**95% CI**	***p*-value**
Total Time (s) *	−0.460	0.083	−0.63, −0.29	<0.001
Sex #	0.589	0.240	0.10, 1.07	0.018
Weight (lbs)	0.012	0.003	0.00, 0.01	<0.001

* Total time is scaled to sample z-scores, # sex is dummy coded using male = 1 and female = 0.

Figure 3 presents a scatterplot of the raw data split by sex. The trendlines for sex-specific data are included. While the effect of sex within the general linear model presented in Table 3 is not significant, there are large effects in the METT time to completion (difference = 32.2 ± 16.6 s, t = 1.95, p = 0.054, Cohen's d = 0.387) between males (mean = 430 ± 83.8 s) and females (mean = 499 ± 64.7 s). Visually, between sexes, there also appears to be a potential difference in the relationship between the baseline METT performance and combat readiness. For these reasons, the authors determined that sex, as a control variable, would be carried forward into the analyses evaluating the discriminant validity of the METT.

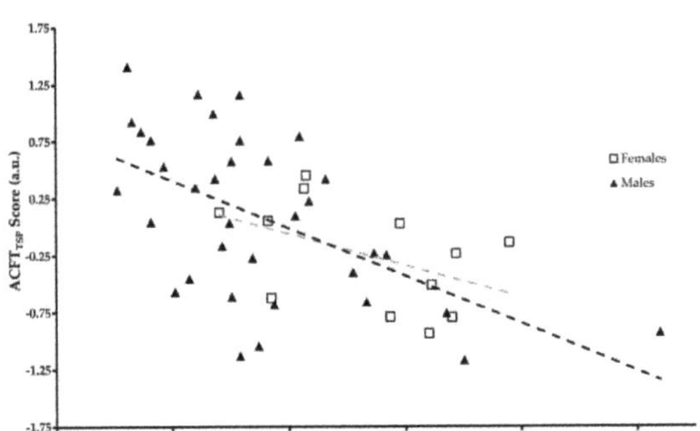

Figure 3. Relationship between baseline ACFT and METT performance. Darker trendline represents the relationship for males and lighter trendline represents the relationship for females.

3.2.3. Construct (Discriminant) Validity

Table 4 presents the parameter estimates for a logistic regression model for predicting ACFT "At-risk/Fail" from the METT time to completion, controlling for sex. Within the model, the METT time to completion significantly predicts the probability of being at-risk or failing the ACFT, wherein there is a 1.6% increased risk of failure for every 1-s increase in total test time above the cut-off score(s). Panel A in Figure 4 illustrates both the probability distributions for sensitivity and specificity measures of potential cut-off values. Panel B in Figure 4 illustrates the receiver operator characteristic (ROC) curve for the cut-off probability of 0.95. Using the derived parameter estimates from Table 4, the calculated thresholds for METT time to completion (accounting for measurement error) required to "pass" the ACFT are less than 536 ± 11 s and 572 ± 12 s for males and females, respectively. Additionally, the cutoff scores demonstrate a reasonable degree of diagnostic utility (e.g., sensitivity, specificity, etc.) as evidenced in Table 4.

Table 4. Logistic regression model output and sensitivity analyses for predicting At-risk/Fail on ACFT ($n = 47$).

Overall Model Test			$R^2_{McF} = -0.227$	$X^2_{(2,44)} = 8.16$	$p = 0.017$
Parameter		**Coefficient**	**SE**	**95% CI**	***p*-value**
Intercept		9.8515	3.560	2.881, 15.897	0.006
Total Time (s)		−0.0166	0.007	−0.029, −0.003	0.021
Sex: Female-Male		0.6096	1.118	−1.581, 2.799	0.586
2 × 2 Classification Table				**Predictive Measures**	
	Predicted			Accuracy	0.553
Observed	At-risk/Fail	Pass	% Correct	Specificity	1.000
At-risk/Fail	6	0	1.00	Sensitivity	0.488
Pass	21	20	48.8	Area Under the Curve	0.817

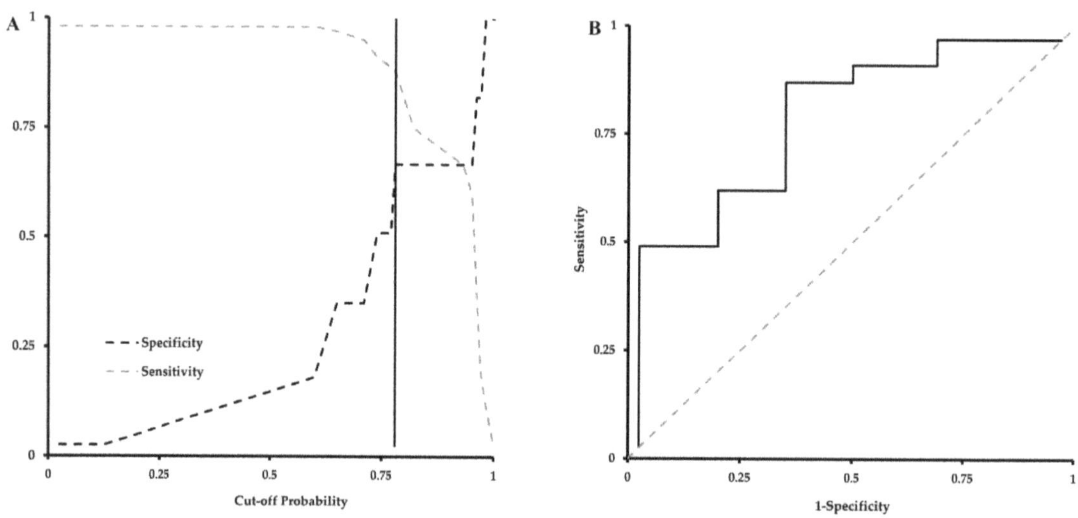

Figure 4. Sensitivity and Specificity Analyses Supporting Figures. Panel (**A**) illustrates the sensitivity and specificity values across the cut-off probability distribution. The vertical line highlights the cut-off value (0.95) which maximizes these metrics. Panel (**B**) is the associated ROC curve for the 0.95 value.

3.3. METT Responsiveness

Following the 11-week HIFT intervention (designed to improve the work capacity), the mean change in the METT time to completion was −5.69 ± 8.9% (95%CI: −8.33, −3.05%). Figure 5 displays the individual-level change in the METT time to completion across the baseline time to completion z-score distribution. Across the study sample, 32 out of 47 (65.3%) cadets improved their METT performance beyond the measurement error, with a maximum improvement of approximately 27.5%. Conversely, 9 out of 47 (19.1%) cadets regressed their METT performance beyond the measurement error, with a maximum regression of approximately 25%. These proportions of individual response heterogeneity align with published data from large-scale exercise interventions [11]. Additionally, there is no significant relationship ($F_{1,46}$ = 0.885, p = 0.352, R^2 = 0.019) between change scores and the baseline METT performance, indicating no bias in responsivity due to the baseline METT performance status.

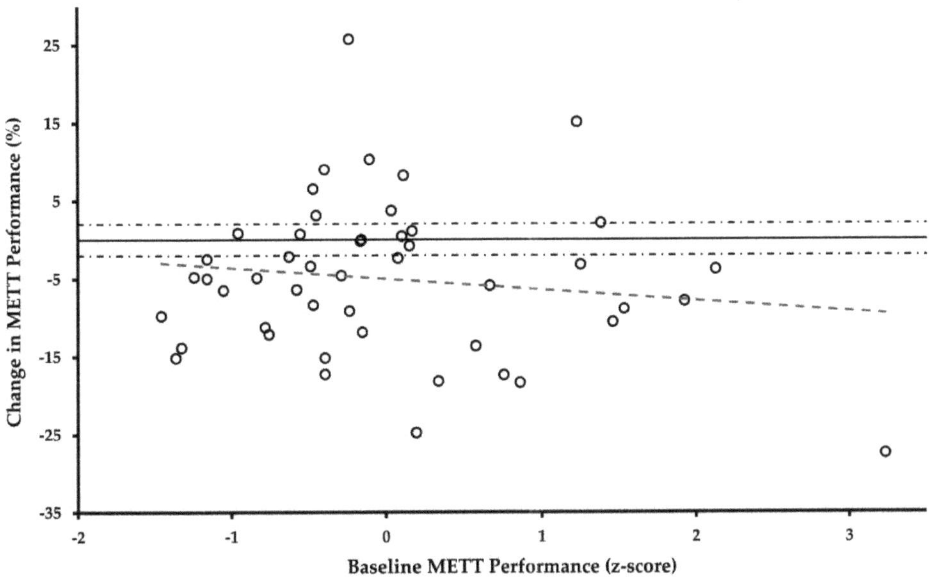

Figure 5. Relationship between Changes in METT Time to Completion and Baseline Performance. Solid line indicates change of 0%. Dashed and dotted lines represent the thresholds of measurement error (i.e., 1.3% within-subject variation + 0.73% inter-rater variation = 2.03% error).

4. Discussion

This study sought to develop and preliminarily evaluate a METT of physical work capacity capable of predicting combat readiness in a collegiate Army ROTC cadet. By employing the Instrument Development Process [5], we designed a time-efficient, single test capable of delivering a valid, reliable, and responsive proxy measure of combat readiness.

At the time of writing, we are aware of only one other attempt to develop a single test capable of serving as a proxy measure of combat readiness. Moore et al. (2022) designed and assessed the reliability of a test named the Combat Readiness Assessment (CRA) [12]. The CRA consists of seven physical task "zones" spread across the field space within a 400-m track and field complex. These zones are made up, in order, of a 10-m sprint zone, 30-m loaded carry zone, 20-m weight drag zone, another 10-m sprint zone, a 15-m "agility box" zone, and a final 60-m sprint zone. While the authors should be commended for their efforts in conceptualizing the CRA, there are ultimately limitations in its construction and assessment that restrict its utility for serving as a proxy measure of combat readiness.

First, compared to the METT designed in the present study, the CRA does not appear to assess the domains of *lower and upper extremity strength/power* or *cardiovascular endurance*. While the CRA does include a loaded carry task, unfortunately the loading scheme is not noted, making determination of its ability to challenge strength and/or power difficult. The METT includes both lower (i.e., deadlift) and upper extremity (i.e., push press) exercise tasks specifically optimized at loading schemes designed to maximize physical work. With respect to cardiovascular endurance, the mean time to completion of the CRA was 208 ± 21 s. Conversely, the mean time to completion of the METT was 464 ± 73 s across both sexes. While it takes approximately 3 min to achieve steady state oxygen consumption, tests of cardiovascular endurance typically take much longer (i.e., 8–12 min) [13]. Maximal tests like critical power typically last no longer than 3 min, yet these tests are designed to capture an individual anerobic rather than aerobic capacity [14]. Thus, when a cadet is instructed to give maximal effort from the onset of a test it can be reasonably assumed that a longer duration effort will better represent cardiovascular endurance/capacity. Such is the case comparing the CRA to the METT.

Second, in evaluating the CRA, the authors only choose to investigate the test's reliability. Conversely, herein we report the reliability, validity, and responsiveness of the METT. To compound this limitation, Moore et al. (2022) also note that the findings regarding the short-term reliability of the CRA are inconclusive given that the test time to completion yielded relatively high coefficients of variation (i.e., 10%) across familiarization sessions. In contrast, the coefficients of variation observed in beta testing of the METT were much smaller for test-retest (i.e., 1.3%), intra-rater (i.e., 0.02%), and inter-rater (i.e., 0.73%) reliability. One reason for this discrepancy in reliability may be found in the tests' duration. With the METT being nearly twice as long as the CRA, it may be that its time to completion is less prone to acute changes in motivation, hydration, sleep, etc., leading up to the testing session.

The results of this study have provided a valid, reliable, and ecologically sensitive test that can serve as a proxy measure of combat readiness in lieu of having cadets complete the lengthy ACFT. The METT demonstrates a reasonable degree of measurement error (i.e., 2.03%) across multiple repeated assessments at the same relative timepoint (i.e., back-to-back weeks) and between observers administering the test. Furthermore, the METT exhibited good content validity as there were significant moderate correlations between the individual components of the test and those of the ACFT. It also demonstrated concurrent validity as baseline scores on the METT were able to significantly predict performance on the ACFT at the baseline. As a diagnostic tool, the METT was able to discriminate between cadets who were at-risk for, or failed, the ACFT from those who were not with a high degree of sensitivity (100%). We also provide sex-specific cut-off scores for time to completion (i.e., males = 536 ± 11 s, females = 572 ± 12 s) on the METT that, above which, ROTC administrators can be confident that cadets would likely not pass the ACFT.

Practically, our recommendation is that this newly developed METT be used as a monitoring tool within ROTC programs to make more informed decisions with respect to cadets' individual training plans. For example, due to the ease of implementation within existing training schedules, the METT could be conducted monthly to determine overall cadre progress toward a target training objective such as "x percent of cadets are predicted to pass the ACFT". Alternatively, these monthly assessments could also determine if individual cadets need additional training beyond what is currently planned if they are classified as at-risk of failing the ACFT. With some minor changes in the test administration (i.e., recording of time to completion for each task), it would even be possible to use the METT as a prescriptive tool by identifying relative deficiencies and highlighting them within training programming. The time-efficient nature of the METT would indeed provide a degree of flexibility when looking to adjust training programs at the individual level.

The present study has several key considerations. Chief among the relative strengths is the comprehensive evaluation of METT reliability, validity, and responsiveness. Another strength is that the practicality of our assessment of discriminant validity provides actionable insights on using the METT to classify cadets based on their predicted performance on the ACFT. Two limitations of this study should be noted. First, the sex distribution in this study is skewed in favor of male cadets. Therefore, there is limited ability to generalize the findings of this study to females. However, even though we chose to carry forward sex as a predictor variable in the logistic regression analyses of discriminant validity, it should be noted that sex was a non-significant factor within the original general linear model. Second, the reliability analyses conducted within the present study used pilot data from the research team rather than from the cadet sample. It is plausible that measurement error within this group is different from that observed in our research staff. Future research should look to correct these limitations by repeating the present study using a larger, more balanced cadre that includes more formalized reliability evaluation such as in the study assessing the CRA. Such a study will have the potential to further refine the cut-off scores presented in this study for determining predicted ACFT performance.

5. Conclusions

This study developed and evaluated the METT for predicting combat readiness within a collegiate Army ROTC cadre. Using the Instrument Development Process, we constructed a time-efficient, singular test that provides a valid, reliable, and responsive proxy measure of ACFT performance. The METT has the potential to provide a means to monitor progress, identify areas for improvement, and guide informed decision-making regarding individualization of cadet training plans. While acknowledging the current study's limitations in sex distribution and reliability analyses, this preliminary evaluation of the METT can guide further investigation and refinement of this tool.

Author Contributions: D.A.C., E.K., A.B., E.W., N.Y., A.W., M.F. and A.J.W. conceptualized, constructed, and optimized the multimodal exercise tolerance test. D.A.C. and B.S. collected and analyzed the data. D.A.C. drafted the original manuscript. B.S., K.M.H., C.K.H., W.S.C.P., R.S.D., C.K. and A.J.W. designed the research, and reviewed and edited the manuscript. All authors have read and agreed to the published version of the manuscript.

Funding: This research received no external funding.

Institutional Review Board Statement: The study was conducted in accordance with the Declaration of Helsinki and approved by the Institutional Review Board of the University of Central Missouri (Protocol# 2176, approved on 11 August 2022) for studies involving humans.

Informed Consent Statement: Informed consent was obtained from all subjects involved in the study.

Data Availability Statement: The de-identified data that support the findings of this study are available on request from the corresponding author. Any use of these data should be accompanied by appropriate attribution to this published report.

Conflicts of Interest: The authors declare no conflict of interest.

References

1. Roberts, B.M.; Rushing, K.A.; Plaisance, E.P. Sex Differences in Body Composition and Fitness Scores in Military Reserve Officers' Training Corps Cadets. *Mil. Med.* **2023**, *188*, e1–e5. [CrossRef] [PubMed]
2. Army Combat Fitness Test. Available online: https://www.army.mil/acft/ (accessed on 28 August 2023).
3. Crawford, D.A.; Drake, N.B.; Carper, M.J.; Deblauw, J.; Heinrich, K.M. Are Changes in Physical Work Capacity Induced by High-Intensity Functional Training Related to Changes in Associated Physiologic Measures? *Sports* **2018**, *6*, 26. [CrossRef] [PubMed]
4. Feito, Y.; Heinrich, K.M.; Butcher, S.J.; Carlos Poston, W.S. High-Intensity Functional Training (Hift): Definition and Research Implications for Improved Fitness. *Sports* **2018**, *6*, 76. [CrossRef] [PubMed]
5. Davis, A.E. Instrument Development: Getting Started. *J. Neurosci. Nurs.* **1996**, *28*, 204–208. [CrossRef] [PubMed]
6. Lentz, J. Prescription Exercise Programming in Preparation for the Army Combat Fitness Test. *NSCA TSAC Rep.* **2022**, *67*, 20–24.
7. Jamovi. *The Jamovi Project*; Jamovi: Burton on Trent, UK, 2021.
8. R Core Team. R: A Language and Environment for Statistical Computing. 2021. Available online: https://cran.r-project.org (accessed on 26 April 2023).
9. Gallucci, M. *GAMLj: General Analyses for Linear Models*; Jamovi: Burton on Trent, UK, 2019.

10. Sing, T.; Sander, O.; Beerenwinkel, N.; Lengauer, T. ROCR: Visualizing the Performance of Scoring Classifiers. 2015. Available online: https://cran.r-project.org/package=ROCR (accessed on 26 April 2023).
11. Bouchard, C.; Rankinen, T. Individual Differences in Response to Regular Physical Activity. *Med. Sci. Sport Exerc.* **2001**, *33*, S446–S451. [CrossRef] [PubMed]
12. Moore, D.; Tayler, M.; Moore, S. The Short-Term Reliability of the Conceptualised 'Combat Readiness Assessment'. *Int. J. Environ. Res. Public Health* **2022**, *19*, 6486. [CrossRef] [PubMed]
13. Ehrman, J.; Liguori, G.; Magal, M. Health-Related Physical Fitness Testing and Interpretation. In *ACSM's Guidelines for Exercise Testing and Prescription*; Lippincott Williams & Wilkins: Philadelphia, PA, USA, 2018; pp. 66–105.
14. Morton, R.H. The Critical Power and Related Whole-Body Bioenergetic Models. *Eur. J. Appl. Physiol.* **2006**, *96*, 339–354. [CrossRef] [PubMed]

Journal of
Functional Morphology and Kinesiology

Article

Transversus Abdominis Ultrasound Thickness during Popular Trunk–Pilates Exercises in Young and Middle-Aged Women

Ioannis Tsartsapakis [1], Maria Gerou [1], Aglaia Zafeiroudi [2] and Eleftherios Kellis [1,*]

[1] Laboratory of Neuromechanics, Department of Physical Education and Sport Sciences at Serres, Aristotle University of Thessaloniki, 62100 Serres, Greece; ioantsar@phed-sr.auth.gr (I.T.)
[2] Department Physical Education & Sport Science, University of Thessaly, 42100 Trikala, Greece
* Correspondence: ekellis@phed-sr.auth.gr

Abstract: The transversus abdominis (TrA) is a core muscle that contributes to functional mobility and lumbar stability. This study aimed to compare the changes in TrA thickness during different Pilates exercises, and to identify the exercise that elicited the greatest TrA activation. Forty-four healthy women were divided into two groups: young (25–35 years old) and middle-aged (36–55 years old). TrA thickness was assessed by ultrasound while the participants performed five Pilates exercises: basic position, hundred, hip roll, side plank, and dead bug. A repeated measures analysis of variance revealed that the dead bug exercise induced a significantly higher increase in TrA thickness (relative to rest) than the other exercises ($p < 0.05$). The young group also showed a significantly higher overall TrA thickness than the middle-aged group ($p < 0.05$). The findings suggest that the dead bug exercise is the most effective for enhancing TrA activation among the Pilates exercises tested. The basic position and the hundred exercises can be used as warm-up exercises before performing more challenging exercises such as the hip roll, the side plank, and the dead bug. The sequence of exercises can be similar for both young and middle-aged women.

Keywords: transversus abdominis; abdominal draw-in maneuver; ultrasound imaging; TrA tthickness; kinetic and functional stabilization

Citation: Tsartsapakis, I.; Gerou, M.; Zafeiroudi, A.; Kellis, E. Transversus Abdominis Ultrasound Thickness during Popular Trunk–Pilates Exercises in Young and Middle-Aged Women. *J. Funct. Morphol. Kinesiol.* **2023**, *8*, 110. https://doi.org/10.3390/jfmk8030110

Academic Editor: Gianpiero Greco

Received: 3 July 2023
Revised: 29 July 2023
Accepted: 2 August 2023
Published: 4 August 2023

1. Introduction

Core stability and trunk control are essential for maintaining postural alignment, preventing injuries, and enhancing performance in various physical activities [1]. The core musculature consists of the muscles of the pelvic floor, the abdominal and back muscles, the diaphragm, and the transversus abdominis (TrA) [2]. The TrA is considered to be the primary stabilizer of the lumbar spine and the pelvis, as it is activated prior to any movement of the limbs [3]. The TrA also reduces the laxity of the sacroiliac joint and contributes to flattening the abdomen [4]. However, the TrA is often underutilized or dysfunctional in many individuals, especially those with low back pain or core instability [4]. Therefore, training the TrA and improving its activation during various movements is important for enhancing core function and reducing pain [5].

One of the methods to assess the function of the TrA is ultrasound (US) imaging, which can measure the thickness of the muscle during rest and contraction [6]. US imaging has been shown to be a reliable and valid technique to evaluate TrA activation, as it reflects the changes in muscle fiber length and pennation angle [7]. US imaging also has some advantages over other methods of measuring TrA function, such as electromyography (EMG) or pressure biofeedback, as it is non-invasive, easy to use, and provides real-time feedback [8]. However, US imaging also has some limitations, such as being dependent on operator skill, requiring standardized positioning and calibration, and being influenced by factors such as hydration status and body fat [9].

Pilates is a popular exercise method developed by Joseph Pilates with its own philosophy and basic principles. The roots of Pilates come from ancient Greek and Eastern philosophy about mind body and spirit connection [10,11]. Today Pilates is divided into two types, the classic and the modern or contemporary, with many differences between them [11]. Classical Pilates exercises focus on posterior pelvic tilt, and they are taught as Joseph Pilates originally invented them without any modification and in the same order every time [11]. In contrast, contemporary Pilates incorporated new exercises or modifications of the existing ones whilst they are performed with a neutral pelvis position. There are suggestions that contemporary Pilates consider latest scientific developments to make the method more appropriate, functional, and safer for the participants [11]. In fact, in contemporary Pilates, any movement and exercise can be incorporated according to the basic principles and philosophy of the method.

The Pilates method constitutes a fundamental component in the movement, health and fitness, and rehabilitation industry. It focuses on training the core musculature, especially the TrA [12]. Pilates exercises are based on six principles: centering, concentration, control, precision, breath, and flow [13]. Exercises that are used in Pilates programs involve performing movements with a neutral spine alignment and a co-contraction of the deep abdominal and pelvic floor muscles [14]. Some examples of common exercises are the supine hook lying abdominal drawing-in maneuver (ADIM) [15], the hundred A and B exercises, which involve holding a static position with arm and leg movements while breathing deeply [16], and the leg raise and roll up exercises, which challenge the trunk stability and mobility while moving the legs or the upper body [17]. The ADIM is a slow and gentle abdominal hollowing [18] maneuver where individuals gently pull the umbilicus towards the spine, hold the contraction, and breathe normally [19–21] for up to 10 s. Originally, the ADIM is performed after the participants assume a supine position with their hips at 40–60° and their knees are flexed between 90° and 100° and their arms are placed along their torso [18]. Since then, the ADIM is performed simultaneously with other exercises to increase TrA contraction [19–21].

Due to its deep anatomical location, non-invasive examination of TrA activation is difficult. For this reason, ultrasound (US) thickness measurements have been used as an indirect index of muscle size at rest as well as an index of muscle recruitment during exercise [22,23]. Core stability exercises have been shown to increase TrA thickness in healthy women and improve low back pain in women with chronic pain [24]. However, there is limited evidence on which Pilates exercises produce the greatest activation of the TrA and whether this activation differs according to the age of the participants. Previous studies have reported conflicting results on which exercises elicit higher TrA recruitment, such as upper or lower limb lifts from the quadruped position [25], prone plank [26], bridge exercises with abdominal bracing [27,28], or planks with opposite arm–leg elevation [29]. Moreover, some studies have suggested that there may be age-related differences in TrA activation [30,31]. A study by Kellis et al. [6] showed that young adults had the greatest relative transversus abdominis thickness during contraction compared to middle-aged adults, adolescents, and children. The aim of this study was to compare TrA thickness during five common exercises (basic position, hundred, hip roll (or bridge), side plank, and dead bug) that are used in Pilates programs and to examine whether there are differences in TrA thickness between younger and middle-aged (but more experienced) participants. It was hypothesized that (1) different Pilates exercises would result in different levels of TrA activation and (2) young participants would have higher TrA activation than middle-aged participants.

2. Materials and Methods

2.1. Participants

A total of 44 adult women mean age 33.2 ± 8.7 (25 to 55 years of age) participated in this study. The participants were divided into two groups: the young group (N = 29, 27.7 ± 2.4 years) and the middle-aged group (N = 15, 44.0 ± 5.7 years). The participants did not report any problems (pain or chronic low back pain) in the area of the core and the trunk. They also had at least three years of experience with Pilates programs.

The study was conducted in accordance with the ethical guidelines of Aristotle University of Thessaloniki, and all procedures followed the most recent version of the Declaration of Helsinki. All participants were informed about the purpose of the research and provided their written consent to participate.

2.2. Instrumentation

All TrA measurements were collected with an Aloka Prosound SSD-3500SV US system (Aloka Inc, Tokyo, Japan). The transducer head had a length of 6 cm, and its frequency was 13 MHZ.

2.3. Exercise Protocol

The duration of the entire procedure was 50 min for each participant to avoid fatigue in the trunk area. The participants first received relevant information on how to perform each of the exercises and then performed several trials of each exercise to gain familiarization. Following familiarization, the main measurements were collected.

First, the participants assumed the relaxed position (Figure 1A) by lying on the mat with hands on their sides and their knees flexed 90°. TrA muscle thickness was measured at rest in this position. Then, a representative set of five classical Pilates mat exercises were performed. The examiner first asked the participants to assume one of the five exercise postures.

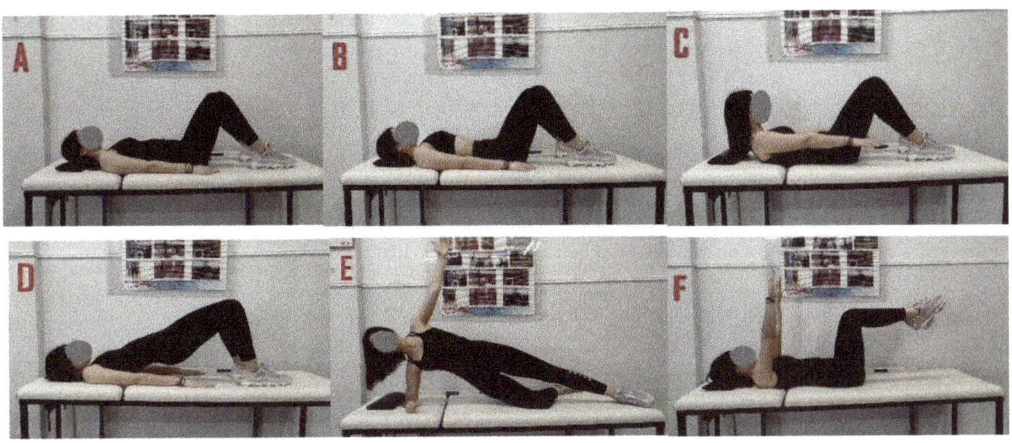

Figure 1. Illustration of the examined exercises: (**A**) relax position, (**B**) basic position, (**C**) hundred, (**D**) hip roll, (**E**) side plank, and (**F**) dead bug.

In particular, the following instructions were given to the participants:

(1) Relax and basic Pilates position (Figure 1A,B) "lie on your mat with your legs bent, feet flat on the ground, chin in toward chest, pelvis in a neutral position. Feel the spine on your mat keeping the natural curve of the lumbar spine. Shoulders are relaxed away from the ears; arms are relaxed with the palms touching the ground". In the basic Pilates position, participants were asked to perform the ADIM for voluntary TrA activation three times.

(2) Hundred (Figure 1C), "lie on your mat with your legs bent, feet flat on the ground and lengthen your spine, pelvis in neutral position. Inhale activate your abs. Exhale lift your head and shoulders off the mat with your eyes between your legs. Arms are off the mat next to the sides of the body, palms facing down, fingers outstretched, and shoulders fixed away from the ears. Arms pump vigorously, lifting up and down no higher than the hips. While pumping arms, inhale and exhale 5 times to complete one repetition. The exercise is performed 10 times with 5 inhales and 5 exhales equaling 100".

(3) Hip roll (Figure 1D), "lie on your back with your knees bent and your legs hip-width apart. Knees are bent at about 90 degrees. Arms are straight and palms down on the mat by your sides. Pelvis should be in a neutral position. This means that your pelvis and bum is neither tucked under (so that your back is flat) nor is it duck-like and sticking out. Take a deep, full inhale and create space in your spine by imagining it lengthening. Then start to exhale slowly through an open mouth. Press into your feet and start to peel your spine up into the bridge position starting from your tailbone. Only bridge up to the point where your shoulder blades are resting on the mat. Pause at the top of your bridge and take an inhale here. Exhale and slowly start to bridge back down. To initiate this part of the movement, first allow your chest to soften. Then allow the rest of the spine to trickle down segmentally to the mat vertebra by vertebra. Your bridge is complete when your body is back resting on the mat with your pelvis in neutral position. Three repetitions will be performed".

(4) Side plank (Figure 1E), "lie on your left side with one leg straight and the other with the knee on the mat. Place your left elbow on the mat. The elbow of your left arm is directly under your shoulder. Spine is in neutral position. Ensure your head is directly in line with your spine. Stretch the right arm toward the ceiling. Engage your abdominal muscles, drawing your navel toward your spine. Your torso is straight in line with no sagging or bending. Hold the position for 3 breaths. Repeat on the other side. Three repetitions will be performed".

(5) Dead bug (Figure 1F), "lie on the mat with your arms extended straight over your chest so they form a perpendicular angle with your torso. Bend your hips and knees 90-degrees, lifting your feet from the ground. Your torso and thighs should form a right angle, as should your thighs and shins (table top). Engage your core, maintaining contact between your lower back and the mat. Your spine maintains in neutral position throughout the exercise. Three repetitions will be performed". All instructions were given by the same instructor who is a certified Pilates teacher.

Except the resting position, every participant was asked to perform the ADIM while they executed each exercise for a period of ten seconds.

2.4. Muscle Thickness Measurements

The US head was placed 2.5 cm above the iliac crest and along the axillary line [32]. The position of the head was standardized by placing the anterior origin of the fascia 2 cm to the left of the middle of the US image when relaxed [33]. US images were used for analysis during the rest condition and while participants performed the ADIM during each exercise. Using the manufacturer's US device software (v2.0, Aloka Inc, Tokyo, Japan), the US image was frozen approximately between 4 and 6 s of the 10 s rest condition or ADIM contraction. TrA was measured on the US device screen as the distance from the superior to inferior fascia of the muscle 2.5 cm from the anterior origin of the fascia (Figure 2). Three repetitions were analyzed, and an average muscle thickness measurement was calculated. In addition to absolute thickness (measured in mm), TrA relative thickness ratio during each exercise was expressed as a percentage of resting thickness, (TrA active − TrA rest)/TrA rest × 100, [34] for each exercise (Figure 3).

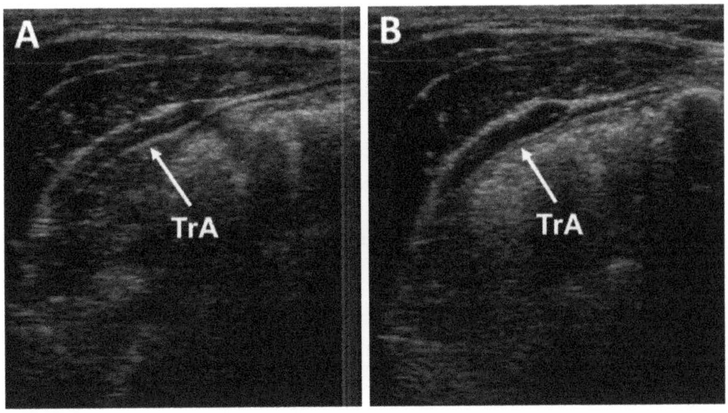

Figure 2. Ultrasound screenshot of TrA measurement. (**A**) TrA at rest prior to the application of ADIM. (**B**) TrA during a contraction after the application of ADIM.

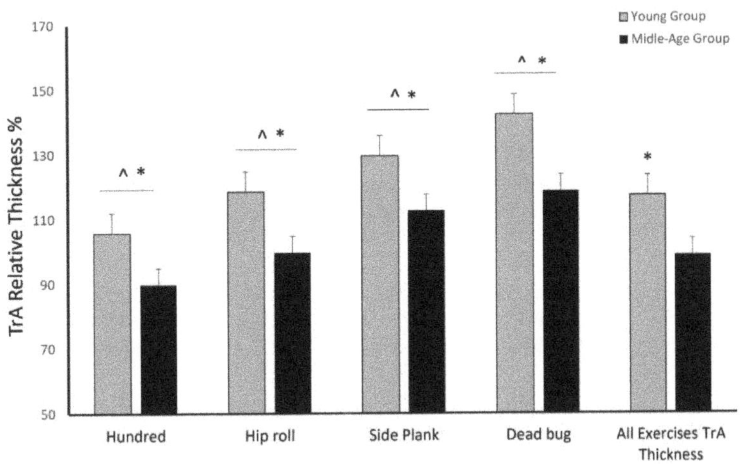

Figure 3. Mean (±SE) TrA relative thickness in each exercise for both groups, expressed as a percentage of the thickness at rest. * Young group had a significantly higher relative mean TrA thickness in all exercises than the middle-aged group (p =< 0.001); ^ each exercise differed compared to other exercises, ($p < 0.01$).

In a previous study, the inter-examiner and intra-examiner reliability of TrA muscle thickness at rest and contraction was examined, and the reliability was high with intraclass correlation coefficients ranging from 0.86 to 0.97 at rest, from 0.89 to 0.97 during ADIM, and from 0.77 to 0.98 for the relative thickness values [6].

2.5. Statistical Analysis

All statistical analyses were conducted using IBM SPSS Statistics ver. 26.0 (IBM Co., Armonk, NY, USA). Normal distribution of the collected data was verified by using the Kolmogorov–Smirnov test. An independent sample t-test was performed to evaluate whether there was a statistically significant difference in anthropometric characteristics and years of Pilates training between the two groups. A two-way repeated measures ANOVA was applied to examine the effects of exercise (basic position, hundred, hip roll, side plank, and dead bug) and group (young vs. middle-aged) on absolute and relative TrA thickness. The Greenhouse–Geisser correction was used when the assumption of sphericity was violated. The degrees of freedom (df), mean square error (MSE), F or t values, and effect sizes (η^2 or Cohen's d) were reported for each test. Post hoc comparisons were performed using the Bonferroni correction. The level of significance was set at $p < 0.05$.

3. Results

3.1. Descriptives

The anthropometric characteristics and years of Pilates training of the entire sample and each group are shown in Table 1. No significant differences were found in anthropometric characteristics between the two groups ($p > 0.05$).

Table 1. Mean (±SD) anthropometric characteristics of each group (BMI = body mass index).

	Total Sample	Young	Middle Age
N	44	29	15
Age (years)	33.2 ± 8.6	27.7 ± 2.4	44.0 ± 5.7
Height (cm)	166.1 ± 6.3	166.6 ± 7.0	165.1 ± 4.9
Mass (kg)	59.0 ± 5.6	58.3 ± 5.5	60.3 ± 5.7
BMI	214 ± 1.9	21.0 ± 1.7	22.1 ± 2.0

3.2. Absolute Thickness

The mean absolute thickness descriptive values for each exercise and group are presented in Table 2. A two-way repeated measures ANOVA revealed a significant main effect of exercise on TrA muscle absolute thickness ($F_{(4, 168)} = 230.37$, $p < 0.001$, $\eta_p^2 = 0.84$), indicating that TrA thickness varied across different exercises. Post hoc Bonferroni analysis indicated that the dead bug exercise had a significantly greater mean TrA absolute thickness score than the side plank, hip roll, hundred, and the basic position exercises, respectively, ($p < 0.001$). Also, the side plank exercise had a significantly greater mean TrA thickness score than the hip roll, hundred, and the basic position exercises ($p < 0.001$). Likewise, the hip roll exercise had a significantly greater mean TrA thickness score than hundred and the basic position exercises ($p < 0.001$). Lastly, the hundred exercise had a significantly greater mean TrA thickness score than the basic position exercise ($p < 0.001$).

Table 2. Mean (± SD) group absolute TrA thickness values for each exercise in the entire sample, the young participants group (Young) and the middle-aged participants group (Middle-Aged). N = number of participants.

	Total Sample	Young	Middle-Aged
N	44	29	15
Basic position	6.68 ± 0.70 ^	6.92 ± 0.70 *	6.23 ± 0.47
Hundred	7.25 ± 0.73 ^	7.47 ± 0.72 *	6.83 ± 0.55
Hip roll	7.64 ± 0.68 ^	7.89 ± 0.64 *	7.17 ± 0.50
Side plank	8.07 ± 0.64 ^	8.29 ± 0.62 *	7.64 ± 0.46
Dead bug	8.41 ± 0.68 ^	8.70 ± 0.60 *	7.86 ± 0.48
All exercises TrA thickness	7.61 ± 0.68	7.85 ± 0.70 *	7.15 ± 0.65

* Young group had a significantly higher absolute mean TrA thickness in all exercises than the middle-aged group ($p < 0.001$), ^ significantly different compared to other exercises, ($p < 0.01$).

A significant main effect of group on TrA muscle absolute thickness was also found ($F_{(1, 42)} = 16.14$, $p < 0.001$, $\eta_p^2 = 0.27$), with the young group had a significantly greater mean TrA thickness score in all exercises than the middle-aged group ($p < 0.001$).

No significant interaction effect between exercise and group on TrA muscle absolute thickness was found ($F_{(4, 168)} = 0.75$, $p = 0.55$), indicating that the effect of exercise on TrA thickness was similar for both groups.

3.3. Relative Thickness

The mean relative thickness descriptive values for each exercise and group are presented in Figure 3. A two-way repeated measures ANOVA revealed a significant main effect of exercise on TrA muscle relative thickness ($F_{(4, 168)} = 142.84$, $p < 0.001$, $\eta_p^2 = 0.87$), indicating that TrA relative thickness varied across different exercises. Post hoc Bonferroni analysis indicated that the dead bug exercise had a significantly greater mean TrA relative thickness score than the side plank, hip roll, hundred and the basic position exercises ($p < 0.001$). Also, the side plank exercise had a significantly greater mean TrA relative thickness score than the hip roll, hundred, and the basic position exercises ($p < 0.001$). Likewise, the hip roll exercise had a significantly greater mean TrA relative thickness score than hundred and the basic position exercises ($p < 0.001$). Lastly, the hundred exercise had a significantly greater mean TrA relative thickness score than the basic position exercise ($p < 0.001$).

A significant main effect of group on TrA muscle relative thickness was also found ($F_{(1, 42)} = 7.01$, $p < 0.05$, $\eta_p^2 = 0.14$), with the young group having a significantly greater mean TrA thickness score in all exercises than the middle-aged group ($p = 0.011$).

No significant interaction effect between exercise and group on TrA muscle relative thickness was found ($F_{(4, 168)} = 0.75$, $p = 0.55$), indicating that the effect of exercise on TrA relative thickness was similar for both groups.

4. Discussion

The purpose of the present study was to examine TrA thickness in a series of exercises that are an integral part of the Pilates exercise programs. Further, it was examined whether a difference in TrA thickness during each exercise exists between the younger and middle-aged participants. The main findings of this study: (a) the dead bug exercise resulted in the highest TrA activation, followed by the side plank, hip roll, hundred and basic position exercises; and (b) the young group had higher TrA activation than the middle-aged group in all exercises.

4.1. Differences between Exercises

Our results showed that there was a ranking of the exercises in terms of TrA activation, which was the same for both groups. The dead bug exercise elicited the highest TrA activation, followed by the side plank, hip roll, hundred, and basic position exercises. This ranking suggests that exercises that require the co-activation of other muscle groups besides the core (dead bug) or exercises that involve lifting the trunk off the ground (side plank and hip roll) induce greater TrA activation than exercises that keep the trunk in contact with the ground and do not require co-activation of large muscle groups (basic position and hundred). This finding is consistent with previous studies that have reported higher TrA activation during exercises that challenge the trunk stability and mobility, such as planks [26], hip roll [27], or limb lifts [25], compared to exercises that involve less trunk movement or load, such as curl-ups [26] or hook lying [27].

One possible explanation for this finding is that the TrA plays a key role in stabilizing the lumbar spine and pelvis during movements or perturbations that impose high loads or forces on these regions [35]. The TrA can stabilize the spine by increasing the intra-abdominal pressure [36] or by resisting the rotational and translational forces during trunk movements [37]. Therefore, exercises that involve lifting or moving the trunk or limbs may require higher TrA activation to maintain spinal stability and alignment than exercises that keep the trunk in a neutral position. Another possible explanation is that Pilates exercises are based on six principles: centering, concentration, control, precision, breath, and flow [11]. These principles emphasize performing movements with a neutral spine alignment and a co-contraction of the deep abdominal and pelvic floor muscles [14]. Therefore, Pilates exercises may facilitate higher TrA activation by enhancing the awareness and coordination of these muscles during various movements.

Our results are partly in agreement with previous studies that have examined which core stability exercises produce the greatest TrA activation [25–27,29]. However, some studies have reported different results, such as higher TrA activation during prone plank [26], hip roll with abdominal bracing [27], or plank with opposite arm-leg elevation [29] than during other exercises. These discrepancies may be due to several factors, such as the use of different methods of measuring TrA activation (US vs. EMG), the use of different populations (healthy vs. low back pain), or the use of different types of exercises (Pilates vs. non-Pilates). Therefore, more studies are needed to compare TrA activation during various Pilates and non-Pilates exercises using both US and EMG methods in different populations.

4.2. Differences between Groups

Our results showed that there was no difference in TrA thickness at rest between the two groups. This finding is in line with two previous studies that have shown that age-related atrophy is less pronounced in deep trunk muscles such as the transversus abdominis and lumbar multifidus [38,39]. However, our results also show that young adults had significantly greater relative average TrA thickness than the middle-aged group in all exercises. This finding is consistent with previous research [6,30,31] as well as with a systematic review that has shown that younger individuals can recruit TrA higher than older individuals [40]. Our findings may be explained by several factors, such as differences in neuromuscular control, muscle fiber type composition, or hormonal status between younger and older individuals [40]. Also, it may be possible that other factors, such as genetic predisposition, lifestyle habits, or injury history, may have influenced TrA activation. Therefore, more studies are needed to examine the effects of Pilates experience on TrA activation using larger samples and longitudinal designs.

4.3. Implications and Applications

The results of this study have some implications and applications for clinical practice and future research. First, our results suggest that exercises that are part of Pilates programs are effective in activating the TrA during various movements. This is important because previous studies have shown that such exercises can improve core stability and function [12], reduce low back pain [41], and enhance quality of life [10] in different populations. Therefore, Pilates programs including such exercises may be beneficial for individuals who want to improve their core health and performance. Second, our results suggest that different Pilates exercises result in different levels of TrA activation. This is important because it can be used in the design and progression of Pilates programs for different purposes and populations. For example, exercises that elicit lower TrA activation (basic position and hundred) may be suitable for beginners or individuals with low back pain who need to learn how to activate their core muscles properly. Exercises that elicit higher TrA activation (dead bug, side plank, and hip roll) may be suitable for advanced or healthy individuals who want to challenge their core stability and mobility. Third, our results suggest that younger individuals can activate their core muscles higher than older individuals regardless of their Pilates experience. This is important because it indicates that age may be a more influential factor than experience on core muscle function. Therefore, more attention should be paid to training older individuals who may have reduced core muscle function due to aging.

4.4. Limitations

The present study has several limitations. First, the study was conducted with recreationally active females with no musculoskeletal injuries. This limits the generalizability of the results to other ages, genders, and populations who may have different levels of core muscle function or pathology. Second, the study examined only one muscle (TrA) using one method (US). This limits the comprehensiveness of the assessment of core muscle function as there are other muscles involved in core stability (such as internal oblique and multifidus) and other methods to measure muscle activity (such as EMG). Third, the study examined only static exercises performed on a stable surface. This limits the ecological validity of the assessment of core muscle function as there are many dynamic movements performed on unstable surfaces in daily life or sports activities. Further, US muscle thickness measurements may be influenced by body fluid shifts [42]. In the present study, the participants were instructed to maintain standard hydration whilst exercises were performed from a supine position, which most likely involves minimal body fluid shifts [42], and, hence, it is likely that the effect of body fluids on muscle thickness measurements was minimal.

5. Conclusions

We examined TrA thickness during five common exercises that are part of Pilates programs performed by young and middle-aged women with Pilates experience. Of these exercises, those that elicited higher TrA activation were dead bug exercise followed by side plank exercise followed by hip roll exercise followed by hundred exercise followed by basic position exercise. Younger women had higher TrA activation than middle-aged women. These findings could be used to adjust exercise progression during a core stabilization exercise program based on age and purpose. Future studies should examine more core muscles using other methods during dynamic movements performed on stable and unstable surfaces in different populations.

Author Contributions: Conceptualization, M.G., I.T. and E.K.; methodology, I.T. and E.K.; statistical analysis, I.T. and E.K.; investigation, M.G. and I.T.; data curation, I.T.; writing—original draft preparation, I.T. and E.K.; writing—review and editing, I.T., E.K., M.G. and A.Z.; visualization, I.T.; supervision, I.T., A.Z. and E.K.; project administration, I.T. and E.K.; All authors have read and agreed to the published version of the manuscript.

Funding: This research received no external funding.

Institutional Review Board Statement: The study was conducted in accordance with the Declaration of Helsinki and approved by the Institutional Ethics Committee of the Aristotle University of Thessaloniki (ERC06/2020 and 25 April 2020).

Informed Consent Statement: Informed consent was obtained from all subjects involved in the study.

Data Availability Statement: The data presented in this study are available on request from the corresponding author.

Acknowledgments: We are incredibly grateful to the Pilates participants for their time, effort, and willingness to participate in this study.

Conflicts of Interest: The authors declare no conflict of interest.

References

1. Smith, M.D.; Russell, A.; Hodges, P.W. Disorders of Breathing and Continence Have a Stronger Association with Back Pain than Obesity and Physical Activity. *Aust. J. Physiother.* **2006**, *52*, 11–16. [CrossRef] [PubMed]
2. Hodges, P.W.; Richardson, C.A. Feedforward Contraction of Transversus Abdominis Is Not Influenced by the Direction of Arm Movement. *Exp. Brain Res.* **1997**, *114*, 362–370. [CrossRef] [PubMed]
3. Ehsani, F.; Sahebi, N.; Shanbehzadeh, S.; Arab, A.M.; ShahAli, S. Stabilization Exercise Affects Function of Transverse Abdominis and Pelvic Floor Muscles in Women with Postpartum Lumbo-Pelvic Pain: A Double-Blinded Randomized Clinical Trial Study. *Int. Urogynecol. J.* **2020**, *31*, 197–204. [CrossRef]
4. Lynders, C. The Critical Role of Development of the Transversus Abdominis in the Prevention and Treatment of Low Back Pain. *HSS J.* ® **2019**, *15*, 214–220. [CrossRef]
5. Lee, C.-W.W.; Hyun, J.; Kim, S.G. Influence of Pilates Mat and Apparatus Exercises on Pain and Balance of Businesswomen with Chronic Low Back Pain. *J. Phys. Ther. Sci.* **2014**, *26*, 475–477. [CrossRef]
6. Kellis, E.; Ellinoudis, A.; Intziegianni, K.; Kofotolis, N. Muscle Thickness During Core Stability Exercises in Children and Adults. *J. Hum. Kinet.* **2020**, *71*, 131–144. [CrossRef]

7. Johnson, A.W.; Adams, L.; Kho, J.B.; Green, D.M.; Pace, N.B.; Mitchell, U.H. Extended Field-of-View Ultrasound Imaging Is Reliable for Measuring Transversus Abdominis Muscle Size at Rest and during Contraction. *BMC Musculoskelet. Disord.* **2021**, *22*, 282. [CrossRef] [PubMed]
8. Whittaker, J.L.; Warner, M.B.; Stokes, M. Comparison of the Sonographic Features of the Abdominal Wall Muscles and Connective Tissues in Individuals With and Without Lumbopelvic Pain. *J. Orthop. Sports Phys. Ther.* **2013**, *43*, 11–19. [CrossRef] [PubMed]
9. Teyhen, D.S.; Gill, N.W.; Whittaker, J.L.; Henry, S.M.; Hides, J.A.; Hodges, P. Rehabilitative Ultrasound Imaging of the Abdominal Muscles. *J. Orthop. Sports Phys. Ther.* **2007**, *37*, 450–466. [CrossRef]
10. Zafeiroudi, A.; Kouthouris, C. Somatic Education and Mind-Body Disciplines: Exploring the Effects of the Pilates Method on Life Satisfaction, Mindfulness and Self-Compassion. *J. Educ. Soc. Res.* **2022**, *12*, 1. [CrossRef]
11. Shedden, M.; Kravitz, L. Pilates. *ACSMs Health Fit. J.* **2007**, *11*, 7–12. [CrossRef]
12. Kofotolis, N.; Kellis, E.; Vlachopoulos, S.P.; Gouitas, I.; Theodorakis, Y. Effects of Pilates and Trunk Strengthening Exercises on Health-Related Quality of Life in Women with Chronic Low Back Pain. *J. Back Musculoskelet. Rehabil.* **2016**, *29*, 649–659. [CrossRef] [PubMed]
13. Anderson, B.D.; Spector, A. Introduction to Pilates-Based Rehabilitation. *Orthop. Phys. Ther. Clin. N. Am.* **2000**, *9*, 395–410.
14. Wells, C.; Kolt, G.S.; Marshall, P.; Bialocerkowski, A. The Definition and Application of Pilates Exercise to Treat People With Chronic Low Back Pain: A Delphi Survey of Australian Physical Therapists. *Phys. Ther.* **2014**, *94*, 792–805. [CrossRef]
15. Richardson, C.A.; Jull, G.A.; Hides, J.A. *A New Clinical Model of the Muscle Dysfunction Linked to the Disturbance of Spinal Stability: Implications for Treatment of Low Back Pain;* Churchill Livingstone: London, UK, 2000.
16. Endleman, I.; Critchley, D.J. Transversus Abdominis and Obliquus Internus Activity During Pilates Exercises: Measurement With Ultrasound Scanning. *Arch. Phys. Med. Rehabil.* **2008**, *89*, 2205–2212. [CrossRef] [PubMed]
17. Phrompaet, S.; Paungmali, A.; Pirunsan, U.; Sitilertpisan, P. Effects of Pilates Training on Lumbo-Pelvic Stability and Flexibility. *Asian J. Sports Med.* **2011**, *2*, 16. [CrossRef]
18. Richardson, C.; Jull, G.; Hides, J.; Hodges, P. *Therapeutic Exercise for Spinal Segmental Stabilization in Low Back Pain;* Churchill Livingstone: London, UK, 1999; ISBN 0443058024.
19. Kaping, K.; Äng, B.O.; Rasmussen-Barr, E. The Abdominal Drawing-in Manoeuvre for Detecting Activity in the Deep Abdominal Muscles: Is This Clinical Tool Reliable and Valid? *BMJ Open* **2015**, *5*, e008711. [CrossRef]
20. McGalliard, M.K.; Dedrick, G.S.; Brismée, J.M.; Cook, C.E.; Apte, G.G.; Sizer, P.S., Jr. Changes in Transversus Abdominis Thickness with Use of the Abdominal Drawing-in Maneuver during a Functional Task. *PM&R* **2010**, *2*, 187–194. [CrossRef]
21. Park, S.-D.; Yu, S.-H. The Effects of Abdominal Draw-in Maneuver and Core Exercise on Abdominal Muscle Thickness and Oswestry Disability Index in Subjects with Chronic Low Back Pain. *J. Exerc. Rehabil.* **2013**, *9*, 286–291. [CrossRef]
22. Costa, L.O.P.; Maher, C.G.; Latimer, J.; Hodges, P.W.; Shirley, D. An Investigation of the Reproducibility of Ultrasound Measures of Abdominal Muscle Activation in Patients with Chronic Non-Specific Low Back Pain. *Eur. Spine J.* **2009**, *18*, 1059–1065. [CrossRef]
23. Costa, L.O.P.; Maher, C.G.; Latimer, J.; Smeets, R.J.E.M. Reproducibility of Rehabilitative Ultrasound Imaging for the Measurement of Abdominal Muscle Activity: A Systematic Review. *Phys. Ther.* **2009**, *89*, 756–769. [CrossRef] [PubMed]
24. Miyamoto, G.C.; Costa, L.O.P.; Galvanin, T.; Cabral, C.M.N. Efficacy of the Addition of Modified Pilates Exercises to a Minimal Intervention in Patients With Chronic Low Back Pain: A Randomized Controlled Trial. *Phys. Ther.* **2013**, *93*, 310–320. [CrossRef] [PubMed]
25. Emami, F.; Pirouzi, S.; Taghizadeh, S. Comparison of Abdominal and Lumbar Muscles Electromyography Activity During Two Types of Stabilization Exercises. *Zahedan J. Res. Med. Sci.* **2015**, *17*, 1–7. [CrossRef]
26. Imai, A.; Kaneoka, K.; Okubo, Y.; Shiina, I.; Tatsumura, M.; Izumi, S.; Shiraki, H. Trunk Muscle Activity During Lumbar Stabilization Exercises on Both a Stable and Unstable Surface. *J. Orthop. Sports Phys. Ther.* **2010**, *40*, 369–375. [CrossRef]
27. Moghadam, N.; Ghaffari, M.S.; Noormohammadpour, P.; Rostam, M.; Zarei, M.; Moosavi, M.; Kordi, R.; Rostami, M.; Zarei, M.; Moosavi, M.; et al. Comparison of the Recruitment of Transverse Abdominis through Drawing-in and Bracing in Different Core Stability Training Positions. *J. Exerc. Rehabil.* **2019**, *15*, 819–825. [CrossRef]
28. Moon, J.-H.; Hong, S.-M.; Kim, C.-W.; Shin, Y.-A. Comparison of Deep and Superficial Abdominal Muscle Activity between Experienced Pilates and Resistance Exercise Instructors and Controls during Stabilization Exercise. *J. Exerc. Rehabil.* **2015**, *11*, 161–168. [CrossRef]
29. Okubo, Y.; Kaneoka, K.; Mai, A.; Shiina, I.; Tatsumura, M.; Izumi, S.; Miyakawa, S.; Imai, A.; Shiina, I.; Tatsumura, M.; et al. Electromyographic Analysis of Transversus Abdominis and Lumbar Multifidus Using Wire Electrodes during Lumbar Stabilization Exercises. *J. Orthop. Sports Phys. Ther.* **2010**, *40*, 743–750. [CrossRef]
30. Gaudreault, N.; Benoît-Piau, J.; van Wingerden, J.P.; Stecco, C.; Daigle, F.; Léonard, G. An Investigation of the Association between Transversus Abdominis Myofascial Structure and Activation with Age in Healthy Adults Using Ultrasound Imaging. *Int. J. Sports Phys. Ther.* **2021**, *16*, 1093–1103. [CrossRef]
31. Davies, P.; Grace, F.M.; Lewis, M.P.; Sculthorpe, N. Observation of Age-Related Decline in the Performance of the Transverse Abdominis Muscle. *PM&R* **2016**, *8*, 45–50. [CrossRef]
32. Teyhen, D.S.; Miltenberger, C.E.; Deiters, H.M.; Del Toro, Y.M.; Pulliam, J.N.; Childs, J.D.; Boyles, R.E.; Flynn, T.W. The Use of Ultrasound Imaging of the Abdominal Drawing-in Maneuver in Subjects with Low Back Pain. *J. Orthop. Sports Phys. Ther.* **2005**, *35*, 346–355. [CrossRef]

33. Ferreira, P.H.; Ferreira, M.L.; Hodges, P.W. Changes in Recruitment of the Abdominal Muscles in People with Low Back Pain: Ultrasound Measurement of Muscle Activity. *Spine* **2004**, *29*, 2560–2566. [CrossRef]
34. Teyhen, D.S.; Bluemle, L.N.; Dolbeer, J.A.; Molloy, J.M.; Whittaker, J.; Childs, J.D. Changes in Lateral Abdominal Muscle Thickness during the Abdominal Drawing-in Maneuver in Those with Lumbopelvic Pain. *J. Orthop. Sports Phys. Ther.* **2009**, *39*, 791–798. [CrossRef] [PubMed]
35. Kibler, W.B.; Press, J.; Sciascia, A. The Role of Core Stability in Athletic Function. *Sports Med.* **2006**, *36*, 189–198. [CrossRef] [PubMed]
36. Watanabe, M.; Kaneoka, K.; Okubo, Y.; Shiina, I.; Tatsumura, M.; Miyakawa, S. Trunk Muscle Activity While Lifting Objects of Unexpected Weight. *Physiotherapy* **2013**, *99*, 78–83. [CrossRef]
37. Motomura, Y.; Tateuchi, H.; Komamura, T.; Yagi, Y.; Nakao, S.; Ichihashi, N. Effects of Trunk Lean and Foot Lift Exercises in Sitting Position on Abdominal Muscle Activity and the Contribution Rate of Transversus Abdominis. *Eur. J. Appl. Physiol.* **2021**, *121*, 173–181. [CrossRef]
38. Ikezoe, T.; Mori, N.; Nakamura, M.; Ichihashi, N. Effects of Age and Inactivity Due to Prolonged Bed Rest on Atrophy of Trunk Muscles. *Eur. J. Appl. Physiol.* **2012**, *112*, 43–48. [CrossRef] [PubMed]
39. Ota, M.; Ikezoe, T.; Kaneoka, K.; Ichihashi, N. Age-Related Changes in the Thickness of the Deep and Superficial Abdominal Muscles in Women. *Arch. Gerontol. Geriatr.* **2012**, *55*, e26–e30. [CrossRef]
40. Cuellar, W.A.A.; Wilson, A.; Blizzard, C.L.L.; Otahal, P.; Callisaya, M.L.L.; Jones, G.; Hides, J.A.A.; Winzenberg, T.M.M. The Assessment of Abdominal and Multifidus Muscles and Their Role in Physical Function in Older Adults: A Systematic Review. *Physiotherapy* **2017**, *103*, 21–39. [CrossRef]
41. Goldberg, N.; Weisman, A.; Schuster, S.; Dar, G.; Masharawi, Y. Effect of a Full Pilates Group Exercise Program on Transversus Abdominis Thickness, Daily Function and Pain in Women with Chronic Low Back Pain. *Kinesiology* **2021**, *53*, 318–325. [CrossRef]
42. Naruse, M.; Trappe, S.; Trappe, T.A. Human Skeletal Muscle Size with Ultrasound Imaging: A Comprehensive Review. *J. Appl. Physiol.* **2022**, *132*, 1267–1279. [CrossRef]

Journal of
Functional Morphology and Kinesiology

MDPI

Article

Effects of Physical Activity in the High School Curriculum on Cardiovascular Health, Cognitive and Physical Performance

Tobias Jagomast [1,2], Theresa Mohr [1,2], Paul Niklas Axt [1,2], Kai Mortensen [3,4], Folke Brinkmann [2,5], Markus Weckmann [2,5], Gordon Ring [6], Michael Reppel [4,7], Daniel Drömann [1,2] and Klaas F. Franzen [1,2,*]

1 Medical Clinic III, University Clinic Schleswig-Holstein Campus Luebeck, Ratzeburger Alle 160, 23562 Luebeck, Germany; tobias.jagomast@uksh.de (T.J.); themohr@t-online.de (T.M.); paul.axt@student.uni-luebeck.de (P.N.A.); daniel.dromann@uksh.de (D.D.)
2 Airway Research Center North (ARCN), German Center for Lung Research (DZL), 22927 Großhansdorf, Germany; folke.brinkmann@uksh.de (F.B.); markus.weckmann@uni-luebeck.de (M.W.)
3 Cardiology Kiel, 24116 Kiel, Germany; kaimortensen@yahoo.de
4 Clinic for Rhythmology, Campus Lübeck, University Hospital Schleswig-Holstein, 23562 Lübeck, Germany; reppel@kardiologie-landsberg.de
5 Section for Pulmonary Pediatrics, Campus Lübeck, University Hospital Schleswig-Holstein, 23562 Lübeck, Germany
6 DRK Krankenhaus Mölln-Ratzeburg, Anästhesie, Röpersberg 2, 23909 Ratzeburg, Germany; g.ring@drk-krankenhaus.de
7 Cardiology Landsberg, 86899 Landsberg, Germany
* Correspondence: klaas.franzen@uni-luebeck.de

Abstract: Cardiovascular health at a young age has implications for preventing cardiovascular disease, and it is associated with improved physical and cognitive performance during the aging process. Sports are well known to prevent cardiovascular disease; however, school-based interventions have mostly been neglected. This cross-sectional study aimed to compare groups of high school students, stratified by the amount of physical activity in their high school curriculum and downtime. Comparisons concerning physical and cognitive performance and arterial stiffness were made. A total of 63 senior-year students were investigated. Arterial stiffness was assessed using the oscillometric technique with Arteriograph™ detection. Three-kilometer and pendulum runs were conducted as typical training loads. Cognitive performance was evaluated via the visual and verbal memory and number connection tests. Regarding cognitive skills, extracurricular physical activity improved the number connection test in male participants ($p = 0.004$). For physical performance, female students with a sports-focused curriculum were faster in the 3 km run ($p < 0.001$). Concerning arterial stiffness, the measurements yielded a lower mean arterial pressure ($p = 0.015$) and aortic pulse wave velocity ($p = 0.04$) in male students with a sports-focused curriculum. In summary, extracurricular physical activity and enrollment in a sports-focused curriculum may be associated with lower cardiovascular risk due to lower arterial stiffness and better physical and cognitive abilities.

Keywords: arterial stiffness; pupils; students; prevention; sports; cognitive performance

Citation: Jagomast, T.; Mohr, T.; Axt, P.N.; Mortensen, K.; Brinkmann, F.; Weckmann, M.; Ring, G.; Reppel, M.; Drömann, D.; Franzen, K.F. Effects of Physical Activity in the High School Curriculum on Cardiovascular Health, Cognitive and Physical Performance. *J. Funct. Morphol. Kinesiol.* **2023**, *8*, 101. https://doi.org/10.3390/jfmk8030101

Academic Editors: Cristina Cortis and Gianpiero Greco

Received: 20 April 2023
Revised: 11 July 2023
Accepted: 18 July 2023
Published: 24 July 2023

1. Introduction

In recent decades, the prevention, diagnosis, and treatment of cardiovascular diseases (CVDs) have become increasingly meaningful in patient care. CVDs are the most common chronic diseases of the 21st century, and their risk factors are highly prevalent in youths [1,2]. CVDs in adolescents have multidirectional implications.

First, CVDs and associated conditions still have high mortality [3,4]. Especially in industrial countries, overweight and obesity tend to occur early in childhood [5,6]. Other features of the CVD cluster are also widely prevalent in youths, such as pre-hypertension, pre-diabetes, and early development of atherosclerosis [7–9]. These medical conditions are assumed to be the first steps in the development of metabolic syndrome in adulthood [10].

Second, CVDs are associated with cognitive performance. In older subjects, it has been shown that even subclinical manifestations of CVDs are associated with impaired cognitive performance [11,12]. In young people, cardiovascular health is related to improved cognitive performance [13,14]. Looking into specific cognitive functions, a large study conducted by Crichton et al. revealed an association between visual-spatial memory, working memory, scanning and tracking, executive function, and cardiovascular health [15]. More generally a study by King et al. found that there is an overproportioned decline in fluid relative to crystallized intelligence in the presence of cardiovascular risk factors [16]. Reduced brain perfusion and chronic low-grade inflammation due to CVD risk factors are discussed as possible pathophysiological links [17,18].

Third, healthcare systems and providers are increasingly confronted with major logistical, financial, and medical challenges in CVD treatment [1,19]. Associated conditions and risk factors, among which are diabetes mellitus and obesity, require complex therapy and consume many resources [20].

Consequently, the prevention of CVDs has gained momentum. Advancements in this field are driven by politics, researchers, healthcare providers, and other players in the field. Harmful behaviors such as smoking and high-caloric diets act as independent risk factors and are widely prevalent in Western society [21–23]. Research has identified physical activity as one of the most important modifiable lifestyle factors to prevent CVDs and to also improve cognitive performance [24–28]. Early intervention has been linked to reduced CVDs in later adulthood [29,30]. Prevention programs in adolescents, therefore, comprise education, lifestyle interventions, and physical activity promotion [31,32].

One of the interventions at the intersection of education and physical activity is the restructuring of secondary education in German high schools. Since 2008/2009, students in Schleswig-Holstein can choose a focus in their curriculum, starting in grade 11 through to grade 13. This focus goes along with a set of adjacent subjects from a holistic approach. One of these focuses is sports. The overall benefits of sports, in general, have been extensively studied [33]. However, the objectifiable effects of participation in the so-called sports curriculum regarding cardiovascular health and physical and cognitive performance have not yet been investigated in Germany, and there are a lack of studies in the international context that confirm the hoped-for benefits of an increased frequency of school sports [34].

This study aimed to close the above-mentioned knowledge gap. In an exploratory cross-sectional study, different parameters were considered, including cardiovascular health, such as arterial stiffness, physical performance, and cognitive performance. Under the assumption of beneficial outcomes in participants in the sports curriculum, we investigated the aforementioned parameters and argue that physical activity in school is of great importance. The results might generate questions for future studies regarding the importance of school sports in the overall well-being of adolescents.

2. Materials and Methods

2.1. Data Collection

This study was a cooperation between three secondary schools (Luebeck, Bad Oldesloe, and Ratzeburg; Schleswig-Holstein, Germany), the Medical Clinic III of the University Hospital Schleswig-Holstein Luebeck, and the Ministry of Education and Science Schleswig-Holstein. Data were prospectively collected from April to May 2012. All schools within a reasonable area that offered sports curricula were asked to participate. A total of 63 senior-year students were finally enrolled, based on voluntary participation. An examination was carried out for hemodynamic parameters and physical and cognitive performance. Groups were stratified by their curriculum, which focused on sports, language, or science. The resulting groups were further defined as "sports curriculum students" (SCS) or "other curricula students" (OCS). SCS had five hours of physical education per week. In comparison, OCS attended only two hours of physical education per week. Furthermore, the cohort was dichotomized by extracurricular physical activity. More than 300 min of sports per week at a moderate intensity was termed as being physically active

(PAS); otherwise, participants were classified as physically inactive (PIS). Based on the World Health Organization Guidelines (WHO), 150–300 min are recommended; however, a large majority of subjects (90.5%) fulfilled this criterion, which caused the adaption of the chosen cut-off for statistical analysis [25].

Data collection took place in total for one to two days at each school and was conducted by an attending doctor in internal medicine and one medical student. On day 1, all participants at each school first had to answer a questionnaire on their medical background, lifestyle habits, and type, duration and frequency of physical activity apart from high school. Following the first part of the study, we employed two standardized tests on the subjects' cognitive skills. The time to conduct the number connection test (NCT) inversely correlates with the intelligence quotient (IQ) and displays perceptual speed [35,36]. The visual and verbal memory test (VVM) indicates associative memory [37]. In the second part, on day 1 or 2, depending on the number of participants at each school, physical performance was assessed using two tests. The pendulum run reflects speed, in which the distance between two targets 10 m apart must be covered as many times as possible within a 1 min interval. A 3 km run was carried out to test endurance. There was break of at least 120 min between the two tests. Before the tests, the subjects' arterial stiffness at rest in a lying position was measured for at least 10 min using an Arteriograph^{TM} (TensioMed^{TM}, Budapest, Hungary). Data for aortic pulse wave velocity (PWVao), systolic blood pressure (SBP), diastolic blood pressure (DBP), and mean arterial pressure (MAP) were collected [38–41].

2.2. Statistical Analysis

The statistical analysis was carried out using the pseudonymized data set with R [42]. All comparisons on continuous variables were performed using a Wilcoxon rank-sum test, since the data were imbalanced and non-normally distributed according to the Shapiro–Wilk test. Two-level ordinal variables were compared by Fisher's exact test. For an overview of the coherences of the different variables, a correlation matrix was created and graphically depicted using Spearman's rank correlation coefficient. Smoking and alcohol consumption were excluded from the inferential statistics due to the small percentages of smokers (7.9%) and heavy alcohol consumers (1.7%), which were defined as smoking or consuming alcohol multiple times per week.

We performed post-hoc power analysis on the given sample sizes. For the comparisons regarding cognitive testing, we assumed medium effect size, hence power for comparison of the entire cohort was 73%, respectively 41% for the female subgroup, and 38% male subgroup stratified by curriculum. When stratified by physical activity power was 37% for male and 45% for female subgroup. For comparisons of physical performance and hemodynamics, we assumed a large effect size yielding power of 82% for the female subgroup and 74% for the male subgroup.

3. Results

3.1. Characteristics of the Test Groups

Our cohort comprised 63 students, of which 33 were female and 30 were male (Table 1). Of these 63 students, 42 were enrolled in the sports curriculum and 21 in other curricula. Regarding extracurricular physical activity, 35 of the 63 students stated that they participated in sports for at least five hours a week and were assigned to the physically active group; 20 students did not fulfill this criterion and were termed physically inactive, while eight students did not provide information about sports performed in their downtime. The mean age of our cohort was 18.9 years. Their mean body mass index (BMI) was normal (22.32 kg/m^2). There was a slight but significant difference between males and females, with males showing a higher BMI (p = 0.011). Half of the participants self-reported that they were aware of healthy nutrition. This effect was significant for sports curriculum students (SCS) compared with other curricula students (OCS) (p = 0.031), and was pronounced for physically active students (PAS) compared to physically inactive students (PIS) (p = 0.086). A large majority of the participants neither smoked nor consumed alcohol regularly, defined as daily and multiple times a week, respectively (Table 1). Interestingly, alcohol consumption was inversely correlated with physical activity (as defined in the Section 2) in the female cohort (Figure 1).

Table 1. Cohort characteristics by (**a**) sex, (**b**) curriculum, and (**c**) physical activity.

(a) Sex	Female (n = 33)	Male (n = 30)	Total (N = 63)	p-Value
Age (years)				0.136
Mean (SD)	18.697 (1.630)	19.167 (0.648)	18.921 (1.274)	
Size (m)				<0.001
Mean (SD)	1.698 (0.062)	1.834 (0.072)	1.763 (0.096)	
Weight (kg)				<0.001
Mean (SD)	63.556 (11.905)	76.231 (7.620)	69.592 (11.876)	
BMI (kg/m^2)				0.011
Mean (SD)	22.006 (3.881)	22.658 (1.869)	22.316 (3.084)	
Healthy nutrition				0.612
N-Miss	2	0	2	
No	14 (45.2%)	16 (53.3%)	30 (49.2%)	
Yes	17 (54.8%)	14 (46.7%)	31 (50.8%)	
Smoking (multiple times a week)				0.183
No	32 (97.0%)	26 (86.7%)	58 (92.1%)	
Yes	1 (3.0%)	4 (13.3%)	5 (7.9%)	
Alcohol (multiple times a week)				0.483
N-Miss	2	1	3	
No	31 (100.0%)	28 (96.6%)	59 (98.3%)	
Yes	0 (0.0%)	1 (3.4%)	1 (1.7%)	
(b) Sports curriculum (all)	**OSC (n = 21)**	**SCS (n = 42)**	**Total (N = 63)**	**p-Value**
Age (years)				0.898
Mean (SD)	19.048 (0.384)	18.857 (1.539)	18.921 (1.274)	
Size (m)				0.443
Mean (SD)	1.748 (0.095)	1.771 (0.096)	1.763 (0.096)	
Weight (kg)				0.838
Mean (SD)	69.750 (13.381)	69.513 (11.221)	69.592 (11.876)	
BMI (kg/m^2)				0.737
Mean (SD)	22.834 (4.223)	22.057 (2.341)	22.316 (3.084)	
Healthy nutrition				0.031
N-Miss	1	1	2	
No	14 (70.0%)	16 (39.0%)	30 (49.2%)	
Yes	6 (30.0%)	25 (61.0%)	31 (50.8%)	
Smoking (multiple times a week)				1.000
No	19 (90.5%)	39 (92.9%)	58 (92.1%)	
Yes	2 (9.5%)	3 (7.1%)	5 (7.9%)	
Alcohol (multiple times a week)				0.333
N-Miss	1	2	3	
No	19 (95.0%)	40 (100.0%)	59 (98.3%)	
Yes	1 (5.0%)	0 (0.0%)	1 (1.7%)	
(c) Physical Activity (all)	**PIS (n = 20)**	**PAS (n = 35)**	**Total (N = 55)**	**p-Value**
Age (years)				0.160
Mean (SD)	19.200 (0.523)	18.771 (1.646)	18.927 (1.359)	
Size (m)				0.227
Mean (SD)	1.736 (0.098)	1.778 (0.096)	1.763 (0.098)	
Weight (kg)				0.274
Mean (SD)	66.412 (11.418)	71.263 (12.334)	69.499 (12.133)	
BMI (kg/m^2)				0.612
Mean (SD)	21.923 (2.522)	22.530 (3.585)	22.309 (3.227)	

Table 1. *Cont.*

Healthy nutrition				0.086
N-Miss	2	0	2	
No	12 (66.7%)	14 (40.0%)	26 (49.1%)	
Yes	6 (33.3%)	21 (60.0%)	27 (50.9%)	
Smoking (multiple times a week)				0.285
No	20 (100.0%)	31 (88.6%)	51 (92.7%)	
Yes	0 (0.0%)	4 (11.4%)	4 (7.3%)	
Alcohol (multiple times a week)				1.000
N-Miss	0	2	2	
No	20 (100.0%)	32 (96.7%)	52 (98.1%)	
Yes	0 (0.0%)	1 (3.3%)	1 (1.9%)	

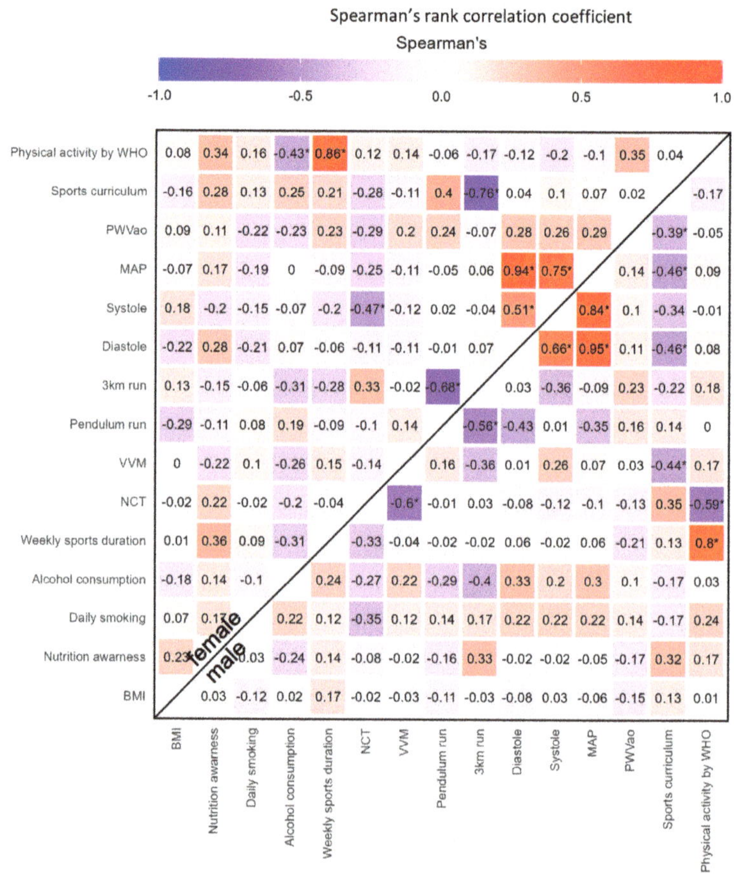

Figure 1. Correlation matrix of the investigated variables stratified by sex for overview (using Spearman's rank correlation coefficient). Nutrition awareness and daily smoking were encoded as 1 for "yes" and 0 for "no". Alcohol consumption had five levels: 5 = daily, 4 = weekly, 3 = weekends, 4 = monthly, 1 = less than monthly. School curriculum was encoded as 1 for SCS and 0 for OCS, while physical activity was encoded using WHO guidelines as 1 for ≥300 min per week (PAS) and 0 for <300 min per week (PIS). * $p < 0.05$.

3.2. Cognitive Performance

Comparing the results of the number connection test (NCT), there was no significant difference between OCS and SCS. However, OCS showed significantly better performance in the visual and verbal memory test (VVM) (p = 0.044) (Table 2a). This difference was observed to be sex-specific in the male subgroup (p = 0.018) (Table 2b). Our analysis based on physical activity in general revealed no difference between PAS and PIS in either of the tests. Interestingly, a sex-specific comparison of male PAS and PIS students revealed significantly better performance by PAS in the NCT (p = 0.004) (Table 2d). No differences were observed between all male and female participants in the VVM or NCT.

Table 2. Cognitive performance of the (**a**) entire cohort by curriculum, (**b**) male students by curriculum, (**c**) female students by curriculum, (**d**) male students by physical activity, and (**e**) female students by physical activity.

(a) Curriculum (all)	OSC (n = 21)	SCS (n = 42)	Total (N = 63)	p-Value
NCT (s)				0.923
N-Miss	0	1	1	
Mean (SD)	58.469 (17.240)	55.005 (7.439)	56.178 (11.682)	
VVM (points)				0.044
Mean (SD)	35.643 (7.013)	30.833 (7.888)	32.437 (7.889)	
(b) Curriculum (male)	**OSC (n = 9)**	**SCS (n = 21)**	**Total (N = 30)**	**p-Value**
NCT (s)				0.066
N-Miss	0	1	1	
Mean (SD)	52.829 (14.677)	57.273 (6.746)	55.894 (9.839)	
VVM (points)				0.018
Mean (SD)	37.333 (6.083)	30.524 (6.969)	32.567 (7.333)	
(c) Curriculum (female)	**OSC (n = 12)**	**SCS (n = 21)**	**Total (N = 33)**	**p-Value**
NCT (s)				0.108
Mean (SD)	62.698 (18.390)	52.846 (7.577)	56.429 (13.240)	
VVM (points)				0.524
Mean (SD)	34.375 (7.643)	31.143 (8.876)	32.318 (8.474)	
(d) Physical activity (male)	**PIS (n = 8)**	**PAS (n = 18)**	**Total (N = 26)**	**p-Value**
NCT (s)				0.004
N-Miss	1	0	1	
Mean (SD)	66.210 (10.686)	53.055 (7.690)	56.738 (10.334)	
VVM (points)				0.403
Mean (SD)	29.812 (6.871)	32.750 (7.735)	31.846 (7.471)	
(e) Physical activity (female)	**PIS (n = 17)**	**PAS (n = 12)**	**Total (N = 29)**	**p-Value**
NCT (s)				0.535
Mean (SD)	57.454 (14.680)	53.620 (10.793)	55.867 (13.138)	
VVM (points)				0.465
Mean (SD)	33.265 (8.722)	31.125 (9.303)	32.379 (8.867)	

3.3. Physical Activity

On average, the participants engaged in physical activity for approximately 450 min a week, with no significant difference between sexes. Interestingly, there was also no difference in the weekly sports duration of the SCS and OCS. Physical ability in the 3 km and pendulum runs was greater in the male participants ($p < 0.001$). Therefore, sex-stratified comparisons were carried out regarding OCS and SCS, as well as PAS and PIS, to avoid bias due to different sex ratios in these groups. For the male group, no difference was observed in the tests, either comparing OCS and SCS, or PAS and PIS. However, in the female subjects, SCS showed superior performance in the 3 km run ($p < 0.001$) (Table 3), while a comparison of female PAS and PIS yielded no significant difference.

Table 3. Comparison of physical tests in (**a**) female students and (**b**) male students.

(a) Curriculum (female)	OSC (n = 12)	SCS (n = 21)	Total (N = 33)	p-Value
Pendulum run (repetitions)				0.061
N-Miss	2	8	10	
Mean (SD)	18.600 (0.966)	19.462 (1.664)	19.087 (1.443)	
3 km run (s)				<0.001
N-Miss	1	4	5	
Mean (SD)	1203.848 (177.048)	970.398 (68.789)	1062.111 (167.016)	
(b) Curriculum (male)	**OSC (n = 9)**	**SCS (n = 21)**	**Total (N = 30)**	**p-Value**
Pendulum run (repetitions)				0.626
N-Miss	7	9	16	
Mean (SD)	20.500 (2.121)	21.250 (0.754)	21.143 (0.949)	
3 km run (s)				0.286
N-Miss	3	3	6	
Mean (SD)	798.483 (67.569)	747.831 (88.150)	760.494 (85.075)	

3.4. Hemodynamics and Arterial Stiffness

Concerning the hemodynamic data (diastolic and systolic blood pressure (DBP and SBP), mean arterial pressure (MAP), and aortic pulse wave velocity (PWVao)) in the entire cohort, there was no difference according to sex, OCS, or SCS, nor PAS and PIS. However, in the male subcohort, SCS tended to have more favorable measurements for DBP ($p = 0.015$), MAP ($p = 0.015$), and PWVao ($p = 0.04$) (Table 4a). These differences were not observed when comparing PAS and PIS males. Female students showed no significant differences in either comparison.

Table 4. Comparison of hemodynamic measurements in (**a**) male students and (**b**) female students.

(a) Curriculum (Male)	OSC (n = 9)	SCS (n = 21)	Total (N = 30)	p-Value
DBP (mmHg)				0.015
N-Miss	0	1	1	
Mean (SD)	74.222 (9.418)	64.450 (9.237)	67.483 (10.218)	
SBP (mmHg)				0.073
N-Miss	0	1	1	
Mean (SD)	135.333 (16.000)	122.350 (14.214)	126.379 (15.735)	
MAP (mmHg)				0.015
N-Miss	0	1	1	
Mean (SD)	94.778 (10.814)	83.750 (9.408)	87.172 (10.974)	
PWVao (m/s)				0.040
N-Miss	0	1	1	
Mean (SD)	7.600 (1.482)	6.410 (1.007)	6.779 (1.276)	
(b) Curriculum (female)	**OSC (n = 12)**	**SCS (n = 21)**	**Total (N = 33)**	**p-Value**
DBP (mmHg)				0.815
N-Miss	0	1	1	
Mean (SD)	68.333 (8.845)	68.700 (7.035)	68.562 (7.624)	
SBP (mmHg)				0.585
N-Miss	0	1	1	
Mean (SD)	123.083 (14.761)	125.250 (7.663)	124.438 (10.698)	
MAP (mmHg)				0.682
N-Miss	0	1	1	
Mean (SD)	86.500 (10.140)	87.550 (5.916)	87.156 (7.629)	
PWVao (m/s)				0.907
N-Miss	0	1	1	
Mean (SD)	6.650 (1.286)	6.530 (1.008)	6.575 (1.102)	

4. Discussion

Cardiovascular risk factors include diabetes mellitus and arterial hypertension, but also modifiable behaviors such as alcohol and tobacco consumption and physical inactivity [43]. Today's medicine increasingly focuses on the earliest detection and reduction of these risk factors. In addition to improved treatment of diabetes mellitus and high blood pressure, primary prophylactic measures are offered, creating incentives to change lifestyle, nutrition, and physical activity level [44]. This study was carried out under the assumption that increased physical activity in adolescents goes along with benefits to physical and mental performance and arterial vascular stiffness. The results can be summarized as follows.

Sex-wise, our cohort was balanced. However, we investigated twice as many SCS as OCS students. The participants showed normative BMI and overall high health awareness, with only a small proportion of smokers and regular alcohol consumers. There were no self-reported major health concerns present in the cohort. Interestingly, SCS had more nutrition awareness than OCS, possibly because SCS are more interested in nutrition to enhance physical performance and therefore chose their specific curriculum. Moreover, they are exposed to the theoretical background of physical performance and nutrition science in their classes. Other studies that have investigated this topic argue that, generally, athletes might get advice from their coaches and teammates, aside from formal education [45,46]. Still, studies about athletes' nutrition knowledge are rare and largely descriptive. The underlying causes remain elusive thus far. On the other hand, studies show health benefits from nutrition intervention programs in school children [47,48]. This underlines the importance of establishing nutritional education in early childhood and adolescence.

Our examination of physical capability revealed no difference in weekly sports duration between SCS and OCS students. Since male students had better results on the 3 km and pendulum runs, we carried out sex-specific data analysis, because SCS and OCS had different sex ratios. SCS females were faster on the 3 km run than OCS females, while the status of physical activity in general showed no effect. In the male subcohort, neither curriculum choice nor stated general physical activity level influenced the results. Overall, SCS students did not show superior results on the physical tests. However, it must be considered that the comparison of weekly time spent in at least moderate-intensity sports between the SCS and OCS showed no significant difference. Apparently, students that lack physical education in school make up for it in their leisure time. Despite this, we hypothesize that the observed effect in SCS females might be due to the specific training. In our questionnaire, we assessed what specific sports the students participated in. Despite SCS and OCS spending the same amount of time engaged in physical activity per week, not all sports might prepare as well for a 3 km run (e.g., sports that demand less endurance). SCS students will train over this distance more often as part of the curriculum, thereby potentially acquiring a specific advantage.

In the subcohort of males, regarding cognitive performance, OCS outperformed SCS in terms of the VVM. Moreover, male PAS showed better results in the NCT than inactive males. For the female cohort, such results were not observed. It is possible that students enrolled in other curricula are more frequently challenged to memorize facts, since humanities and natural sciences make up a larger part of their study plan. However, we showed that physical activity in general goes along with improved scores in the NCT, confirming our hypothesis. Numerous studies have shown the positive effects of physical activity on cognitive function [27,28,49–51]. The results presented here suggest that the NCT in particular might be sensitive to the level of athleticism. The NCT measures perceptual speed, one aspect that underlines all qualities of intelligence and therefore correlates with IQ [36]. Perceptual speed plays a major role in sports [52]. In an elderly cohort, Oswald et al. showed superior improvements in cognitive tests such as the NCT when subjects received physical and cognitive training combined [53]. The sex-specific effect was previously observed by Legault et al. in adolescent athletes when testing the perceptual–cognitive abilities of the participants [52]. A biological cause still needs to be identified. However, Legault et al. argued that the investigated female athletes were not on an equal level of training compared to their male counterparts. Additionally, the type of sport plays a role in improving specific cognitive functions [54]. The VVM in our study, as a test of associative memory, seemed to be less affected by physical activity. Perhaps memory and recall play a minor role in the sports played by the cohort. Further research is warranted to investigate the relationships between specific qualities of intelligence and different kinds of sports.

Evaluation of arterial stiffness yielded significant differences only in the male subcohort. Male SCS had lower DBP, MAP, and PWVao. Due to their curriculum, these students regularly engage in endurance sports. Research shows that this type of physical activity has a positive effect on the arteries. Physical activity in general may therefore be of secondary importance, while the kind of sport is more relevant [55]. There is also a significant negative association between physical fitness and the occurrence of arterial hypertension in adolescents [56]. The risk of hypertension decreases as fitness level improve [57,58]. Other studies have proven that reduced physical activity and high BMI lead to an increase in PWV and thus to increased arterial stiffness [59,60]. Both results suggest that students would benefit from additional physical education classes. The sex-specific effect observed in our study has previously been reported. A review article by DuPont et al. summarized the current state of knowledge [61]. A priori, women have lower baseline PWV [62]. After short bursts of exercise, the effects on PWV are only observed in men [63,64]. Moreover, PWV inversely correlates with cardiorespiratory endurance, but only in men [65]. Men are believed to have greater testosterone exertion during exercise than women [66]. Testosterone is known to lower PWV in the short and long terms [67–69]. In their review article, Moreau et al. argued that these effects are due to structural changes in the endothelium, as well as acute changes in nitric oxide signaling [70,71]. Perhaps due to the elevated PWV baseline in men, changes due to exercise are more pronounced, caused by higher testosterone release, compared to women. However, most results were obtained by observational studies. Testosterone signaling pathways of vascular function have only been extensively characterized in preclinical models [70]. Further identification of corresponding human signaling pathways is warranted to link observations to biological mechanisms.

Our study has some limitations. A power analysis revealed insufficient power, less than 80%, especially for the subgroup comparisons of cognitive performance. However applicable sample size was limitedsince all eligible students within a reasonable regional area were included. Therefore, our study has pilot trial character, and statements are preliminary and further research is needed. Prospective analysis of a larger cohort, augmented by differentiated measures of physical and cognitive ability, would therefore be desirable. Additionally, questionnaires were employed to assess nutrition awareness and weekly time spent engaged in physical activity. A well-known bias of this approach is social desirability, which might have led to overestimating the actual time spent engaged in physical activity [72] as, in our study, nearly all students reported that they participated in at least 150 min of intermediate-to-high levels of physical activity per week, which is the amount recommended by the WHO.

5. Conclusions

The data reported showed the benefits of the German sports curriculum in terms of cardiovascular health and physical performance. Physical activity in general was associated with improved cognitive performance. However, due to the small number of subjects, this study is limited. Overall, enrollment in the sports curriculum correlated with performance on the 3 km run, DBP, MAP, and PWVao in a sex-specific manner. This might be due to specific endurance training, which is not a mandatory part of general physical activity. However, for cognitive performance on the NCT, the exact kind and nature of the sport seems of secondary importance, and better results were achieved by physically active students. To be able to demonstrate the long-term effectiveness of physical activity in schools on cardiovascular health in adolescents, a multi-center longitudinal study is warranted and different interventions should be compared. Moreover, research needs to focus on understanding underlying sex-specific changes in physiology caused by exercise.

Author Contributions: Conceptualization, K.F.F., M.R. and K.M.; methodology, K.F.F.; software, K.F.F., T.M. and P.N.A.; validation, K.F.F. and T.J.; formal analysis, T.J.; investigation, T.J., T.M., P.N.A., F.B., M.W., G.R. and K.F.F.; resources, F.B., M.W., D.D., M.R., K.M. and K.F.F.; data curation, K.F.F., T.M., P.N.A., G.R. and T.J.; writing—original draft preparation, T.J. and K.F.F.; writing—review and editing, K.F.F., T.M., P.N.A., G.R., F.B., M.W., T.J., K.M., M.R. and D.D.; visualization, T.J.; supervision, K.M., D.D. and K.F.F.; project administration, F.B., M.W., D.D., K.M., M.R. and K.F.F.; funding acquisition, K.M., M.R., D.D. and K.F.F. All authors have read and agreed to the published version of the manuscript.

Funding: This research received no external funding.

Institutional Review Board Statement: This study was conducted in accordance with the Declaration of Helsinki and approved by the Institutional Ethics Committee of the University of Luebeck (main protocol: File number 11-051).

Informed Consent Statement: Informed consent was obtained from all subjects involved in the study.

Data Availability Statement: Due to privacy restrictions, the authors have omitted public data availability.

Acknowledgments: The authors thank the responsible persons of the participating schools and ministries.

Conflicts of Interest: The authors declare no conflict of interest. The funders had no role in the design of the study; in the collection, analyses, or interpretation of data; in the writing of the manuscript, or in the decision to publish the results.

Abbreviations

BMI	Body mass index
CVD	Cardiovascular diseases
DBP	Diastolic blood pressure
IQ	Intelligence quotient
MAP	Mean arterial pressure
NCT	Number connection test
OCS	Other curricula students
PAS	Physically active students
PIS	Physically inactive students
PWVao	Aortic pulse wave velocity
SBP	Systolic blood pressure
SCS	Sports curriculum students
VVM	Visual and verbal memory test
WHO	World Health Organization

References

1. Chapel, J.M.; Ritchey, M.D.; Zhang, D.; Wang, G. Prevalence and Medical Costs of Chronic Diseases Among Adult Medicaid Beneficiaries. *Am. J. Prev. Med.* **2017**, *53*, S143–S154. [CrossRef]
2. May, A.L.; Kuklina, E.V.; Yoon, P.W. Prevalence of Cardiovascular Disease Risk Factors Among US Adolescents, 1999−2008. *Pediatrics* **2012**, *129*, 1035–1041. [CrossRef]
3. Amini, M.; Zayeri, F.; Salehi, M. Trend Analysis of Cardiovascular Disease Mortality, Incidence, and Mortality-to-Incidence Ratio: Results from Global Burden of Disease Study 2017. *BMC Public Health* **2021**, *21*, 401. [CrossRef] [PubMed]
4. Roth, G.A.; Mensah, G.A.; Johnson, C.O.; Addolorato, G.; Ammirati, E.; Baddour, L.M.; Barengo, N.C.; Beaton, A.Z.; Benjamin, E.J.; Benziger, C.P.; et al. Global Burden of Cardiovascular Diseases and Risk Factors, 1990–2019. *J. Am. Coll. Cardiol.* **2020**, *76*, 2982–3021. [CrossRef] [PubMed]
5. Schienkiewitz, A.; Brettschneider, A.-K.; Damerow, S.; Schaffrath Rosario, A. Overweight and Obesity among Children and Adolescents in Germany. Results of the Cross-Sectional KiGGS Wave 2 Study and Trends. *J. Health Monit.* **2018**, *3*, 15–22. [CrossRef]
6. Sanyaolu, A.; Okorie, C.; Qi, X.; Locke, J.; Rehman, S. Childhood and Adolescent Obesity in the United States: A Public Health Concern. *Glob. Pediatr. Health* **2019**, *6*, 2333794X19891305. [CrossRef]
7. Strong, J.P.; Malcom, G.T.; McMahan, C.A.; Tracy, R.E.; Newman, W.P.; Herderick, E.E.; Cornhill, J.F. Prevalence and Extent of Atherosclerosis in Adolescents and Young Adults: Implications for Prevention from the Pathobiological Determinants of Atherosclerosis in Youth Study. *JAMA* **1999**, *281*, 727–735. [CrossRef] [PubMed]

8. Li, C.; Ford, E.S.; Zhao, G.; Mokdad, A.H. Prevalence of Pre-Diabetes and Its Association With Clustering of Cardiometabolic Risk Factors and Hyperinsulinemia Among U.S. Adolescents. *Diabetes Care* **2009**, *32*, 342–347. [CrossRef] [PubMed]
9. Hansen, M.L.; Gunn, P.W.; Kaelber, D.C. Underdiagnosis of Hypertension in Children and Adolescents. *JAMA* **2007**, *298*, 874–879. [CrossRef]
10. Kelishadi, R. Childhood Overweight, Obesity, and the Metabolic Syndrome in Developing Countries. *Epidemiol. Rev.* **2007**, *29*, 62–76. [CrossRef]
11. Ihle-Hansen, H.; Ihle-Hansen, H.; Sandset, E.C.; Hagberg, G. Subclinical Carotid Artery Atherosclerosis and Cognitive Function: A Mini-Review. *Front. Neurol.* **2021**, *12*, 705043. [CrossRef]
12. Lin, F.; Pa, J.; Karim, R.; Hodis, H.N.; Han, S.D.; Henderson, V.W.; St John, J.A.; Mack, W.J. Subclinical Carotid Artery Atherosclerosis and Cognitive Function in Older Adults. *Alzheimer's Res. Ther.* **2022**, *14*, 63. [CrossRef] [PubMed]
13. Kulshreshtha, A.; Goetz, M.; Alonso, A.; Shah, A.J.; Bremner, J.D.; Goldberg, J.; Vaccarino, V. Association Between Cardiovascular Health and Cognitive Performance: A Twins Study. *J. Alzheimers Dis.* **2019**, *71*, 957–968. [CrossRef] [PubMed]
14. Reis, J.P.; Loria, C.M.; Launer, L.J.; Sidney, S.; Liu, K.; Jacobs, D.R.; Zhu, N.; Lloyd-Jones, D.M.; He, K.; Yaffe, K. Cardiovascular Health through Young Adulthood and Cognitive Functioning in Midlife. *Ann. Neurol.* **2013**, *73*, 170–179. [CrossRef] [PubMed]
15. Crichton, G.E.; Elias, M.F.; Davey, A.; Alkerwi, A. Cardiovascular Health and Cognitive Function: The Maine-Syracuse Longitudinal Study. *PLoS ONE* **2014**, *9*, e89317. [CrossRef] [PubMed]
16. King, D.L.O.; Henson, R.N.; Kievit, R.; Wolpe, N.; Brayne, C.; Tyler, L.K.; Rowe, J.B.; Tsvetanov, K.A. Distinct Components of Cardiovascular Health Are Linked with Age-Related Differences in Cognitive Abilities. *Sci. Rep.* **2023**, *13*, 978. [CrossRef] [PubMed]
17. Alosco, M.L.; Gunstad, J.; Jerskey, B.A.; Xu, X.; Clark, U.S.; Hassenstab, J.; Cote, D.M.; Walsh, E.G.; Labbe, D.R.; Hoge, R.; et al. The Adverse Effects of Reduced Cerebral Perfusion on Cognition and Brain Structure in Older Adults with Cardiovascular Disease. *Brain Behav.* **2013**, *3*, 626–636. [CrossRef]
18. Kipinoinen, T.; Toppala, S.; Rinne, J.O.; Viitanen, M.H.; Jula, A.M.; Ekblad, L.L. Association of Midlife Inflammatory Markers With Cognitive Performance at 10-Year Follow-Up. *Neurology* **2022**, *99*, e2294–e2302. [CrossRef]
19. Tarride, J.-E.; Lim, M.; DesMeules, M.; Luo, W.; Burke, N.; O'Reilly, D.; Bowen, J.; Goeree, R. A Review of the Cost of Cardiovascular Disease. *Can. J. Cardiol.* **2009**, *25*, e195–e202. [CrossRef]
20. Buddeke, J.; Bots, M.L.; van Dis, I.; Visseren, F.L.; Hollander, M.; Schellevis, F.G.; Vaartjes, I. Comorbidity in Patients with Cardiovascular Disease in Primary Care: A Cohort Study with Routine Healthcare Data. *Br. J. Gen. Pract.* **2019**, *69*, e398–e406. [CrossRef]
21. Akbartabartoori, M.; Lean, M.E.J.; Hankey, C.R. Smoking Combined with Overweight or Obesity Markedly Elevates Cardiovascular Risk Factors. *Eur. J. Cardiovasc. Prev. Rehabil.* **2006**, *13*, 938–946. [CrossRef] [PubMed]
22. Schienkiewitz, A.; Kuhnert, R.; Blume, M.; Mensink, G.B.M. Overweight and Obesity among Adults in Germany—Results from GEDA 2019/2020-EHIS. *J. Health Monit.* **2022**, *7*, 21–28. [CrossRef] [PubMed]
23. Lampert, T.; von der Lippe, E.; Müters, S. Prevalence of smoking in the adult population of Germany: Results of the German Health Interview and Examination Survey for Adults (DEGS1). *Bundesgesundheitsblatt Gesundheitsforschung Gesundheitsschutz* **2013**, *56*, 802–808. [CrossRef] [PubMed]
24. Piercy, K.; Troiano, R. Physical Activity Guidelines for Americans From the US Department of Health and Human Service Office of Disease Prevention and Health Promotion; US Department of Health and Human Services. *Circ. Cardiovasc. Qual. Outcomes* **2018**, *11*, e005263. [CrossRef] [PubMed]
25. Bull, F.C.; Al-Ansari, S.S.; Biddle, S.; Borodulin, K.; Buman, M.P.; Cardon, G.; Carty, C.; Chaput, J.-P.; Chastin, S.; Chou, R.; et al. World Health Organization 2020 Guidelines on Physical Activity and Sedentary Behaviour. *Br. J. Sports Med.* **2020**, *54*, 1451–1462. [CrossRef]
26. Rippe, J.M. Lifestyle Strategies for Risk Factor Reduction, Prevention, and Treatment of Cardiovascular Disease. *Am. J. Lifestyle Med.* **2018**, *13*, 204–212. [CrossRef]
27. Mandolesi, L.; Polverino, A.; Montuori, S.; Foti, F.; Ferraioli, G.; Sorrentino, P.; Sorrentino, G. Effects of Physical Exercise on Cognitive Functioning and Wellbeing: Biological and Psychological Benefits. *Front. Psychol.* **2018**, *9*, 509. [CrossRef]
28. Biddle, S.J.H.; Ciaccioni, S.; Thomas, G.; Vergeer, I. Physical Activity and Mental Health in Children and Adolescents: An Updated Review of Reviews and an Analysis of Causality. *Psychol. Sport. Exerc.* **2019**, *42*, 146–155. [CrossRef]
29. da Silva, G.C.R.; Tebar, W.R.; Saraiva, B.T.C.; Farah, B.Q.; Vanderlei, L.C.M.; Ferrari, G.; Christofaro, D.G.D. Association of Early Sports Practice with Cardiovascular Risk Factors in Community-Dwelling Adults: A Retrospective Epidemiological Study. *Sports Med.-Open* **2023**, *9*, 15. [CrossRef]
30. Gero, K.; Iso, H.; Kitamura, A.; Yamagishi, K.; Yatsuya, H.; Tamakoshi, A. Cardiovascular Disease Mortality in Relation to Physical Activity during Adolescence and Adulthood in Japan: Does School-Based Sport Club Participation Matter? *Prev. Med.* **2018**, *113*, 102–108. [CrossRef]
31. Eliasson, A.; Kashani, M.; Vernalis, M. Results of a Prospective Cardiovascular Disease Prevention Program. *Prev. Med. Rep.* **2021**, *22*, 101344. [CrossRef] [PubMed]
32. Aljutaili, M.; Becker, C.; Witt, S.; Holle, R.; Leidl, R.; Block, M.; Brachmann, J.; Silber, S.; Bestehorn, K.; Stollenwerk, B. Should Health Insurers Target Prevention of Cardiovascular Disease?: A Cost-Effectiveness Analysis of an Individualised Programme in Germany Based on Routine Data. *BMC Health Serv. Res.* **2014**, *14*, 263. [CrossRef]

33. Sequi-Dominguez, I.; Mavridis, D.; Cavero-Redondo, I.; Saz-Lara, A.; Martinez-Vizcaino, V.; Núñez de Arenas-Arroyo, S. Comparative Effectiveness of Different Types of Exercise in Reducing Arterial Stiffness in Children and Adolescents: A Systematic Review and Network Meta-Analysis. *Br. J. Sports Med.* **2023**, *57*, 15. [CrossRef]
34. Wassenaar, T.M.; Wheatley, C.M.; Beale, N.; Nichols, T.; Salvan, P.; Meaney, A.; Atherton, K.; Diaz-Ordaz, K.; Dawes, H.; Johansen-Berg, H. The Effect of a One-Year Vigorous Physical Activity Intervention on Fitness, Cognitive Performance and Mental Health in Young Adolescents: The Fit to Study Cluster Randomised Controlled Trial. *Int. J. Behav. Nutr. Phys. Act.* **2021**, *18*, 47. [CrossRef] [PubMed]
35. Vernon, P.A. Der Zahlen-Verbindungs-Test and Other Trail-Making Correlates of General Intelligence. *Person. Ind. Differ.* **1993**, *14*, 35–40. [CrossRef]
36. Oswald, W.D.; Roth, E. Der Zahlen-Verbindungs-Test (ZVT). In *Hogrefe Verlag fuer Psychologie*; Springer: Berlin/Heidelberg, Germany, 1987.
37. Schellig, D. *Handbook of Neuropsychological Tests—Attention, Memory, Executive Functions*; Hogrefe Verlag: Göttingen, Germany, 2009; ISBN 978-3-8017-1857-2.
38. Baulmann, J.; Nürnberger, J.; Slany, J.; Schmieder, R.; Schmidt-Trucksäss, A.; Baumgart, D.; Cremerius, P.; Hess, O.; Mortensen, K.; Weber, T. Arterial Stiffness and Pulse Wave Analysis. *DMW* **2010**, *135*, 4–14. [CrossRef] [PubMed]
39. Baulmann, J.; Schillings, U.; Rickert, S.; Uen, S.; Düsing, R.; Illyes, M.; Cziraki, A.; Nickering, G.; Mengden, T. A New Oscillometric Method for Assessment of Arterial Stiffness: Comparison with Tonometric and Piezo-Electronic Methods. *J. Hypertens.* **2008**, *26*, 523–528. [CrossRef]
40. O'Rourke, M.F.; Seward, J.B. Central Arterial Pressure and Arterial Pressure Pulse: New Views Entering the Second Century after Korotkov. *Mayo Clin. Proc.* **2006**, *81*, 1057–1068. [CrossRef] [PubMed]
41. Rajzer, M.W.; Wojciechowska, W.; Klocek, M.; Palka, I.; Brzozowska-Kiszka, M.; Kawecka-Jaszcz, K. Comparison of Aortic Pulse Wave Velocity Measured by Three Techniques: Complior, SphygmoCor and Arteriograph. *J. Hypertens.* **2008**, *26*, 2001–2007. [CrossRef]
42. R Core Team. *R: A Language and Environment for Statistical Computing*; R Foundation for Statistical Computing: Vienna, Austria, 2023. Available online: https://Www.R-Project.Org/ (accessed on 14 February 2023).
43. Ng, R.; Sutradhar, R.; Yao, Z.; Wodchis, W.P.; Rosella, L.C. Smoking, Drinking, Diet and Physical Activity—Modifiable Lifestyle Risk Factors and Their Associations with Age to First Chronic Disease. *Int. J. Epidemiol.* **2020**, *49*, 113–130. [CrossRef]
44. Lancarotte, I.; Nobre, M.R. Primordial and Primary Prevention Programs for Cardiovascular Diseases: From Risk Assessment through Risk Communication to Risk Reduction. A Review of the Literature. *Clinics (Sao Paulo)* **2016**, *71*, 667–678. [CrossRef]
45. Cupisti, A.; D'Alessandro, C.; Castrogiovanni, S.; Barale, A.; Morelli, E. Nutrition Knowledge and Dietary Composition in Italian Adolescent Female Athletes and Non-Athletes. *Int. J. Sport. Nutr. Exerc. Metab.* **2002**, *12*, 207–219. [CrossRef]
46. Heaney, S.; O'Connor, H.; Michael, S.; Gifford, J.; Naughton, G. Nutrition Knowledge in Athletes: A Systematic Review. *Int. J. Sport Nutr. Exerc. Metab.* **2011**, *21*, 248–261. [CrossRef] [PubMed]
47. Alzaben, A.S.; Alnashwan, N.I.; Alatr, A.A.; Alneghamshi, N.A.; Alhashem, A.M. Effectiveness of a Nutrition Education and Intervention Programme on Nutrition Knowledge and Dietary Practice among Princess Nourah Bint Abdulrahman University's Population. *Public Health Nutr.* **2021**, *24*, 1854–1860. [CrossRef] [PubMed]
48. Kendel Jovanović, G.; Janković, S.; Pavičić ŽeŽelj, S. The Effect of Nutritional and Lifestyle Education Intervention Program on Nutrition Knowledge, Diet Quality, Lifestyle, and Nutritional Status of Croatian School Children. *Front. Sustain. Food Syst.* **2023**, *7*, 1019849. [CrossRef]
49. Schlaffke, L.; Lissek, S.; Lenz, M.; Brüne, M.; Juckel, G.; Hinrichs, T.; Platen, P.; Tegenthoff, M.; Schmidt-Wilcke, T. Sports and Brain Morphology—A Voxel-Based Morphometry Study with Endurance Athletes and Martial Artists. *Neuroscience* **2014**, *259*, 35–42. [CrossRef]
50. Nakata, H.; Yoshie, M.; Miura, A.; Kudo, K. Characteristics of the Athletes' Brain: Evidence from Neurophysiology and Neuroimaging. *Brain Res. Rev.* **2010**, *62*, 197–211. [CrossRef] [PubMed]
51. Rasberry, C.N.; Lee, S.M.; Robin, L.; Laris, B.A.; Russell, L.A.; Coyle, K.K.; Nihiser, A.J. The Association between School-Based Physical Activity, Including Physical Education, and Academic Performance: A Systematic Review of the Literature. *Prev. Med.* **2011**, *52* (Suppl. 1), S10–S20. [CrossRef] [PubMed]
52. Legault, I.; Sutterlin-Guindon, D.; Faubert, J. Perceptual Cognitive Abilities in Young Athletes: A Gender Comparison. *PLoS ONE* **2022**, *17*, e0273607. [CrossRef] [PubMed]
53. Oswald, W.D.; Gunzelmann, T.; Rupprecht, R.; Hagen, B. Differential Effects of Single versus Combined Cognitive and Physical Training with Older Adults: The SimA Study in a 5-Year Perspective. *Eur. J. Ageing* **2006**, *3*, 179. [CrossRef]
54. Yongtawee, A.; Park, J.; Kim, Y.; Woo, M. Athletes Have Different Dominant Cognitive Functions Depending on Type of Sport. *Int. J. Sport Exerc. Psychol.* **2022**, *20*, 1–15. [CrossRef]
55. Said Ouamer, D.; Guerchani Mohamed Karim, M.K.; Djermane, D.; Benkhedda, S. Pulse Wave Velocity and Blood Pressure in Athletes Performing Endurance and Intense Resistance Training. *Eur. Heart J.* **2020**, *41*, ehaa946.2716. [CrossRef]
56. Scherr, C.; Fabiano, L.C.C.; Guerra, R.L.; Belém, L.H.J.; Câmara, A.C.G.; Campos, A. Sports Practices and Cardiovascular Risk in Teenagers. *Arq. Bras. Cardiol.* **2018**, *110*, 248–255. [CrossRef] [PubMed]

57. Dong, Y.; Jan, C.; Zou, Z.; Dong, B.; Hu, P.; Ma, Y.; Yang, Z.; Wang, X.; Li, Y.; Gao, D.; et al. Comprehensive Physical Fitness and High Blood Pressure in Children and Adolescents: A National Cross-Sectional Survey in China. *J. Sci. Med. Sport* **2020**, *23*, 800–806. [CrossRef] [PubMed]
58. Janssen, I.; Leblanc, A.G. Systematic Review of the Health Benefits of Physical Activity and Fitness in School-Aged Children and Youth. *Int. J. Behav. Nutr. Phys.* **2010**, *7*, 40. [CrossRef]
59. Sakuragi, S.; Abhayaratna, K.; Gravenmaker, K.J.; O'Reilly, C.; Srikusalanukul, W.; Budge, M.M.; Telford, R.D.; Abhayaratna, W.P. Influence of Adiposity and Physical Activity on Arterial Stiffness in Healthy Children: The Lifestyle of Our Kids Study. *Hypertension* **2009**, *53*, 611–616. [CrossRef]
60. Wójtowicz, J.; Łempicka, A.; Łuczyński, W.; Szczepański, W.; Zomerfeld, A.; Semeran, K.; Bossowski, A. Central Aortic Pressure, Arterial Stiffness and Echocardiographic Parameters of Children with Overweight/Obesity and Arterial Hypertension. *Adv. Clin. Exp. Med.* **2017**, *26*, 1399–1404. [CrossRef]
61. DuPont, J.J.; Kenney, R.M.; Patel, A.R.; Jaffe, I.Z. Sex Differences in Mechanisms of Arterial Stiffness. *Br. J. Pharmacol.* **2019**, *176*, 4208–4225. [CrossRef]
62. Mitchell, G.F.; Parise, H.; Benjamin, E.J.; Larson, M.G.; Keyes, M.J.; Vita, J.A.; Vasan, R.S.; Levy, D. Changes in Arterial Stiffness and Wave Reflection with Advancing Age in Healthy Men and Women: The Framingham Heart Study. *Hypertension* **2004**, *43*, 1239–1245. [CrossRef]
63. Doonan, R.J.; Mutter, A.; Egiziano, G.; Gomez, Y.-H.; Daskalopoulou, S.S. Differences in Arterial Stiffness at Rest and after Acute Exercise between Young Men and Women. *Hypertens. Res.* **2013**, *36*, 226–231. [CrossRef]
64. Perdomo, S.J.; Moody, A.M.; McCoy, S.M.; Barinas-Mitchell, E.; Jakicic, J.M.; Gibbs, B.B. Effects on Carotid–Femoral Pulse Wave Velocity 24 h Post Exercise in Young Healthy Adults. *Hypertens. Res.* **2016**, *39*, 435–439. [CrossRef]
65. Chung, J.; Kim, M.; Jin, Y.; Kim, Y.; Hong, J. Fitness as a Determinant of Arterial Stiffness in Healthy Adult Men: A Cross-Sectional Study. *J. Sports Med. Phys. Fit.* **2018**, *58*, 150–156. [CrossRef]
66. Poderoso, R.; Cirilo-Sousa, M.; Júnior, A.; Novaes, J.; Vianna, J.; Dias, M.; Leitão, L.; Reis, V.; Neto, N.; Vilaça-Alves, J. Gender Differences in Chronic Hormonal and Immunological Responses to CrossFit®. *Int. J. Environ. Res. Public. Health* **2019**, *16*, 2577. [CrossRef] [PubMed]
67. Yaron, M.; Greenman, Y.; Rosenfeld, J.B.; Izkhakov, E.; Limor, R.; Osher, E.; Shenkerman, G.; Tordjman, K.; Stern, N. Effect of Testosterone Replacement Therapy on Arterial Stiffness in Older Hypogonadal Men. *Eur. J. Endocrinol.* **2009**, *160*, 839–846. [CrossRef] [PubMed]
68. Dockery, F.; Bulpitt, C.J.; Donaldson, M.; Fernandez, S.; Rajkumar, C. The Relationship between Androgens and Arterial Stiffness in Older Men. *J. Am. Geriatr. Soc.* **2003**, *51*, 1627–1632. [CrossRef] [PubMed]
69. Vlachopoulos, C.; Ioakeimidis, N.; Miner, M.; Aggelis, A.; Pietri, P.; Terentes-Printzios, D.; Tsekoura, D.; Stefanadis, C. Testosterone Deficiency: A Determinant of Aortic Stiffness in Men. *Atherosclerosis* **2014**, *233*, 278–283. [CrossRef]
70. Moreau, K.L.; Babcock, M.C.; Hildreth, K.L. Sex Differences in Vascular Aging in Response to Testosterone. *Biol. Sex. Differ.* **2020**, *11*, 18. [CrossRef] [PubMed]
71. Campelo, A.E.; Cutini, P.H.; Massheimer, V.L. Testosterone Modulates Platelet Aggregation and Endothelial Cell Growth through Nitric Oxide Pathway. *J. Endocrinol.* **2012**, *213*, 77–87. [CrossRef]
72. Vesely, S.; Klöckner, C.A. Social Desirability in Environmental Psychology Research: Three Meta-Analyses. *Front. Psychol.* **2020**, *11*, 1395. [CrossRef]

Journal of
Functional Morphology and Kinesiology

Article

A Chair-Based Music–Kinetic Combined Exercise Program as an Alternative Approach for Increasing Health, Functional Capacity, and Physical Fitness Indices in Middle-Aged Pre-Menopausal Women

Konstantina Karatrantou *, Theodoros Papavasiliou, Christos Batatolis, Theodora Vasilopoulou, Panagiotis Ioakimidis and Vassilis Gerodimos

Department of Physical Education and Sports Science, University of Thessaly, 42100 Trikala, Greece; vasilopoulouphys@gmail.com (T.V.); ioakeimidis@uth.gr (P.I.)
* Correspondence: kokaratr@uth.gr

Abstract: Lately, chairs have been widely used as a cheap, easily accessible, safe, and effective training means in different settings (e.g., in gyms, the house, workplaces, and in rehabilitation). This study investigated the effectiveness of a 10-week chair-based music–kinetic integrated combined exercise program on health, functional capacity, and physical fitness indicators of middle-aged pre-menopausal women. A total of 40 healthy women (40–53 years) were assigned to two groups: exercise (EG) and control (CG). The EG followed a 10-week (3 times/weekly; 30 training sessions) chair-based exercise program including aerobic dance, flexibility, coordination, and strength exercises with body weight or auxiliary means. Selected indicators of health, functional capacity, and physical fitness were evaluated before and after the 10 weeks. Following the program, the EG significantly reduced their body fat (−2.5%), blood pressure (by −4.5 to −5.5%), the time during the timed up-and-go (TUG) test (by −10.27%), heart rate (by −6.35 to −13.78%), and the rate of perceived exertion (by −24.45 to −25.88%), while increasing respiratory function (3.5–4%), flexibility (12.17%), balance (50.38–51.07%), maximal handgrip strength (10–12.17%), and endurance strength (43.87–55.91%). The chair-based combined music–kinetic exercise program was effective and could be safely used in different settings to improve health, functional capacity, and physical fitness in middle-aged women.

Keywords: aerobic dance; flexibility; balance; strength; integrated concurrent training; aging

Citation: Karatrantou, K.; Papavasiliou, T.; Batatolis, C.; Vasilopoulou, T.; Ioakimidis, P.; Gerodimos, V. A Chair-Based Music–Kinetic Combined Exercise Program as an Alternative Approach for Increasing Health, Functional Capacity, and Physical Fitness Indices in Middle-Aged Pre-Menopausal Women. *J. Funct. Morphol. Kinesiol.* **2023**, *8*, 81. https://doi.org/10.3390/jfmk8020081

Academic Editor: Gianpiero Greco

Received: 23 May 2023
Revised: 13 June 2023
Accepted: 14 June 2023
Published: 15 June 2023

1. Introduction

Middle age (40–64 years old) is one of the most important periods of women's life and marks the transition from young adulthood to older age [1]. This period of life is associated with various physical, mental, cognitive, and social changes, which affect women's health-related quality of life (HRQOL) [1,2]. The World Health Organization (WHO) defines HRQOL as "perfect physical, mental, and social health and well-being", which is affected by different daily lifestyle behaviors [3]. The reduced physical activity and the adoption of other unhealthy behaviors (i.e., smoking, alcohol consumption, and unhealthy eating habits) are considered important risk factors related to (a) the development of chronic diseases (obesity, hypertension, cardiovascular diseases, diabetes, etc.), (b) a reduction in independent living, (c) the deterioration of HRQOL, and (d) the decrease of life expectancy in middle-aged and older individuals [4–6]. Despite the current recommendations of the WHO and the American College of Sports Medicine (ACSM) for regular physical activity and exercise to improve or maintain physical and mental health, many middle-aged and older individuals have not adopted a physically active lifestyle [4,5]. The low availability and accessibility of safe exercise programs and training means according to the individual's possibilities, high costs and time constraints are considered the main contributing factors to the reduced participation of the population in exercise activities [4,6]. Taking all the above into consideration, several organizations all over the world suggest the design and implementation of appropriate exercise programs for untrained middle-aged and older individuals [4–6], using safe, cheap, easily applicable, and accessible training means.

For this reason, during the last few decades, chairs have been used as an alternative training means for implementing various exercise programs (flexibility, balance, strength, and aerobic capacity) in different populations (i.e., healthy older individuals, young and middle-aged employees, individuals with chronic diseases or mobility difficulties, pregnant women, and untrained individuals) [7–22] and have several advantages. First of all, the use of a chair minimizes the risk of falls and injury during exercise by offering better stability, support of the human body, and safety to the trainees [7,10,15]. Other important advantages of chairs are their low cost and easy accessibility. Moreover, exercise programs using chairs as a basic training means can be easily adapted and implemented in any indoor or outdoor place (without requiring particularly large space), such as in the gym, at home, in the workplace, and in a classroom, courtyard, park, rehabilitation center, or hospital room. In the scientific literature, several studies have examined the effect of chair-based exercise programs in different populations reporting promising results in various cardiovascular and neuromuscular health-related parameters (i.e., gait, balance strength, flexibility, blood pressure, heart rate, and musculoskeletal pain) [7–22]. It should be mentioned that the vast majority of the aforementioned studies (a) were performed in elderly frail people or individuals with chronic diseases [7–12,15–22], while there is limited information on healthy middle-aged individuals and (b) were focused on improving single or specific indices of health and physical fitness. To the best of our knowledge, no previous study has examined the effectiveness of a "holistic" chair-based exercise approach focusing on all the important functional and physical fitness parameters (aerobic capacity, strength, flexibility, and coordination abilities). However, according to the ACSM and the WHO, middle-aged individuals should engage in specifically designed combined exercise programs at least 3 times per week, which should entail cardiorespiratory and neuromuscular exercises (balance, strength, and flexibility) aiming to improve or preserve physical fitness and health [4,5].

Furthermore, to the best of our knowledge, no previous study has investigated the effectiveness of a music–kinetic chair-based exercise program in healthy middle-aged individuals, while several studies have used music–kinetic exercise programs (different dance training programs) without a chair, reporting beneficial effects in physical and mental health in middle-aged individuals [23–28]. During the last few decades, several studies have addressed the impact of music either as an ergogenic aid or as a means by which to adjust and control the intensity of exercise, causing the appropriate adaptations to the human body [29,30]. Previous studies in the scientific literature have reported a significant interaction between exercise intensity (heart rate and rate of perceived exertion responses throughout exercise workout) and music tempo in different exercise modalities (e.g., cycling and treadmill walking) [31,32]. Additionally, the use of music throughout exercise programs has been shown to (a) reduce the perception of fatigue and exertion through dissociation and distraction during exercise, (b) increase arousal and neural activity, and as a result, improve exercise performance, and (c) increase motivation and effort, mood, exercise enjoyment, and feelings of power [33–37]. For this reason, it is of interest to design, implement and evaluate the efficacy of a music–kinetic chair-based combined exercise program that can be used in different exercise and rehabilitation settings to improve health, functional capacity, and overall fitness in middle-aged untrained individuals.

Thus, the present study aimed to examine the effectiveness of a 10-week chair based music–kinetic integrated (where the exercise goals were repeatedly altered during the main part of the training session) combined exercise program (aerobic dance, flexibility, coordination, and strength exercises with body weight or auxiliary means) on health (body fat, blood pressure, and respiratory function), functional capacity (lower back and hamstrings flexibility, static and dynamic balance), and physical fitness (strength and aerobic capacity) indicators of healthy middle-aged pre-menopausal women.

2. Materials and Methods

2.1. Participants

Firstly, 50 premenopausal middle-aged women, following announcements in mass media (e-magazines and e-newspapers) and on social media (Facebook and Twitter), were recruited to participate in this study and were assessed for eligibility. Six of them were excluded because they did not meet some of the inclusion criteria (they had chronic health problems, such as diabetes, cardiovascular disease, and hypertension) and four of them were excluded because they were unable to complete the initial functional capacity and physical fitness measurements due to musculoskeletal discomfort in the knee joint and the lumbar spine. Thus, the final sample of the present study was 40 pre-menopausal middle-aged untrained women (40–53 years old), who were divided into two equal groups: the exercise group (EG; n = 20) and the control group (CG; n = 20) (Table 1). Before the study, the subject's medical history and activity status were assessed using a specific questionnaire. All the final participants of the present study (a) were healthy without injury or disease and were free of any illness, (b) did not report the use of any medication and (c) did not participate in any organized physical activity for at least six months before the study. In addition, before the study, the participants were informed about the experimental procedures and the possible risks during the study and signed an informed consent form. The conduction of the study took place according to the Declaration of Helsinki and ethical approval was granted by the Ethics Committee of the University of Thessaly.

Table 1. Age and somatometric characteristics of the middle-aged women per group (mean ± sd).

Variables	EG (n = 20)	CG (n = 20)
Age (years old)	46.80 ± 4.70	46.35 ± 3.85
Height (m)	1.64 ± 0.08	1.65 ± 0.07
Body mass (kg)	66.34 ± 7.79	67.26 ± 6.82
Body mass index (kg/m^2)	24.66 ± 3.10	24.73 ± 3.55

EG: exercise group; CG: control group.

2.2. Study Design

Primarily, a pilot study was performed to determine the final testing and training procedures. One to two weeks before the start of the study, the participants performed two–three familiarization sessions to become accustomed to the instrumentation and the experimental (testing and training) procedures. Subsequently, the baseline measurements were performed in the total sample. Following the pre-training measurements, the participants were randomly assigned to two equal groups: the EG and the CG. A computer-generated list of random numbers was used for the allocation of the sample in one of the two groups, exercise or control. It should also be mentioned that the main investigator and the outcome assessors were blinded to the allocated intervention during the entire period of data collection. During the study, the EG participated in a 10-week (3 times per week) music–kinetic chair-based integrated combined training program; while the CG did not perform any systematically organized training program during the 10 weeks. It would be important to mention that no adverse effects or injuries were reported during the 10-week exercise program. The training program was supervised by an exercise instructor, and special exercise attendance books were filled in to confirm the participants' exercise adherence (all of the participants of the study completed 30 training sessions in total). Exercise adherence was also reinforced using different motivation strategies (i.e., think positive, make a commitment, and set short-term goals) [38]. Two days after the end of the training session, the pre-training measurements were repeated in the same order and at the same time of day. The EG was instructed not to engage in any other activities during the research. In addition, the participants were instructed to continue their regular diet during the study, avoid the consumption of caffeine, alcohol, and tobacco at least 24 h before the test, avoid any intense activity before the test, and rest sufficiently the night before the test.

2.3. Training Program

The EG followed a 10-week (3 days/week; 30 training sessions in total) music–kinetic integrated combined chair-based exercise program (flexibility, balance, strength, and aerobic capacity). Each training session lasted about 50–60 min and included 15-min warm-up and flexibility training, a 30–40-min main part (integrated combined balance, strength, and aerobic training using chair-based seated and chair-assisted standing exercises), and 5-min recovery. During the main part of the training program, the balance, strength, and aerobic training were altered in a predetermined order (2–2.5-min aerobic dance/1–1.5-min strength or balance exercises). Throughout each exercise session of the 10-week exercise program, real-time monitoring of the participants' heart rate was performed using the Polar Team Solution system (Science Technologies, Kempele, Finland), and the rating of perceived exertion (RPE) was assessed using the 20-point Borg scale after each exercise session to ensure the safety of the participants. The basic training mean of the program was the chair. It should be mentioned that special emphasis was placed on the selection of the appropriate chair used for the program. In more detail, the criteria for choosing the appropriate chair were as follows: (a) a stable chair without wheels, (b) a chair without armrests so that the movements are not hindered, (c) a chair with a back for better lumbar spine support (not a softback), and (d) the chair height adjusted depending on the height of the participants, so that the feet could be flat on the floor with a knee angle approximately at 90°.

The main part of the training program included:

(a) Aerobic training: The aerobic training program included low-impact aerobic dance movements from a sitting position in the chair or from an upright position around the chair (i.e., knee lift, heel up, kick, lateral lunges, squats, and V step) in conjunction with continuous arm movements at the shoulder level as well as above the head. We selected a low-impact aerobic dance because it is safe and is widely used in fitness and rehabilitation centers for improving indices of health and overall fitness in middle-aged and older individuals. During the aerobic dance choreography, the women hold a medium resistance anti-stress ball or a hand gripper in each hand and squeezed it simultaneously according to the specific aerobic dance movements. The intensity (65–80% of the age-predicted HR_{max}; music rhythm 110–120 beats/min) and the duration (16–25 min) of aerobic training progressively increased during the training program, according to the recommendation of the ACSM [5].

(b) Strength training: The strength training program included chair-based seated and chair-assisted standing exercises with body weight as well as exercises with auxiliary means (dumbbells, Pilates mini balls, rings, anti-stress balls, and hand grippers) for all major muscle groups. In more detail, the program consisted of exercises for the lower limbs (i.e., sit-to-stand exercise, adductor ball squeeze from sitting position, standing lateral hip raises with chair support, and calf raises with chair support), the upper limbs (i.e., tricep extensions, lateral raises, and bicep curls from the sitting position), as well as for the abdominal and dorsal trunk muscles (i.e., modified chair sit-ups, sitting twists, the seated cat–cow exercise, and seated knee lifts). The training load of strength exercises, throughout the 10-week exercise program, was modified by progressively increasing the number of sets (1–3), repetitions (8–15 RM), and the resistance of the dumbbells (1–3 kg), according to the recommendation of the ACSM [5]. All strength exercises were performed following the music rhythm (100–110 beats/min).

(c) Balance training: The balance training program included static (two-leg and one-leg stance exercises) and dynamic balance exercises with dynamic motion in lower and/or upper limbs (i.e., calf raises, standing hip extensions, and standing hip abductions) as well as dynamic balance exercises with different ways of locomotion (i.e., heel-to-toe forward walking, backward walking, lateral walking, heel walking, and toe walking). The static balance exercises were initially performed, with the support of one or two hands on the chair and without auxiliary means, and then performed without the support of the hands on the chair using small auxiliary means (Pilates mini balls and rings, anti-stress balls, and hand grippers). The training load of balance exercises, throughout the 10-week exercise program, was modified by progressively increasing the number of sets (1–3), the repetitions/duration (8–15 reps or 10–30 s), and the distance in dynamic balance exercises with locomotion (3–5 m), according to the recommendation of the ACSM [5]. All balance exercises were performed following the music rhythm (100–110 beats/min).

The training load characteristics during the 10-week intervention are analytically presented in Table 2.

Table 2. Progression of training load during the 10 weeks.

	Weeks			
	1–2	3–4	5–7	8–10
Total duration of the training session (min)	50	50–55	57	60
Total duration of the main part (min)	30	30–35	37	40
Aerobic dance/strength balance ratio during the main part	2 min/ 1 min	2–2.20 min/ 1 min	2.5 min/ 1.20 min	2.5 min/ 1.5 min
		Aerobic training		
Music rhythm (beats/min)	110	110–115	115	115–120
Intensity (% HRmax)	65–70%	70–75%	70–75%	75–80%
Duration (set x time)	8 × 2 min = 16 min total	10 × 2 − 2.20 min = 20–22 min total	10 × 2.5 min = 25 min total	10 × 2.5 min = 25 min total
Training contents	Seated aerobic dance	Seated aerobic dance (14 min)—standing aerobic dance around the chair (6–8 min)	Seated aerobic dance (15 min)—standing aerobic dance around the chair (10 min)	Seated aerobic dance (12.5 min)—standing aerobic dance around the chair (12.5 min)
Equipment	Anti-stress balls	Anti-stress balls	Hand grippers	Hand grippers
		Strength training		
Music rhythm (beats/min)	100–105	105–108	108	108–110
Sets	1–2	2	2	2–3
Reps/set	8–10	10–12	12	15
Equipment	Mini balls, dumbbells 1–2 kg, and anti-stress balls	Mini balls, dumbbells 1–2 kg, and anti-stress balls	Pilates ring, dumbbells 2–3 kg, and hand grippers	Pilates ring, dumbbells 2–3 kg, and hand grippers
		Balance training		
Music rhythm (beats/min)	100–105	105–108	108	108–110
Sets	1–2	2	2	2–3
Reps or duration (s) or distance (m)/set	8–10 reps/10–15 s/3 m	10–12 reps/15–20 s/3–4 m	12–15 reps/20–25 s/4–5 m	15–20 reps/25–30 s/5 m
Equipment	-	-	Mini balls and anti-stress balls	Pilates ring and hand grippers

Additionally, an indicative training session (the ninth training session) of the 10-week intervention program is analytically presented in Table 3.

Table 3. An indicative training session of the 10-week intervention program.

	Total duration of the ninth training session: 50 min
Warm-up-Flexibility (15 min)	Low-impact chair-based seated aerobic dance lower and upper limb movements (5 min). Dynamic and static stretching exercises (chair-based seated and chair-assisted standing) for the whole body (12 exercises; 2 sets × 15 s for static/15 reps for dynamic exercise).
Main part (30 min)	
	Block 1. Seated aerobic dance (2 min)/2 balance strength exercises: (a) one-leg stance with the leg bent forward at 90° (1 set × 15 s/leg) and (b) calf raises with simultaneous tricep extensions with a mini ball (1 set × 10 reps). **Block 2**. Seated aerobic dance (2 min)/2 balance strength exercises: (a) one-leg stance with the leg bent forward at 90° (1 set × 15 s/leg) and (b) calf raises with simultaneous tricep extensions with a mini ball (1 set × 10 reps). **Block 3**. Standing aerobic dance (2 min)/2 balance exercises: (a) heel-to-toe forward walking (1 set × 3 m) and (b) backward walking (1 set × 3m). **Block 4**. Seated aerobic dance (2 min)/2 balance exercises: (a) heel-to-toe forward walking (1 set × 3 m), and (b) backward walking (1 set × 3m). **Block 5**. Seated aerobic dance (2 min)/2 strength exercises: (a) lateral raises with dumbbells from a sitting position (1 set × 10 reps) and (b) bicep curls with dumbbells from a sitting position (1 set × 10 reps). **Block 6**. Standing aerobic dance (2 min)/2 strength exercises: (a) lateral raises with dumbbells from a sitting position (1 set × 10 reps) and (b) bicep curls with dumbbells from a sitting position (1 set × 10 reps). **Block 7**. Seated aerobic dance (2 min)/2 strength exercises: (a) sit-to-stand exercise (1 set × 10 reps) and (b) adductor mini ball squeeze from the sitting position (1 set × 10 reps). **Block 8**. Seated aerobic dance (2 min)/2 strength exercises: (a) sit-to-stand exercise (1 set × 10 reps) and (b) adductor mini ball squeeze from the sitting position (1 set × 10 reps). **Block 9**. Standing aerobic dance (2 min)/2 strength exercises: (a) sitting twists (1 set × 10 reps) and (b) seated cat–cow exercise (1 set × 10 reps). **Block 10**. Seated aerobic dance (2 min)/2 strength exercises: (a) sitting twists (1 set × 10 reps) and (b) seated cat–cow exercise (1 set × 10 reps).
Cool down (5 min)	Low-impact chair-based seated aerobic dance lower and upper limb movements (2 min) and chair-based seated static stretching exercises for the whole body in conjunction with breathing exercises (3 min).

2.4. Testing Procedures

Health, functional capacity, and physical fitness indices were measured in both the EG and the CG before and after the 10 weeks. Before the functional capacity and physical fitness testing, a 10-min warm-up was performed by the participants including 5-min stationary cycling and 5-min static-dynamic stretching exercises for all major muscle groups.

2.4.1. Health Indices

(a) The percentage of body fat (%BF) was assessed using the bioelectrical impedance method (Maltron 900) and then the fat-free mass (FFM) was calculated; (b) blood pressure and (c) respiratory function (FVC; FEV_1) were also measured using an electronic blood pressure monitor (A&D-UA-851) and a portable spirometer (Micro, Medical, Micro), respectively [39,40].

2.4.2. Functional Capacity Indices

The lower back and hamstrings' flexibility was assessed with the sit and reach test using a special box (sit and reach flex tester, Novel Products Inc., Rockton, IL, USA) following the instructions of the ACSM [34]. The participants were instructed to lean forward slowly as far as possible (while exhaling), without bending their knees, and to hold at the final position for at least 2 s [39]. The participants performed three trials with a rest period of 15 s, and the best score (in cm) was considered for analysis, while the static and dynamic balance were also evaluated using the 1-min single limb stance and the timed up and go test, as previously described by Douris et al. [41] and Rikli and Jones [42]. During the static balance test, the participants were asked to stand on a firm surface and look straight ahead. The stopwatch began after the participants raised one leg and stopped when the participants became unstable and placed the flexed leg on the ground or at the completion of 1-min [41]. Both legs were tested in a random order, and the mean score (in s) of three trials of each leg was considered for analysis. While during the TUG test, the participants were instructed to stand up from a chair, walk as quickly as possible for 3 m, turn around, walk back, and sit down in the chair [42]. The participants performed three trials (with 30 s rest between the trials), and the best score (in s) was considered for analysis.

2.4.3. Physical Fitness Indices

The muscular strength and endurance of the upper body were assessed using three reliable tests: (a) the maximal handgrip strength test, (b) the sit-ups test, and (c) the modified knee push-ups test, which are widely used in the scientific literature using different testing protocols and equipment for the evaluation of various populations such as young and middle-aged adults, children, and adolescents [39,43–45]. In more detail, the maximal handgrip strength test was conducted with a hydraulic dynamometer (Jamar 5030J1, Jamar Technologies, Horsham, PA, USA) and performed from the sitting position on a height-adjustable chair with the participants' feet supported, their shoulders adducted and neutrally rotated, their elbow flexed at 90°, and their forearm in the neutral position [43]. The participants performed three maximal isometric contractions (each lasting 5 s) with each hand, with a 1-min rest between trials, and the best score with each hand was considered for analysis. Furthermore, during the sit-up test, the participants were instructed to lie in the supine position with their knees bent at an angle of 100–110° and with both arms folded across their chest. The maximum number of sit-ups was considered for analysis [39]. Additionally, during the push-ups test, the participants were positioned with their knees bent at an angle of 100–110° and their arms extended at a shoulder-width apart. The participants lowered their bodies, bending their elbows at an angle of 90°, and then returned back to the starting position. The maximum number of push-ups was considered for analysis [39].

Finally, cardiorespiratory fitness was assessed using the submaximal treadmill walking test of Ebelling et al., consisting of three 4-min stages [46]. The participants started the 4-min walking test protocol at an initial treadmill velocity that corresponded to 60% of their age-predicted HR_{max} and 0% grade (stage 1). Then, the walking speed remained stable for each participant, and the treadmill incline was increased to 5% (stage 2) and 10% (stage 3). The heart rate of the participants was measured before the walking test protocol, after each stage, and at the first minute following the termination of the walking test using chest belt telemetry (Polar Electro, Kempele, Finland). Additionally, the rating of perceived exertion (RPE) was assessed at the end of each stage using the 20-point Borg scale. Maximal oxygen uptake (VO_{2max}; mL/kg/min) was also estimated using the following equation proposed by Ebbeling et al. [46]: VO_{2max} = 15.1 + 21.8 (speed in mph) −0.327 (heart rate in bpm at 5% grade) −0.263 (speed × age in years) + 0.00504 (heart rate in bpm at 5% grade × age in years) + 5.98 (gender: female = 0, male = 1).

2.5. Statistical Analysis

All statistical analyses were performed using IBM SPSS Statistics v.26 software (IBM Corporation, Armonk, New York, USA), and the results are presented as the means ± standard deviations. A statistical power analysis (software package GPower 3.0) before the initiation of the study indicated that a total number of 36 participants (18 participants in each group) would yield adequate power (>0.85) and a level of significance (<0.05). The total sample of the present study was 40 middle-aged pre-menopausal women (20 participants in each group). The normality of data was examined using the Shapiro–Wilk test (all variables followed the normal distribution). Two-way analysis of variance (ANOVA), 2 groups (EG and CG) × 2 time points (pre and post training), with repeated measures on the "time point" factor and multiple comparisons with the Sidak method, was applied to locate significantly different means within and between the groups. Cohen's effect sizes were calculated using the equation: d = difference between means/pooled SD. One-way ANOVAs were used between the groups to compare the relative changes from pre to post training in all of the tested parameters. The significance level was set at $p < 0.05$.

3. Results

3.1. Health Indices

Two-way ANOVAs indicated significant interaction effects on the percentage of body fat and blood pressure as well as on respiratory function (FVC; FEV_1) ($p < 0.05$). Specifically, the EG body fat and blood pressure values were significantly lower in the post-training measurements versus the pre-training measurements, while the FVC and FEV_1 values were significantly greater in the post-training measurements versus the pre-training measurements ($p < 0.05$; with small–medium effect sizes d = 0.24–0.43), and the FFM values remained stable ($p > 0.05$). In the CG, all the above variables did not change after the 10 weeks ($p > 0.05$) (Table 4). Comparisons between groups revealed that all post-training values for body fat and blood pressure were significantly lower in the EG versus the CG, while the FVC and FEV_1 values were significantly higher in the EG versus the CG ($p < 0.05$). The FFM post-training values did not differ between the EG and the CG ($p > 0.05$). The percent changes from pre to post training for body fat, blood pressure, and respiratory function were significantly greater in the EG vs. the CG ($p < 0.01$). Regarding the pre-training measurements, no significant differences were observed in all health parameters between the two groups ($p > 0.05$).

Table 4. Health indices in the exercise and control group pre and post training (mean ± SD).

Variables	Group	Pre Training	Post Training	Mean % Change
Body fat (%)	EG	29.50 ± 6.90	27.00 ± 7.50 $^{*,\#}$	−2.5 †
	CG	29.09 ± 9.85	29.48 ± 11.84	+1.3
Systolic BP (mmHg)	EG	106.84 ± 10.15	103.64 ± 8.54 $^{*,\#}$	−3.0 †
	CG	110.80 ± 12.80	111.45 ± 11.20	+0.6
Diastolic BP (mmHg)	EG	74.29 ± 8.43	70.84 ± 7.30 $^{*,\#}$	−4.6 †
	CG	76.46 ± 10.50	78.27 ± 9.93	+2.3
FVC (L)	EG	3.32 ± 0.52	3.44 ± 0.51 $^{*,\#}$	+3.6 †
	CG	3.11 ± 0.43	3.10 ± 0.41	−0.3
FEV_1 (L)	EG	2.63 ± 0.43	2.74 ± 0.42 $^{*,\#}$	+4.2 †
	CG	2.59 ± 0.34	2.60 ± 0.32	+0.4

where * $p < 0.05$ statistically significant difference before and after the intervention program in the EG, # $p < 0.05$ statistically significant difference between the EG and the CG in the post-training measurement, and † $p < 0.01$ statistically significant difference between the EG and the CG in the percent change. BP, blood pressure; CG, control group; EG: exercise group; FVC, forced vital capacity; FEV_1, forced expiratory volume in 1 s.

3.2. Functional Capacity Indices

The two-way analyses of variance showed significant interaction effects on all functional capacity indices (flexibility and static and dynamic balance) ($p < 0.001$). More specifically, in the EG, the flexibility and static balance values were significantly higher in the post-training measurements versus the pre-training measurements, while the TUG values were significantly lower in the post-training measurements versus the pre-training measurements ($p < 0.001$; d = 0.70–1.15). In the CG, all of the above variables did not change after the 10 weeks ($p > 0.05$) (Table 5). Comparisons between the groups revealed that all of the post-training flexibility and static balance values were significantly greater in the EG versus the CG, while the TUG values were significantly lower in the EG versus the CG ($p < 0.001$). Regarding the pre-training measurements, no significant differences were observed in all functional capacity parameters between the two groups ($p > 0.05$).

Table 5. Flexibility and balance values in the exercise and control group pre and post training (mean ± SD).

Variables	Group	Pre Training	Post Training	Mean % Change
Flexibility—Sit-and-reach test (cm)	EG	24.61 ± 6.43	27.86 ± 6.36 *,#	+12.2 †
	GG	24.67 ± 6.35	24.00 ± 6.38	−2.7
Static balance—Right leg (s)	EG	56.92 ± 40.28	108.82 ± 55.64 *,#	+51.1 †
	CG	56.91 ± 40.16	56.18 ± 39.93	−1.3
Static balance—Left leg (s)	EG	48.73 ± 39.80	101.73 ± 59.34 *,#	+50.4 †
	CG	47.77 ± 39.62	48.78 ± 39.30	+2.1
Dynamic balance—TUG test (s)	EG	4.90 ± 0.47	4.44 ± 0.37 *,#	−10.3 †
	CG	4.90 ± 0.46	4.91 ± 0.47	+0.2

where * $p < 0.001$ statistically significant difference before and after the intervention program in the EG, # $p < 0.01$ statistically significant difference between the EG and the CG in the post-training measurement, and † $p < 0.001$ statistically significant difference between the EG and the CG in the percent change. CG: control group; EG: exercise group; TUG test: timed up-and-go test.

3.3. Physical Fitness Indices

3.3.1. Strength

The analyses of variance indicated significant two-way interaction effects on all of the strength tests ($p < 0.001$). More specifically, in the EG, the handgrip, push-ups, and sit-ups test values were significantly higher in the post-training measurements versus the pre-training measurements ($p < 0.001$; d = 0.70–1.57). In the CG, the above variables did not change after the 10 weeks ($p > 0.05$) (Table 6). Comparisons between the groups revealed that all post-training strength values were significantly greater in the EG versus the CG ($p < 0.001$). The percent changes from pre to post training for the handgrip, push-ups, and sit-ups test were significantly greater in the EG vs. the CG ($p < 0.001$). Regarding the pre-training measurements, no significant differences were observed in all the upper body strength values between the two groups ($p > 0.05$).

Table 6. Strength values in the exercise and control groups pre and post training (mean ± SD).

Variables	Group	Pre Training	Post Training	Mean % Change
Maximal HG preferred hand (kg)	EG	31.11 ± 5.48	35.36 ± 5.35 *,#	+12.2 †
	CG	31.28 ± 5.54	30.58 ± 5.27	−2.3
Maximal HG non-preferred hand (kg)	EG	30.17 ± 5.09	33.61 ± 5.81 *,#	+10.0 †
	CG	30.22 ± 5.05	29.61 ± 4.97	−2.1
Sit-ups (reps)	EG	14.50 ± 9.78	32.56 ± 13.86 *,#	+55.9 †
	CG	14.67 ± 9.82	14.22 ± 9.08	−2.4
Push-ups (reps)	EG	12.17 ± 7.16	21.00 ± 7.81 *,#	+43.9 †
	CG	12.28 ± 6.94	12.72 ± 6.75	+1.5

where * $p < 0.001$ statistically significant difference before and after the intervention program in the EG, # $p < 0.01$ statistically significant difference between the EG and the CG in the post-training measurement, and † $p < 0.001$ statistically significant difference between the EG and the CG in the percent change. CG, control group; EG: exercise group; HG: handgrip strength.

3.3.2. Aerobic Capacity

The analyses of variance demonstrated significant two-way interaction effects on the heart rate and RPE values ($p < 0.001$; Table 7). Specifically, the EG heart rate and RPE values were significantly lower in the post-training measurements versus the pre-training measurements ($p < 0.001$; d = 0.7–1.15), while the VO_{2max} values were significantly higher. In the CG, the above variables did not change after the 10 weeks ($p > 0.05$). Comparisons between the groups revealed that all heart rates and RPE post-training values were significantly lower in the EG versus the CG ($p < 0.001$), while the VO_{2max} values were significantly higher. The percent changes from pre to post training for heart rate, RPE, and VO_{2max} were significantly greater in the EG vs. the CG ($p < 0.001$). Concerning the pre-training measurements, non-significant differences were observed between the two groups ($p > 0.05$).

Table 7. Cardiorespiratory fitness in the exercise and control groups pre and post training (mean ± SD).

Variables	Group	Pre Training	Post Training	Mean % Change
HR rest (beats/min)	EG	83.50 ± 8.86	73.72 ± 8.50 *,#	−13.8 †
	CG	83.33 ± 8.81	84.44 ± 8.79	+1.3
HR test (beats/min) Stage 1°	EG	114.78 ± 6.12	105.06 ± 8.45 *,#	−9.8 †
	CG	114.33 ± 6.09	115.72 ± 6.72	+1.2
Stage 2°	EG	132.11 ± 9.04	122.67 ± 11.57 *,#	−8.2 †
	CG	131.89 ± 8.71	132.83 ± 9.44	+0.7
Stage 3°	EG	145.06 ± 7.46	137.82 ± 11.40 *,#	−6.4 †
	CG	145.88 ± 7.47	144.50 ± 7.55	−0.9
HR rec (beats/min) 1st min	EG	113.67 ± 11.28	100.83 ± 11.44 *,#	−13.3 †
	CG	113.56 ± 11.11	114.06 ± 11.30	+0.4
RPE (Borg scale) Stage 1°	EG	9.22 ± 2.05	7.44 ± 1.62 *,#	−24.7 †
	CG	9.50 ± 2.19	9.11 ± 2.20	−1.5
Stage 2°	EG	11.83 ± 3.05	9.50 ± 2.64 *,#	−25.9 †
	CG	11.72 ± 2.97	12.17 ± 2.94	+2.6
Stage 3°	EG	13.50 ± 3.12	11.12 ± 2.96 *,#	−25.5 †
	CG	13.19 ± 3.15	13.75 ± 3.44	+2.4
VO_{2max} estimation (mL/kg/min)	EG	36.50 ± 3.1	41.2 ± 3.0 *,#	+11.4 †
	CG	36.89 ± 2.5	36.5 ± 2.4	−1.1

where * $p < 0.001$ statistically significant difference before and after the intervention program in the EG, # $p < 0.01$ statistically significant difference between the EG and the CG in the post-training measurement, and † $p < 0.001$ statistically significant difference between the EG and the CG in the percent change. HRrest: heart values at rest in a sitting position, HR test: heart values during the submaximal exercise, HR rec: heart values following the submaximal exercise, and RPE test: the rating of perceived exertion during the submaximal exercise. VO_{2max} was estimated using the following equation: VO_{2max} = 15.1 + 21.8 (speed in mph) − 0.327 (heart rate in bpm) − 0.263 (speed × age in years) + 0.00504 (heart rate in bpm × age in years) + 5.98 (gender: female = 0, male = 1).

4. Discussion

Biological aging in conjunction with physical inactivity and reduced participation in organized exercise programs may lead to a decline in cardiovascular and neuromuscular function, contributing to physical frailty and deterioration in health-related quality of life [4,5,47,48]. For this reason, all health and exercise organizations such as the ACSM, the WHO, and the CDC recommend the systematic participation of middle-aged and older individuals in combined exercise programs consisting of cardiovascular and neuromuscular activities as the most effective "non-pharmacological" intervention for counteracting the harmful effects of a sedentary lifestyle and aging [4–6]. In this context, during the last few decades, different sports and health professionals all over the world have focused on the design, implementation, and evaluation of different serial and integrated combined exercise programs using various activities and training means [13,14,23,24,26,28,49–55]. Although chair-based exercise programs have gained popularity as an alternative mode of exercise for improving health, functional capacity, and physical fitness, especially in older and frail individuals [7–12,15–22], only a few studies have examined the effects of chair-based exercise programs in healthy middle-aged individuals [13,14]. This study was designed and implemented with success and safety (without adverse side effects or injuries) in middle-aged pre-menopausal women with a 10-week supervised music–kinetic chair-based integrated combined exercise program using chair-based seated and chair-assisted standing flexibility, balance, and strength exercises as well as low-impact aerobic dance movements. The exercise program that was implemented was effective in inducing significant adaptations to all health, neuromuscular, and cardiovascular parameters.

Neuromuscular function (flexibility, balance, and strength) plays an important role in the safe and effective participation of middle-aged and older individuals in daily activities [5]. The progressive loss of flexibility, balance, and strength is an inevitable occurrence of aging [5], contributing to physical frailty and a deterioration in health-related quality of life. This study showed that a 10-week supervised music–kinetic integrated combined exercise program using chair-based seated and chair-assisted standing flexibility, balance, and strength exercises with body weight or small auxiliary means (dumbbells, Pilates mini balls, and rings, anti-stress balls, and hand grippers) resulted in a 12% gain in flexibility of the hamstring and/or lower back muscles, a 50–51% gain in static balance, a 10% gain in dynamic balance, a 10–13% gain in maximal handgrip strength, and a 44–56% gain in upper body endurance strength. The findings of the present study are in line with previous investigations reporting similar gains in neuromuscular parameters (flexibility or static and dynamic balance or lower and upper body strength) after different chair-based exercise programs in older and frail individuals with chronic diseases or injuries [7–12,15–22] as well as in employees of different working environments (i.e., offices and hospitals) [13,14]. The results of previous studies that implemented different combined exercise programs without chairs demonstrate conflicting results. Some of them following the results of the present study reported significant improvements in neuromuscular indices of middle-aged men and women, while others failed to observe significant neuromuscular training adaptations [23,24,27,49,50,56]. According to several previous investigators, the confusing results among studies concerning neuromuscular adaptations may be attributed to differences in subjects' characteristics, loading parameters, and exercise modalities, but mainly to the order of exercises, which may reinforce the so-called "interference effect", diminishing the efficacy of combined strength and aerobic training compared to separately training only strength or endurance [57,58].

Strength and endurance training activate different mechanisms, therefore causing opposite adaptations to the human body. In more detail, strength training causes skeletal muscle hypertrophy and neuromuscular responses by activating the mammalian/mechanistic target of the rapamycin (mTOR) signaling pathway [59,60], whereas aerobic training causes skeletal muscle oxidative and metabolic capacity [61] by activating adenosine monophosphate (AMP)-activated protein kinase (AMPK). It should be mentioned that AMPK interferes with mTOR signaling via tuberous sclerosis complex 2 (TSC2), repressing protein synthesis [62]. Taking all the above into consideration, the combination of those two different modes of training (strength vs. aerobic) in the same training period/session may lead to the so-called "interference effect". Some previous studies have reported that residual fatigue produced by prior aerobic exercise workouts decreases the neural input to the exercised muscle leading to decrements in force output and the rate of force development, as well as attenuation of neuromuscular responses [52]. Conversely, some other studies have demonstrated that the mode of combined training (serial or integrated) and the order of exercises during combined training does not affect neuromuscular responses [53]. In our study, we chose an integrated combined training mode, which according to previous studies may reduce or eliminate the "interference effect" between neuromuscular and aerobic exercise workouts due to less muscle soreness and faster muscle recovery after exercise [63–65].

Cardiorespiratory fitness (CRF) is also an important indication of a person's overall physical health, and it refers to the capacity of the circulatory and respiratory systems to supply oxygen to skeletal muscle mitochondria for the energy production needed during physical activity [53,54]. Low levels of CRF in conjunction with high levels of body fat are strong predictors of cardiovascular disease (CVD) and all-cause mortality in middle-aged and older individuals [66,67]. The present study reported that a music–kinetic chair-based integrated combined exercise program decreased body fat by 2.5% (with a small effect size), blood pressure by 4.5–5.5% (with a small effect size), heart rate by 6.5–14%, and the rate of perceived exertion by 25–26%, while it increased respiratory function by 3.5–4% in middle-aged pre-menopausal women. To the best of our knowledge, very few studies [13,14,68] have examined the efficacy of chair-based exercise programs on body composition and cardiorespiratory function. The results of these studies are in line with those of the present study, reporting significant benefits in body composition and cardiorespiratory fitness of employees or frail older individuals [13,14,68]. Furthermore, the results of the present study revealed similar cardiorespiratory adaptations in comparison with other studies that implemented non-chair combined exercise programs in middle-aged men and women using various activities [23,25–27,50].

The findings of this study are limited to the use of a 10-week music–kinetic chair-based integrated combined exercise program consisting of flexibility, balance, strength, and low-impact aerobic dance exercises using body weight or small auxiliary means (dumbbells, Pilates mini balls, and rings, anti-stress balls, and hand grippers). Future studies could investigate possible training adaptations using other exercise modalities and training interventions of greater program duration (above 10 weeks). Furthermore, our findings are limited to healthy middle-aged pre-menopausal women. Future studies could examine the efficacy and safety of music–kinetic chair-based integrated combined exercise programs in obese individuals, individuals of other age groups (i.e., children or young adults), individuals with different training statuses (trained individuals) as well as in women with different menopause stages (menopause or post-menopause). Finally, in upcoming studies, it would be interesting to examine the efficacy of the chair-based music–kinetic combined exercise program and other health-related factors such as biochemical indicators and evaluation of stress and psychological well-being.

5. Conclusions

In conclusion, a 10-week music–kinetic integrated combined exercise program, using chair-based seated and chair-assisted standing flexibility, balance, and strength exercises as well as low-impact aerobic dance movements, is an effective intervention that induces significant cardiovascular and neuromuscular adaptations in middle-aged pre-menopausal women, without causing adverse side effects or injuries. This study provides perspectives for an alternative and efficient exercise approach that can be used with safety in fitness and rehabilitation centers to ameliorate the age-associated loss of functional capacity and overall fitness in middle-aged women.

Author Contributions: Conceptualization, V.G. and K.K.; methodology, V.G, K.K., T.P. and C.B.; formal analysis, P.I. and T.V.; investigation, T.P., T.V., C.B. and P.I.; data curation, K.K. and V.G.; writing—original draft preparation, K.K. and T.P.; writing—review and editing, V.G.; supervision, V.G.; project administration, V.G. and K.K. All authors have read and agreed to the published version of the manuscript.

Funding: This research received no external funding.

Institutional Review Board Statement: The study was conducted following the Declaration of Helsinki and approved by the Ethics Committee of the University of Thessaly (protocol code: 1930 and date of approval: 25/5/2022).

Informed Consent Statement: Informed consent was obtained from all subjects involved in the study.

Data Availability Statement: Data are unavailable due to privacy or ethical restrictions.

Conflicts of Interest: The authors declare no conflict of interest.

References

1. Thomas, A.J.; Mitchell, E.S.; Woods, N.F. The challenges of midlife women: Themes from the Seattle midlife Women's health study. *Women's Midlife Health* **2018**, *4*, 8. [CrossRef] [PubMed]
2. Kase, N.G. Impact of hormone therapy for women aged 35 to 65 years, from contraception to hormone replacement. *Gend. Med.* **2009**, *6* (Suppl. 1), 37–59. [CrossRef] [PubMed]
3. World Health Organization. *The Constitution of the World Health Organization*; WHO: Washington, DC, USA, 1948.
4. World Health Organization. *Global Recommendations on Physical Activity for Health*; WHO Press: Geneva, Switzerland, 2010.
5. Garber, C.E.; Blissmer, B.; Deschenes, M.R.; Deschenes, M.R.; Franklin, B.A.; Lamonte, M.J.; Lee, I.-M.; Nieman, D.C.; Swain, D.P. Quantity and Quality of Exercise for Developing and Maintaining Cardiorespiratory, Musculoskeletal, and Neuromotor Fitness in Apparently Healthy Adults: Guidance for Prescribing Exercise. *Med. Sci. Sports Exerc.* **2011**, *43*, 1334–1359. [CrossRef] [PubMed]
6. Centers for Disease Control and Prevention. *Steps to Wellness: A Guide to Implementing the 2008 Physical Activity Guidelines for Americans in the Workplace*; U.S. Department of Health and Human Services: Atlanta, GA, USA, 2012.
7. Anthony, K.; Robinson, K.; Logan, P.; Gordon, A.L.; Harwood, R.H.; Masud, T. Chair-Based Exercises for Frail Older People: A Systematic Review. *BioMed Res. Int.* **2013**, *2013*, 309506. [CrossRef]

8. Arslan, T.; Telci, E.A.; Arslan, S. The Effect of Chair-Based Exercises on Exercise Perception and Risk of Falling in Inactive Older Adults Who Live at Nursing Home. *Top. Geriatr. Rehabil.* **2023**, *39*, 2–11. [CrossRef]
9. Cordes, T.; Zwingmann, K.; Rudisch, J.; Voelcker-Rehage, C.; Wollesen, B. Multicomponent exercise to improve motor functions, cognition and well-being for nursing home residents who are unable to walk—A randomized controlled trial. *Exp. Gerontol.* **2021**, *153*, 111484. [CrossRef]
10. Efendi, F.; Tonapa, S.I.; Has, E.M.M.; Ho, K.H.M. Effects of chair-based resistance band exercise on physical functioning, sleep quality, and depression of older adults in long-term care facilities: Systematic review and meta-analysis. *Int. J. Nurs. Sci.* **2022**, *10*, 72–81. [CrossRef]
11. Furtado, G.E.; Carvalho, H.M.; Loureiro, M.; Patrício, M.; Uba-Chupel, M.; Colado, J.C.; Hogervorst, E.; Ferreira, J.P.; Teixeira, A.M. Chair-based exercise programs in institutionalized older women: Salivary steroid hormones, disabilities and frailty changes. *Exp. Gerontol.* **2019**, *130*, 110790. [CrossRef]
12. Furtado, G.E.; Letieri, R.V.; Silva-Caldo, A.; Trombeta, J.C.S.; Monteiro, C.; Rodrigues, R.N.; Vieira-Pedrosa, A.; Barros, M.P.; Cavaglieri, C.R.; Hogervorst, E.; et al. Combined Chair-Based Exercises Improve Functional Fitness, Mental Well-Being, Salivary Steroid Balance, and Anti-microbial Activity in Pre-frail Older Women. *Front. Psychol.* **2021**, *12*, 564490. [CrossRef]
13. Gerodimos, V.; Karatrantou, K.; Papazeti, K.; Batatolis, C.; Krommidas, C. Workplace exercise program in a hospital environment: An effective strategy for the promotion of employees physical and mental health. A randomized controlled study. *Int. Arch. Occup. Environ. Health* **2022**, *95*, 1491–1500. [CrossRef]
14. Karatrantou, K.; Gerodimos, V.; Manouras, N.; Vasilopoulou, T.; Melissopoulou, A.; Mesiakaris, A.F.; Theodorakis, Y. Health-Promoting Effects of a Concurrent Workplace Training Program in Inactive Office Workers (HealPWorkers): A Randomized Controlled Study. *Am. J. Health Promot.* **2020**, *34*, 376–386. [CrossRef]
15. Klempel, N.; Blackburn, N.E.; McMullan, I.L.; Wilson, J.J.; Smith, L.; Cunningham, C.; O'sullivan, R.; Caserotti, P.; Tully, M.A. The Effect of Chair-Based Exercise on Physical Function in Older Adults: A Systematic Review and Meta-Analysis. *Int. J. Environ. Res. Public Health* **2021**, *18*, 1902. [CrossRef]
16. McCaffrey, R.; Taylor, D.; Marker, C.; Park, J. A Pilot Study of the Effects of Chair Yoga and Chair-Based Exercise on Biopsychosocial Outcomes in Older Adults with Lower Extremity Osteoarthritis. *Holist. Nurs. Pract.* **2019**, *33*, 321–326. [CrossRef] [PubMed]
17. Pańczyk, J.; Kamecki, H.; Tchórzewska-Korba, H.; Szulerecki, P.; Rosa, A.; Sosnowski, R. Maintaining physical activity in the era of COVID-19 pandemic: A chair-based exercise program for home-isolated elderly prostate cancer patients. *Central Eur. J. Urol.* **2020**, *73*, 385–386. [CrossRef]
18. Park, J.; Tolea, M.I.; Sherman, D.; Rosenfeld, A.; Arcay, V.; Lopes, Y.; Galvin, J.E. Feasibility of Conducting Nonpharmacological Interventions to Manage Dementia Symptoms in Community-Dwelling Older Adults: A Cluster Randomized Controlled Trial. *Am. J. Alzheimer's Dis. Other Dement.* **2019**, *35*, 1533317519872635. [CrossRef] [PubMed]
19. Robinson, K.R.; Masud, T.; Hawley-Hague, H. Instructors' Perceptions of Mostly Seated Exercise Classes: Exploring the Concept of Chair Based Exercise. *BioMed Res. Int.* **2016**, *2016*, 3241873. [CrossRef] [PubMed]
20. Robinson, K.R.; Long, A.L.; Leighton, P.; Armstrong, S.; Pulikottill-Jacob, R.; Gladman, J.R.F.; Gordon, A.L.; Logan, P.; Anthony, K.A.; Harwood, R.H.; et al. Chair based exercise in community settings: A cluster randomised feasibility study. *BMC Geriatr.* **2018**, *18*, 82. [CrossRef]
21. Shirazi, F.; Nasab, M.N.Z.; Jaberi, A. Comparing the Effects of Virtual Reality and Home Chair-Based Exercises on Balance, Daily Living Activities, and Loneliness Among Older Adults With Balance Disorders. *Res. Gerontol. Nurs.* **2023**, *16*, 33–42. [CrossRef]
22. Stojanović, M.D.; Mikić, M.J.; Milošević, Z.; Vuković, J.; Jezdimirović, T.; Vučetić, V. Effects of Chair-Based, Low–Load Elastic Band Resistance Training on Functional Fitness and Metabolic Biomarkers in Older Women. *J. Sports Sci. Med.* **2021**, *20*, 133–141. [CrossRef]
23. Karatrantou, K.; Gerodimos, V.; Häkkinen, K.; Zafeiridis, A. Health-Promoting Effects of Serial vs. Integrated Combined Strength and Aerobic Training. *Int. J. Sports Med.* **2017**, *38*, 55–64. [CrossRef]
24. Tsourlou, T.; Gerodimos, V.; Kellis, E.; Stavropoulos, N.; Kellis, S. The effects of a calisthenics and a light strength training pro-gram on lower limb muscle strength and body composition in mature women. *J Strength Cond Res.* **2003**, *17*, 590–598. [PubMed]
25. Gillett, P.A.; Eisenman, P.A. The effect of intensity controlled aerobic dance exercise on aerobic capacity of middle-aged, overweight women. *Res. Nurs. Health* **1987**, *10*, 383–390. [CrossRef] [PubMed]
26. Kraemer, W.J.; Keuning, M.; Ratamess, N.A.; Volek, J.S.; McCormick, M.; Bush, J.A.; Nindl, B.C.; Gordon, S.E.; Mazzetti, S.A.; Newton, R.U.; et al. Resistance training combined with bench-step aerobics enhances women's health profile. *Med. Sci. Sports Exerc.* **2001**, *33*, 259–269. [CrossRef] [PubMed]
27. Schiffer, T.; Schulte, S.; Sperlich, B. Aerobic dance: Health and fitness effects in middle-aged premenopausal women. *JEPonline* **2008**, *11*, 25–33.
28. Karatrantou, K.; Gerodimos, V. Does Obesity Affect Neuromuscular and Cardiovascular Adaptations after a 3-Month Combined Exercise Program in Untrained Premenopausal Middle-Aged Women? *Sports* **2023**, *11*, 82. [CrossRef] [PubMed]
29. Edworthy, J.; Waring, H. The effects of music tempo and loudness level on treadmill exercise. *Ergonomics* **2006**, *49*, 1597–1610. [CrossRef]
30. Lim, H.; Atkinson, G.; Karageorghis, C.; Eubank, M. Effects of Differentiated Music on Cycling Time Trial. *Int. J. Sports Med.* **2009**, *30*, 435–442. [CrossRef] [PubMed]

31. Karageorghis, C.I.; Jones, L.; Low, D.C. Relationship between exercise heart rate and music tempo preference. *Res. Q. Exerc. Sport* **2006**, *77*, 240–250. [CrossRef]
32. Karageorghis, C.I.; Jones, L.; Priest, D.-L.; Akers, R.I.; Clarke, A.; Perry, J.M.; Reddick, B.T.; Bishop, D.T.; Lim, H.B. Revisiting the Relationship Between Exercise Heart Rate and Music Tempo Preference. *Res. Q. Exerc. Sport* **2011**, *82*, 274–284. [CrossRef]
33. Boutcher, S.H.; Trenske, M. The Effects of Sensory Deprivation and Music on Perceived Exertion and Affect during Exercise. *J. Sport Exerc. Psychol.* **1990**, *12*, 167–176. [CrossRef]
34. Ballmann, C.G.; Maynard, D.J.; Lafoon, Z.N.; Marshall, M.R.; Williams, T.D.; Rogers, R.R. Effects of Listening to Preferred versus Non-Preferred Music on Repeated Wingate Anaerobic Test Performance. *Sports* **2019**, *7*, 185. [CrossRef]
35. Bishop, D.T.; Wright, M.; Karageorghis, C.I. Tempo and intensity of pre-task music modulate neural activity during reactive task performance. *Psychol. Music* **2014**, *42*, 714–727. [CrossRef]
36. Biagini, M.S.; Brown, L.E.; Coburn, J.W.; Judelson, D.A.; Statler, T.A.; Bottaro, M.; Tran, T.T.; Longo, N.A. Effects of Self-Selected Music on Strength, Explosiveness, and Mood. *J. Strength Cond. Res.* **2012**, *26*, 1934–1938. [CrossRef]
37. Hsu, D.Y.; Huang, L.; Nordgren, L.F.; Rucker, D.D.; Galinsky, A.D. The music of power: Perceptual and behavioral consequences of powerful music. *Soc. Psychol. Pers. Sci.* **2014**, *6*, 75–83. [CrossRef]
38. Brehm, B. *Successful Fitness Motivation Strategies*, 1st ed.; Human Kinetics: Champaign, IL, USA, 2004.
39. American College of Sports Medicine (ACSM). *ACSM's Guidelines for Exercise Testing and Prescription*, 9th ed.; Lippincott Williams & Wilkins: Philadelphia, PA, USA, 2013; pp. 40–107.
40. American Thoracic Society (ATS). Lung Function Testing: Selection of reference values and interpretive strategies. *Am. Rev. Respir. Dis.* **1991**, *144*, 1202–1218. [CrossRef] [PubMed]
41. Douris, P.; Chinan, A.; Gomez, M.; Aw, A.; Steffens, D.; Weiss, S. Fitness levels of middle aged martial art practitioners. *Br. J. Sports Med.* **2004**, *38*, 143–147. [CrossRef] [PubMed]
42. Rikli, R.E.; Jones, C.J. Development and Validation of a Functional Fitness Test for Community-Residing Older Adults. *J. Aging Phys. Act.* **1999**, *7*, 129–161. [CrossRef]
43. Gerodimos, V.; Karatrantou, K.; Psychou, D.; Vasilopoulou, T.; Zafeiridis, A. Static and Dynamic Handgrip Strength Endurance: Test-Retest Reproducibility. *J. Hand Surg.* **2017**, *42*, e175–e184. [CrossRef]
44. Ortega, F.B.; Artero, E.G.; Ruiz, J.R.; Vicente-Rodriguez, G.; Bergman, P.; Hagströmer, M.; Ottevaere, C.; Nagy, E.; Konsta, O.; Rey-López, J.P.; et al. Reliability of health-related physical fitness tests in European adolescents. The HELENA Study. *Int. J. Obes.* **2008**, *32*, S49–S57. [CrossRef] [PubMed]
45. Patti, A.; Maggio, M.C.; Corsello, G.; Messina, G.; Iovane, A.; Palma, A. Evaluation of Fitness and the Balance Levels of Children with a Diagnosis of Juvenile Idiopathic Arthritis: A Pilot Study. *Int. J. Environ. Res. Public Health* **2017**, *14*, 806. [CrossRef] [PubMed]
46. Ebbeling, C.B.; Ward, A.; Puleo, E.M.; Widrick, J.; Rippe, J.M. Development of a single-stage submaximal treadmill walking test. *Med. Sci. Sports Exerc.* **1991**, *23*, 966–973. [CrossRef] [PubMed]
47. American College of Sports Medicine; Chodzko-Zajko, W.J.; Proctor, D.N.; Fiatarone Singh, M.A.; Minson, C.T.; Nigg, C.R.; Salem, G.J.; Skinner, J.S. American College of Sports Medicine position stand. Exercise and Physical Activity for Older Adults. *Med. Sci. Sports Exerc.* **2009**, *41*, 1510–1530. [CrossRef] [PubMed]
48. Nelson, M.E.; Rejeski, W.J.; Blair, S.N.; Duncan, P.W.; Judge, J.O.; King, A.C.; Macera, C.A.; Castaneda-Sceppa, C.; American College of Sports Medicine; American Heart Association. Physical activity and public health in older adults: Recommendation from the American College of Sports Medicine and the American Heart Association. *Circulation* **2007**, *116*, 1094–1105. [CrossRef] [PubMed]
49. Batrakoulis, A.; Jamurtas, A.Z.; Tsimeas, P.; Poulios, A.; Perivoliotis, K.; Syrou, N.; Papanikolaou, K.; Draganidis, D.; Deli, C.K.; Metsios, G.S.; et al. Hybrid-type, multicomponent interval training upregulates musculoskeletal fitness of adults with overweight and obesity in a volume-dependent manner: A 1-year dose-response randomised controlled trial. *Eur. J. Sport Sci.* **2022**, *23*, 432–443. [CrossRef] [PubMed]
50. Grivas, G.V.; Karatrantou, K.; Chasialis, A.; Batatolis, C.; Ioakimidis, P.; Gerodimos, V. Serial vs. Integrated Outdoor Combined Training Programs for Health Promotion in Middle-Aged Males. *Sports* **2022**, *10*, 122. [CrossRef]
51. Ciolac, E.G.; Greve, J.M.D. Exercise-induced improvements in cardiorespiratory fitness and heart rate response to exercise are impaired in overweight/obese postmenopausal women. *Clinics* **2011**, *66*, 583–589. [CrossRef]
52. Eklund, D.; Pulverenti, T.; Bankers, S.; Avela, J.; Newton, R.; Schumann, M.; Häkkinen, K. Neuromuscular Adaptations to Different Modes of Combined Strength and Endurance Training. *Int. J. Sports Med.* **2014**, *36*, 120–129. [CrossRef]
53. Schumann, M.; Küüsmaa, M.; Newton, R.U.; Sirparanta, A.-I.; Syväoja, H.; Häkkinen, A.; Häkkinen, K. Fitness and Lean Mass Increases during Combined Training Independent of Loading Order. *Med. Sci. Sports Exerc.* **2014**, *46*, 1758–1768. [CrossRef]
54. Batrakoulis, A.; Tsimeas, P.; Deli, C.K.; Vlachopoulos, D.; Ubago-Guisado, E.; Poulios, A.; Chatzinikolaou, A.; Draganidis, D.; Papanikolaou, K.; Georgakouli, K.; et al. Hybrid neuromuscular training promotes musculoskeletal adaptations in inactive overweight and obese women: A training-detraining randomized controlled trial. *J. Sports Sci.* **2020**, *39*, 503–512. [CrossRef]
55. Batrakoulis, A.; Jamurtas, A.Z.; Georgakouli, K.; Draganidis, D.; Deli, C.K.; Papanikolaou, K.; Avloniti, A.; Chatzinikolaou, A.; Leontsini, D.; Tsimeas, P.; et al. High intensity, circuit-type integrated neuromuscular training alters energy balance and reduces body mass and fat in obese women: A 10-month training-detraining randomized controlled trial. *PLoS ONE* **2018**, *13*, e0202390. [CrossRef]

56. Blake, A.L.; Miller, W.C.; Brown, D.A. Adiposity does not hinder the fitness response to exercise training in obese women. *J. Sports Med. Phys. Fitness* **2000**, *40*, 170–177. [CrossRef] [PubMed]
57. Cadore, E.L.; Izquierdo, M.; Alberton, C.L.; Pinto, R.S.; Conceição, M.; Cunha, G.; Radaelli, R.; Bottaro, M.; Trindade, G.T.; Kruel, L.F.M. Strength prior to endurance intra-session exercise sequence optimizes neuromuscular and cardiovascular gains in elderly men. *Exp. Gerontol.* **2012**, *47*, 164–169. [CrossRef] [PubMed]
58. Cadore, E.L.; Izquierdo, M.; Pinto, S.S.; Alberton, C.L.; Pinto, R.S.; Baroni, B.M.; Vaz, M.A.; Lanferdini, F.J.; Radaelli, R.; González-Izal, M.; et al. Neuromuscular adaptations to concurrent training in the elderly: Effects of intrasession exercise sequence. *Age* **2012**, *35*, 891–903. [CrossRef] [PubMed]
59. Ogasawara, R.; Kobayashi, K.; Tsutaki, A.; Lee, K.; Abe, T.; Fujita, S.; Nakazato, K.; Ishii, N. MTOR signaling response to re-sistance exercise is altered by chronic resistance training and detraining in skeletal muscle. *J. Appl. Physiol.* **2013**, *114*, 934–940. [CrossRef]
60. Ogasawara, R.; Yasuda, T.; Sakamaki, M.; Ozaki, H.; Abe, T. Effects of periodic and continued resistance training on muscle CSA and strength in previously untrained men. *Clin. Physiol. Funct. Imaging* **2011**, *31*, 399–404. [CrossRef]
61. Holloszy, J.O.; Coyle, E.F. Adaptations of skeletal muscle to endurance exercise and their metabolic consequences. *J. Appl. Physiol. Respir. Environ. Exerc. Physiol.* **1984**, *56*, 831–838. [CrossRef]
62. Inoki, K.; Zhu, T.; Guan, K.-L. TSC2 Mediates Cellular Energy Response to Control Cell Growth and Survival. *Cell* **2003**, *115*, 577–590. [CrossRef]
63. Davis, W.J.; Wood, D.T.; Andrews, R.G.; Elkind, L.M. Concurrent Training Enhances Athletes' Strength, Muscle Endurance, and Other Measures. *J. Strength Cond. Res.* **2008**, *22*, 1487–1502. [CrossRef]
64. Davis, W.J.; Wood, D.T.; Andrews, R.G.; Elkind, L.M. Concurrent Training Enhances Athletes' Cardiovascular and Cardiorespiratory Measures. *J. Strength Cond. Res.* **2008**, *22*, 1503–1514. [CrossRef]
65. Davis, W.J.; Wood, D.T.; Andrews, R.G.; Elkind, L.M. Elimination of Delayed-Onset Muscle Soreness by Pre-resistance Cardioacceleration before Each Set. *J. Strength Cond. Res.* **2008**, *22*, 212–225. [CrossRef]
66. Ross, R.; Blair, S.N.; Arena, R.; Church, T.S.; Despres, J.P.; Franklin, B.A.; Haskell, W.L.; Kaminsky, L.A.; Levine, B.D.; Lavie, C.J.; et al. Importance of Assessing Cardiorespiratory Fitness in Clinical Practice: A Case for Fitness as a Clinical Vital Sign: A Scientific Statement from the American Heart Association. *Circulation* **2016**, *134*, e653–e699. [CrossRef] [PubMed]
67. Caspersen, C.J.; Powell, K.E.; Christenson, G.M. Physical activity, exercise, and physical fitness: Definitions and distinctions for health-related research. *Public Health Rep.* **1985**, *100*, 126–131. [PubMed]
68. Daniel, K. Wii-Hab for Pre-Frail Older Adults. *Rehabil. Nurs.* **2012**, *37*, 195–201. [CrossRef] [PubMed]

Journal of
Functional Morphology and Kinesiology

MDPI

Review

Barriers to Physical Activity for Women with Physical Disabilities: A Systematic Review

Jurgi Olasagasti-Ibargoien [1], Arkaitz Castañeda-Babarro [1], Patxi León-Guereño [1,*] and Naroa Uria-Olaizola [2]

[1] Health, Physical Activity and Sports Science Laboratory, Department of Physical Activity and Sports, Faculty of Education and Sport, University of Deusto, 48007 Bilbao, Spain; jurgi.olasagasti@deusto.es (J.O.-I.); arkaitz.castaneda@deusto.es (A.C.-B.)

[2] Deusto Sports and Society, Department of Physical Activity and Sports, Faculty of Education and Sport, University of Deusto, 48007 Bilbao, Spain; naroa.uria@deusto.es

* Correspondence: patxi.leon@deusto.es

Abstract: Physical activity is essential for women with physical disabilities. This review aims to identify the barriers they face in practicing sport. A systematic review was conducted using the PubMed/Medline, Scopus, and Web of Science databases in January 2023, with an update in March 2023. The eligibility criteria used for inclusion were as follows. (i) Women with physical disabilities; (ii) women who engage in or want to engage in physical activities and/or sport, both adapted and non-adapted; (iii) identification of women's barriers to such practice; (iv) research articles; and (v) papers written in English and published in peer-reviewed journals. The exclusion were as follows. (i) Women with illness, injury or transient physical activity difficulties; (ii) mention of rehabilitative physical activity; and (iii) results showing no differentiation in barrier types by gender. This review identified different barriers, grouped into eight types according to the differentiating factor, thus showing that disable people's participation in physical activity is directly related to some specific barriers which seem to differ according to their gender. Therefore, the success of participation in physical activities depends not only on the user's concern, but also on an inclusive social environment.

Keywords: physical activity; barriers; women; physical disability

Citation: Olasagasti-Ibargoien, J.; Castañeda-Babarro, A.; León-Guereño, P.; Uria-Olaizola, N. Barriers to Physical Activity for Women with Physical Disabilities: A Systematic Review. *J. Funct. Morphol. Kinesiol.* **2023**, *8*, 82. https://doi.org/10.3390/jfmk8020082

Academic Editor: Laura Stefani

Received: 28 April 2023
Revised: 13 June 2023
Accepted: 14 June 2023
Published: 16 June 2023

1. Introduction

An estimated 1.3 billion people, or 16% of the world's population, currently suffer from some form of disability [1]. About 1.5 billion people live with a physical, mental, sensory, or intellectual disability worldwide [2], of which women are the most affected, [3], making up 58.6% of the total. It is well known that regular physical activity is essential for maintaining good health and preventing disease [4–6]; the beneficial effects of exercise and physical activity on numerous aspects of health are now well known and generally accepted [7–9]. The practice of physical activity improves the physical, mental, and social state of the individual [10]. However, only 40% of women take part in the minimum recommended amount of physical activity [4,11], and in general, people with disabilities are in poorer health than the general population [2,12,13]. People with different disabilities such as cerebral palsy or spinal cord injury often face significant barriers to participating in physical activity [14–16], and in particular, women with physical disabilities often face unique and multiple challenges to practicing physical activity, including social, psychological, and physical barriers [17].

There is growing awareness of the importance of physical activity for people with physical disabilities, and as a result, there are several research studies on the benefits of physical activity for people with physical disabilities [18–21], and some suggestions for the adaptation of activities, e.g., for mothers with physical disabilities [22] or interventions for the assistance of people with a spinal cord injury [23]. Physical/sports activities for people with disabilities contribute to their functional independence, improve their physical condition, performance and physical capacity, favor the prevention and correction of deformities and postural defects, reduce stress, and improve self-confidence, emotional states, relationships with others, enjoyment and interest, among other things [24–26]. Within the Spanish population specifically, there is no study on the sporting habits of people with disabilities [27], although there are studies on the low levels of participation in sports practice [28], and on barriers to sport, both for different types of disabilities [14–16,29,30] and for people with physical disabilities in particular. However, the involvement of gender differences in these barriers is not appreciated [31–37]. However, when it comes to participation in physical activity (between women and men with disabilities), [14,16,20] women show poorer levels of participation. Differences gender-wise are found in the perception of barriers to physical activity according to gender [14]. Therefore, it is vitally important to highlight the needs of women with disabilities by identifying the barriers that have been identified in the literature and making this reality visible, in order to encourage participation in physical activity by women with disabilities.

Studies can be found in the literature that examine different types of barriers and their multiple classifications, such as social barriers, including discrimination and stigma; psychological barriers, including low levels of self-esteem and lack of motivation; and physical barriers, such as lack of access to adapted facilities and equipment [38–40]. Moreover, there exist intra-personal barriers, such as poor body image or fear of injury [41], and interpersonal barriers, such as lack of support or disapproval from others [12]. It is worth noting the existence of the differentiation in types of barriers according to gender [42]. Ways to overcome these barriers should be explored and the most effective strategies to increase the participation of women with physical disabilities in physical activity should be discussed.

The aim of this research is to raise awareness of the specific barriers faced by women with physical disabilities in relation to physical activity, and to ensure that they are addressed by management to the greatest extent of their responsibilities, in order to promote greater participation in physical activity. For these reasons, this article presents the results of a systematic review of the literature on barriers to physical activity for women with physical disabilities.

2. Materials and Methods

2.1. Literature Searching Strategies

The present research is a systematic review that seeks to identify the perceived barriers to women with physical disabilities who engage in or want to engage in physical activity. The research was conducted according the Preferred Reporting Items for Systematic Reviews and Meta-Analyses (PRISMA) guidelines [43]. This allowed an adequate structuring of the review, which answers the following question: what are the perceived barriers of women with physical disabilities who engage in or want to engage in physical activity, both adapted and non-adapted?

The following databases were used to conduct a structured search: PUBMED/MEDLINE, Web of Science (WOS) and Scopus. Using these high-quality databases, the search was completed without limitation to any specific year, and results were included up to and including 31 March 2023. Articles were retrieved from electronic databases using the following search strategy (Table 1): Barrier* AND "physical activit*" OR "adapted physical activit*" OR sport* AND disab* AND women OR woman, with these terms appearing in the title or abstract. Keywords were selected based on background reading. Articles considered relevant to this field of activity were obtained using the snowball strategy linked to this equation. In addition, all relevant studies were found by reviewing the titles and abstracts of articles in databases and the results of literature searches. These articles were considered potentially relevant and were analyzed for their compliance with the inclusion criteria for the final analysis. In addition, the reference sections of all articles found were examined, and all titles and abstracts obtained were cross-checked in order to detect possible duplication or lack of actual studies on the topic. Titles and abstracts were also selected for further full-text review. Two different authors searched for previous studies separately (J.O.-I. and N.U.-O.), and possible discrepancies were discussed with a third author (P.L.-G.).

Table 1. Search strategy.

	Articles Found		
	WOS	PUBMED	SCOPUS
1- Barrier* AND physical activit* AND disab* AND women	86	49	361
2- Barrier* AND physical activit* AND disab* AND woman	86	4	361
3- Barrier* AND adapted physical activit* AND disab* AND wom*	8	0	18
4- Barrier* AND sport* AND disab* AND wom* (All Fields)	21	14	71
5- Barrier* AND "physical activity" AND disab* AND wom*	63	48	235
Total without duplicates	97	55	397
		410	

2.2. Inclusion and Exclusion Criteria

No discrimination was made by country, race, or age, in order to obtain the most possible research. Articles published in English or Spanish and only research articles were filtered out.

The eligibility criteria used for inclusion were (i) women with physical disabilities; (ii) women who engage in or want to engage in physical activity and/or sport, both adapted and non-adapted; and (iii) the identification of barriers to women's physical activity and/or sport. The exclusion criteria applied to the research were the following: (i) women with illnesses (i.e., those not identified as a disability, such as women with cancer), injuries or situations of difficulty for physical activity of a specific or transient duration, such as pregnant women; (ii) women engaging in rehabilitation physical activity, as they have access to physical therapy activities; and (iii) results not showing gender differentiation within the type of perceived barrier.

2.3. Quality Criteria

Two authors assessed quality in terms of the methodology used, along with any risk of bias (J.O.-I. and N.U.O.). Lack of consensus was submitted to third party assessment (P.L-G.), following the protocol for search and selection of studies [44]. All the following points of the protocol were carried out. (1) Whether the selected studies met the eligibility criteria or not was determined; (2) all the papers found were compared with each other to find out whether the studies overlapped or not; and (3) the selection process was then carried out. (A) The search results were combined by identifying the DOI of each article (if not available, one was assigned to each article). (B) All the searches were input in a database, and duplicates removed by DOI for a first screening. (C) For the second screening, studies were sorted by title, and publication data were compared to remove duplicates, taking into account the title, authors, journal, year, and number and/or volume of the study. (D) All the identified full texts were recruited for analysis. (E) The decision to include a paper in the study was made considering the favorable opinion of two researchers (J.O.-I. and N.U.-O.); if there was a difference in opinion, it is a third researcher (A.C.-B.) who decides with a third opinion (following point 4 of the protocol, an established process of inclusion criteria in the case of disagreement, and point 5, the reason for the exclusion of the excluded studies).

2.4. Data Processing

All the selected articles had to identify a study outcome that referred specifically to women. These outcomes were grouped according to the type of outcome, corresponding to a differentiating factors which were as a result of an exploratory factor analysis (EFA) that explained 56.5% of the total variance: personal, physical, psychological, leadership, media support, coaching role, economic, others' attitudes, social, and cultural/religious support [17]. The barriers identified in each study were categorized and unified according to each grouping factor. In addition to the results, the profile of the subjects and the type of intervention carried out in these studies were added to obtain the results of each study.

3. Results

3.1. Search Process

Of the 1425 articles found after searching different databases, only 9 articles were identified that met all the inclusion criteria for the purposes of the systematic review, which are presented in the flowchart [45] (Figure 1). Of these 1425 articles, 1015 were removed as duplicates. Of the remaining 410 articles, 369 were eliminated after examination of titles or abstracts. Of the 41 full-text articles assessed for eligibility, a further 33 papers were discarded because they did not identify gender in the type of barrier (n = 8), did not specify the type of barrier (n = 13), did not specify the type of disability of the subjects (n = 3), were systematic reviews of another topic (n = 5), or were not related to the defined object of study (n = 4). On the other hand, one article was found after the citation search [39]. Thus, the present systematic review included nine studies [39,41,46–52].

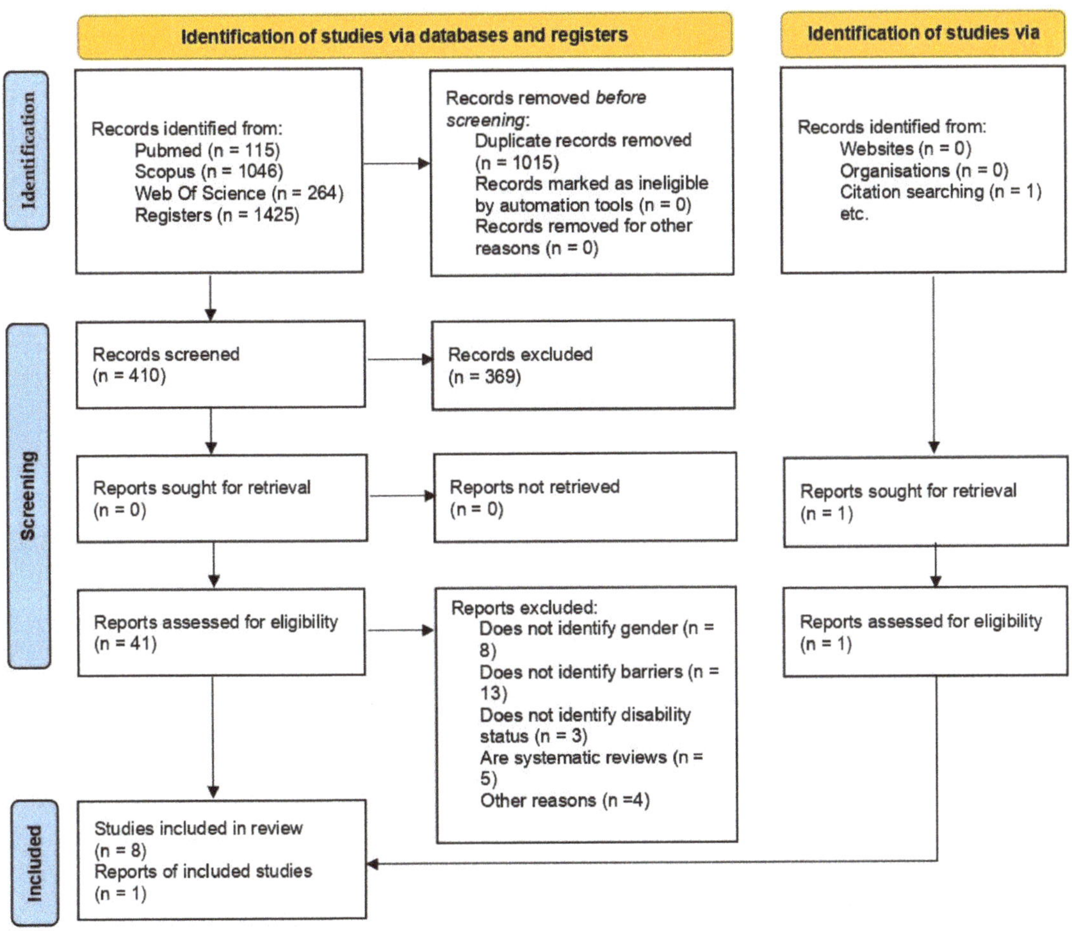

Figure 1. PRISMA flow diagram for study selection.

3.2. Differentiating Factor and Characteristics of Barriers

The different types of barriers identified as differentiating factors were based on the work of Bakhtiary et al.; the characteristics detected in each of them and the studies in which these barriers are mentioned are shown in Table 2.

Table 2. Studies included in the systematic review: characteristics of barriers and relevant studios.

Differentiating Factor	Characteristics	Number of Studies	References
Personal	Age Solitude Lifestyle Being a woman Lack of strategy Fatigue	1 study 1 study 2 studies 1 study 1 study 1 study	[50] [50] [50,52] [50] [50] [47]
Physical	Health Mobility Self-care Dependence	3 studies 2 studies 1 study 1 study	[41,50,52] [47,50] [50] [50]
Psychological	Self-image Motivation Fear Perception of (in)capacity	1 study 6 studies 3 studies 1 study	[39] [41,46,47,49,50,52] [41,50,52] [50]
Managerial	Accessibility or adaptations Transport Communication Political organization	4 studies 4 studies 4 studies 2 studies	[47–51] [47,49,50,52] [47,49,50,52] [49,50]
Coach role	Lack of training	2 studies	[49,51]
Economic	High cost Assistants' expenses	3 studies 1 study	[47,49,52] [48]
Others attitudes	Looks	2 studies	[50,51]
Social support	Family Colleague Society Institution	2 studies 2 studies 4 studies 1 study	[49,50] [41,50] [46,47,49,51] [49]
Cultural/religious support			
The media			

Table 2 shows that there is no study that confirms that there are barriers according to the differentiating factors of media support and cultural/religious support.

Table 3 shows all the studies found with the most complete data on the study subjects, the intervention methodology used, and the types of barriers identified according to the corresponding factor. The most frequently mentioned factor as a barrier was the psychological factor ($n = 7$), with a lack of motivation predominating. This was followed by the management ($n = 6$) of the offers or possibilities to practice sport for women with physical disabilities, and the lack of social support ($n = 6$), understood as the lack of support both from the immediate environment and from other people in society for access to or the possibility of engaging in physical activity.

Table 3. Data extraction and synthesis.

Author/s Year	Population	Intervention	Barriers Factor
Anderson et al., 2008 [41]	Subjects: • 22 women (10–18 years): Type of injury: • Cerebral palsy (7) • Spina bifida (8) • Osteogenesis (2) • Amputee (2) • Reduced mobility (2) • Cerebral anoxia(1)	Semi-structured interviews	1, 3, 9
Cardenas et al., 2021 [49]	Subjects: 49 women	Questionnaire	1, 3, 4, 6, 7, 8, 9
Dlugonski et al., 2012 [46]	Subjects: • 11 women (42.9 years ± 10.2) Type of injury: Multiple Sclerosis	Semi-structured interviews	3, 9
Henderson and Bedini, 1995 [47]	Subjects: • 16 women (29–53 years): Type of injury: • Rheumatoid arthritis (3) • Multiple sclerosis (3) • Spinal cord injury (3) • Cerebral palsy (2) others (5)	In depth interviews	1, 2, 3, 4, 7, 9
Odette et al., 2003 [48]	Subjects: • 45 women (+18 years) (mean 43, 18–80 years) Type of injury: • Rheumatological • Neurological • Musculoskeletal disorders	Focus group	4, 7
Rauch et al., 2013 [50]	Subjects: 13 women (44, 31–75 years)	Focus group and individual interviews	1, 2, 3, 4, 5, 8, 9
Richardos et al., 2017a [51]	Subjects: 8 women (+18 years), (mean 40, 23–60 years)	Focus group and individual interviews	8, 9
Richardos et al., 2017b [39]	Subjects: • 8 women (+18 years), (mean 43 years ± 13)	Semi-structured interviews, videoconferences, telephone interviews	3, 4, 6
Rimmer et al., 2000 [52]	Subjects: • 53 (18–64 years) (4%, 18–34 years; 31%, 35–49 years and 65%, 50–64 years) Type of injury: • Arthritis (30) • Apoplexy (22) • Multiple sclerosis (14) • Diabetes (10) • Lung diseases (8)	Telephone interviews	1, 2, 3, 4, 7

1. Personal; 2. physical; 3. psychological; 4. managerial; 5. the media; 6. coach's role; 7. economic; 8. others' attitudes; 9. social support; 10. cultural/religious.

4. Discussion

The current review aims to identify the perceived barriers of women with disabilities to engaging in physical activity or sport. We did not find any existing studies with such objectives. Therefore, the main objective has been to identify several types of very complex barriers that cover several aspects through which they can be approached; we propose that knowledge of these will help professionals to guide and favor women with physical disabilities in accessing sports or physical activity, as happens in populations with other physical needs [53]. A total of eight types of barriers (personal, physical, psychological, direction, coach's role, economic, others' attitudes, and social support) were identified from nine studies.

This research has yielded many significant insights. First, the results demonstrate that the barriers to physical activity for women with physical disabilities are multiple and complex, and span multiple dimensions. Many women with physical disabilities find it difficult to be physically active [54]; this study has revealed that personal barriers such as age, fatigue, loneliness, lifestyle, or simply being a woman may limit participation in any physical activity. All these factors are responsible for the low participation of women with physical disabilities in sport, since women have been shown to be less likely to participate in sports than men [16].

There is sufficient theoretical evidence on the benefits of sporting activity [55]; in the case of people with disabilities, it contributes to their functional independence, improves their physical condition, performance and physical capacity, favors the prevention and correction of deformities and postural defects, reduces stress, improves self-confidence, emotional state, relationships with others, and enjoyment and interest, among other things [26,56–58]. However, a second important finding of this review is that barriers related to physical disability, such as health, mobility, or the degree of dependence on others, also prevent women from practicing sport, thus reducing the possibility of appropriating all the benefits mentioned above.

Another barrier to participation is often linked to psychological factors. Within the psychological variables, motivation is one of the best known, although it is well known that motivation can be influenced by different factors [59] and is considered the most prominent factor in adherence to physical activity [13,60], The same factors were found in this study, wherein women with disabilities experience different situations that lead to a lack of motivation being a barrier to practicing sport [41,46,47,49,50,52]. In addition to motivation, other psychological factors, such as fear [41,50,52], the perception of not being able to engage in physical activity [50], or a negative self-perception [39], form a barrier for women with physical disabilities.

Such women should have opportunities for physical activity in a safe and adapted environment in accordance with their needs, under the Sport Law 2007 [61]; moreover, society as a whole must be committed to making this a reality [62]. However, this study has shown that these people encounter many management barriers, such as poor accessibility or lack of adaptations to sports centers, lack of transport to sports facilities, lack of co-communication between professionals, and poor organizational management. Confined spaces and equipment that does not easily accommodate mobility limitations also prevent them from making full use of exercise equipment and space [16], and the lack of communication between different professionals is also often one of the main barriers [63] that leads to a lack of opportunities [64]. Therefore, we believe that it is necessary to theorize about the structure of sporting institutions, starting with an inclusive atmosphere that can then be implemented into the wider sporting culture and activities, in which all people belonging to the community can be participants, as also pointed out in another study [62].

The role of a coach is essential for the proper performance of physical activities to ensure the safety of the participant and the benefits of physical activity and sport [65]; the important role of trainers is evident [15]. Therefore, health and physical activity professionals should consider individuals' abilities, needs, limitations, values, personality types and aptitudes in order to customize an adapted program and minimize the effects of possible barriers [53,66]. This study shows that training staff lack training in adapting physical activity or programs to the needs of users. There is a great lack of knowledge about the different sports modalities available for people with disabilities, especially those that are specific (e.g., boccia, slalom and goalball) [67]. Therefore, we believe that personalized attention may be the key to increasing levels of participation in sports, and to keeping programs challenging and attractive for people with physical disabilities. In addition, there should be a variety of offers, so that the user can select a program that best suits his or her needs [64,67].

It is clear that for women with physical disabilities to benefit from sport requires an approach that involves a wider range of programs. However, the economic context of the users must also be considered, as this barrier can have a crucial impact on participation in sport [35]. Taking into account that resources for this group are limited [31], when the financial costs of sporting activities increase, a barrier to participation is formed. In this sense, being a woman can also be an added barrier, as it can be more difficult to obtain sporting sponsors [68]. It is clear that for women with physical disabilities to benefit from sport, an approach that involves a wider range of programs is required. However, the economic context of the users must also be considered, as this barrier can have a crucial impact on participation in sport. Among the benefits of sports practice mentioned above, the improvement of relationships with others is defined by the following [21,26]; however, we should take into account the differentiation between social support in relationships with non-disabled people and in relationships with people with disabilities. Studies have shown an improvement in happiness as a result of perceived social support among people with disabilities [33]; however, this same improvement is not felt as a result of support from people without disabilities [46,47,49,51]. In addition to this, we would have to differentiate between social support from family and from acquaintances and other people. Family support [69] and the support of partners is fundamental, although barriers may exist [41,49,50]; however, the support of society and institutions also has an impact on successful sports practice [14,47,49]. Users are therefore more likely to show reduced adherence to exercise without this support [70,71]. It should also be noted that there are differences in social support according to gender [72]; in one study, it was found that men received more support from family and friends than women [73], just as in this study, wherein a lack of social support can be observed as a barrier to physical activity. Women's participation in physical activity was shown to be lower than the participation of men with disabilities [14,16,20]; these differences are also significant when it comes to the perception of barriers to physical activity, according to gender [14], between men and women.

It is also worth noting that another barrier identified was social attitudes towards people with disabilities. Negative attitudes may become barriers to the full realization of human potential [38], and because physical disabilities are visible to others, they can lead to stigmatizing social experiences [53,74]. It is therefore necessary to eliminate disability stigma, as people with disabilities who perceive stereotyping to a high degree also perceive a lower quality of life [33,75]. A society that does not recognize and value people with functional diversity loses all the potential they have to offer [76]. Other barriers identified as differentiating factors were culture and media [17], but in this research, they were far less represented.

Limitations

As this is a systematic review, our limitations are related to the studies inserted here. Although the selected sample is composed of a specific population (women with disabilities who want to perform or perform physical activity or sport), it is heterogeneous in terms of age, the type of physical limitation within the physical disability, and the context of the physical activity or sport performed by the women in the studies.

5. Conclusions

This review has enabled the identification of the barriers that women with physical disabilities encounter when performing physical activities. These findings highlight that participation in sports practice does not only depend on the participant. Society must know the barriers that women with physical disabilities face in practicing sports; this review publicizes those barriers in order to improve our best practices. Understanding and raising awareness of these barriers will allow interventions to be adapted to address the barriers, and to provide more targeted support and guidance to women with physical disabilities.

As people with physical disabilities themselves have demonstrated and demonstrate every day, we must not forget that they are people with great abilities who want to participate, on equal terms, in physical activity. As active members of the society to which they belong, they have the right to live as independently as possible and with the highest possible quality of life. A society that does not recognize the value of people with functional diversity will lose all the potential they have to offer.

Author Contributions: Conceptualization: N.U.-O. and J.O.-I.; Formal analysis: N.U.-O. and J.O.-I.; Investigation: N.U.-O., J.O.-I., A.C.-B. and P.L.-G.; Methodology: N.U.-O., J.O.-I., A.C.-B. and P.L.-G.; Writing and Reviewing; writing—original draft preparation N.U.-O. and J.O.-I.; Project administration: J.O.-I.; Data curation: A.C.-B. and P.L.-G. All authors have read and agreed to the published version of the manuscript.

Funding: This research received no external funding.

Institutional Review Board Statement: Not applicable.

Informed Consent Statement: Not applicable.

Data Availability Statement: Not applicable.

Conflicts of Interest: The authors declare no conflict of interest.

References

1. OMS. Discapacidad: Datos y Cifras. 2023. Available online: https://www.who.int/es/news-room/fact-sheets/detail/disability-and-health (accessed on 20 April 2023).
2. Ginis, K.A.M.; van der Ploeg, H.P.; Foster, C.; Lai, B.; McBride, C.B.; Ng, K.; Pratt, M.; Shirazipour, C.H.; Smith, B.; Vásquez, P.M.; et al. Participation of people living with disabilities in physical activity: A global perspective. *Lancet* **2021**, *398*, 443–455. [CrossRef]
3. Kolkka, T.; Williams, T. Gender and disability sport participation: Setting a sociological research agenda. *Adapt. Phys. Act. Q.* **1997**, *14*, 8–23. [CrossRef]
4. González, N.F.; Rivas, A.D. Actividad física y ejercicio en la mujer. *Rev. Colomb. Cardiol.* **2018**, *25*, 125–131. [CrossRef]
5. Martin Ginis, K.A.; Ma, J.K.; Latimer-Cheung, A.E.; Rimmer, J.H. A systematic review of review articles addressing factors related to physical activity participation among children and adults with physical disabilities. *Health Psychol. Rev.* **2016**, *10*, 478–494. [CrossRef] [PubMed]
6. Martin, J.J. Benefits and barriers to physical activity for individuals with disabilities: A social-relational model of disability perspective. *Disabil. Rehabil.* **2013**, *35*, 2030–2037. [CrossRef] [PubMed]
7. Blauwet, C.A.; Iezzoni, L.I. From the paralympics to public health: Increasing physical activity through legislative and policy initiatives. *PMR* **2014**, *6*, S4–S10. [CrossRef]
8. de Vries, N.M.; van Ravensberg, C.D.; Hobbelen, J.S.M.; Olde Rikkert, M.G.M.; Staal, J.B.; Nijhuis-van der Sanden, M.W.G. Effects of physical exercise therapy on mobility, physical functioning, physical activity and quality of life in community-dwelling older adults with impaired mobility, physical disability and/or multi-morbidity: A meta-analysis. *Ageing Res. Rev.* **2012**, *11*, 136–149. [CrossRef]
9. Warburton, D.E.R.; Bredin, S.S.D. Health benefits of physical activity: A systematic review of current systematic reviews. *Curr. Opin. Cardiol.* **2017**, *32*, 541–556. [CrossRef]
10. Ozols Rosales, M.A. Editorial—Actividad Física y Discapacidad. *MHSalud Rev. en Ciencias del Mov. Hum. y Salud* **2007**, *4*, 1–5. [CrossRef]
11. Kızar, O.; Demir, G.T.; Genç, H. Examination of the Effect of National and Amateur Disabled Athletes' Disabilty Types on Sports Participation Motivation. *Eur. J. Phys. Educ. Sport Sci.* **2021**, *6*, 1–16. [CrossRef]
12. Úbeda-Colomer, J.; Monforte, J.; Devís-Devís, J. Physical activity of university students with disabilities: Accomplishment of recommendations and differences by age, sex, disability and weight status. *Public Health* **2019**, *166*, 69–78. [CrossRef]
13. Bentzen, M.; Brurok, B.; Roeleveld, K.; Hoff, M.; Jahnsen, R.; Wouda, M.F.; Baumgart, J.K. Changes in physical activity and basic psychological needs related to mental health among people with physical disability during the COVID-19 pandemic in Norway. *Disabil. Health J.* **2021**, *14*, 101126. [CrossRef] [PubMed]
14. Dėdelė, A.; Chebotarova, Y.; Miškinytė, A. Motivations and barriers towards optimal physical activity level: A community-based assessment of 28 EU countries. *Prev. Med.* **2022**, *164*, 107336. [CrossRef] [PubMed]
15. Ferguson, J.J.; Spencer, N.L.I. "A Really Strong Bond": Coaches in Women Athletes' Experiences of Inclusion in Parasport. *Int. Sport Coach. J.* **2021**, *8*, 283–292. [CrossRef]
16. Rolfe, D.E.; Yoshida, K.; Renwick, R.; Bailey, C. Negotiating participation: How women living with disabilities address barriers to exercise. *Health Care Women Int.* **2009**, *30*, 743–766. [CrossRef] [PubMed]

17. Bakhtiary, F.; Noorbakhsh, M.; Noorbakhsh, P.; Sepasi, H. Development and Validation of a Tool for Assessing Barriers to Participation in Team Sports for Women with Physical-Mobility Disabilities. *Ann. Appl. Sport Sci.* **2020**, *8*, e809. [CrossRef]
18. Sañudo Corrales, B. Actividad físico—Deportiva para personas con discapacidad física. In *Actividad Física en Poblaciones Especiales: Salud y Calidad de Vida*; Wanceulen: Sevilla, Spain, 2012; pp. 97–132; ISBN 978-84-9993-260-6.
19. Charron, S.; McKay, K.A.; Tremlett, H. Physical activity and disability outcomes in multiple sclerosis: A systematic review (2011–2016). *Mult. Scler. Relat. Disord.* **2018**, *20*, 169–177. [CrossRef]
20. McCullagh, R.; Fitzgerald, P.; Murphy, R.P.M.; Cooke, G. Long-term benefits of exercising on quality of life and fatigue in multiple sclerosis patients with mild disability: A pilot study. *Clin. Rehabil.* **2008**, *22*, 206–214. [CrossRef]
21. Shephard, R.J. Benefits of sport and physical activity for the disabled: Implications for the individual and for society. *Scand. J. Rehabil. Med.* **1991**, *23*, 51–59. [CrossRef]
22. Walker, L.O.; Becker, H.; Andrews, E.E.; Phillips, C.S. Adapting a health behavioral change and psychosocial toolkit to the context of physical disabilities: Lessons learned from disabled women with young children. *Disabil. Health J.* **2021**, *14*, 100977. [CrossRef]
23. Rezende, L.S.; Lima, M.B.; Salvador, E.P. Interventions for promoting physical activity among individuals with spinal cord injury: A systematic review. *J. Phys. Act. Health* **2018**, *15*, 954–959. [CrossRef] [PubMed]
24. Arbour, K.P.; Latimer, A.E.; Ginis KA, M.; Jung, M.E. Moving beyond the stigma: The impression formation benefits of exercise for individuals with a physical disability. *Adapt. Phys. Act. Q.* **2007**, *24*, 144–159. [CrossRef] [PubMed]
25. Asonitou, K.; Mpampoulis, T.; Irakleous-Paleologou, H.; Koutsouki, D. Effects of an adapted physical activity program on physical fitness of adults with intellectual disabilities. *Adv. Phys. Educ.* **2018**, *8*, 321–336. [CrossRef]
26. Fernando, M.; Duque, R. Beneficios de la práctica de actividad física deportiva en personas con discapacidad física. *Año* **2022**, *20*, 152–172.
27. Perez Tejero, J.; Ocete Calvo, C. Personas con discapacidad y práctica deportiva en España. In *Libro Blanco del Deporte de Personas con Discapacidad en España*; Cermi. Ediciones Cinca: Madrid, Spain, 2019; ISBN 978-84-16668-69-4.
28. Ramírez Muñoz, A.; Sanz de Gabiña, L.; Figueroa de la Paz, A. *Estudio Sobre Los Hábitos Deportivos en Las Personas con Discapacidad en la Provincia de Guipúzcoa*; Gobierno de España, Ministerio de Sanidad, Servicios Sociales e Igualdad: Gipúzcoa, Spain, 2007; ISBN 9788527729833.
29. Alexandra, D.; Rojas, C.; Valentina, J.; Castrillon, D.; Cabrera, V.G.; Marcela, L.; González, E.; Marcela, P.; Garzón, M.; Muñoz-hinrichsen, F.; et al. Estado del arte de la investigación en discapacidad y actividad física en Sudamérica. Una Revisión Narrativa. *Retos* **2023**, *2041*, 945–968.
30. Rincón, F.; Aydé, C.; Giraldo, R.; Alexis, F. Percepción de beneficios, barreras y nivel de actividad física de estudiantes universitarios. *Investig. Andin.* **2015**, *17*, 1391–1406.
31. Braza, D.W.; Iverson, M.; Lee, K.; Hennessy, C.; Nelson, D. Promoting physical activity by creating awareness of adaptive sports and recreation opportunities: An academic–community partnership perspective. *Prog. Community Health Partnersh. Res. Educ. Action* **2018**, *12*, 165–172. [CrossRef]
32. Buffart, L.M.; Westendorp, T.; Van Den Berg-Emons, R.J.; Stam, H.J.; Roebroeck, M.E. Perceived barriers to and facilitators of physical activity in young adults with childhood-onset physical disabilities. *J. Rehabil. Med.* **2009**, *41*, 881–885. [CrossRef]
33. Kim, Y.; Cho, J.; Fuller, D.K.; Kang, M. Correlates of physical activity among people with disabilities in South Korea: A multilevel modeling approach. *J. Phys. Act. Health* **2015**, *12*, 1031–1038. [CrossRef] [PubMed]
34. Mulligan, H.; Miyahara, M.; Nichols-Dunsmuir, A. Multiple perspectives on accessibility to physical activity for people with long-term mobility impairment. *Scand. J. Disabil. Res.* **2017**, *19*, 295–306. [CrossRef]
35. Scelza, W.M.; Kalpakjian, C.Z.; Zemper, E.D.; Tate, D.G. Perceived barriers to exercise in people with spinal cord injury. *Am. J. Phys. Med. Rehabil.* **2005**, *84*, 576–583. [CrossRef] [PubMed]
36. Smith, B.; Papathomas, A.; Martin Ginis, K.A.; Latimer-Cheung, A.E. Understanding physical activity in spinal cord injury rehabilitation: Translating and communicating research through stories. *Disabil. Rehabil.* **2013**, *35*, 2046–2055. [CrossRef] [PubMed]
37. Úbeda-Colomer, J.; Monforte, J.; Granell, J.C.; Goig, R.L.; Cabrera, M.Á.T.; Devis-Devis, J. Reasons for sport practice and drop-out in university students with disabilities: Influence of age and disability grade. *Cult. Cienc. y Deport.* **2018**, *13*, 51–60. [CrossRef]
38. Patricia, J.; Miranda, A.; Yulieth, L.; Urquijo, G. Barreras contextuales para la participación de las personas con discapacidad física. *Salud UIS* **2013**, *45*, 41–51.
39. Richardson, E.V.; Smith, B.; Papathomas, A. Disability and the gym: Experiences, barriers and facilitators of gym use for individuals with physical disabilities. *Disabil. Rehabil.* **2017**, *39*, 1950–1957. [CrossRef] [PubMed]
40. Kim, J.; Kim, J.; Kim, Y.; Han, A.; Nguyen, M.C. The contribution of physical and social activity participation to social support and happiness among people with physical disabilities. *Disabil. Health J.* **2021**, *14*, 100974. [CrossRef] [PubMed]
41. Anderson, D.M.; Wozencroft, A.; Bedini, L.A. Adolescent girls' involvement in disability sport: A comparison of social support mechanisms. *J. Leis. Res.* **2008**, *40*, 183–207. [CrossRef]
42. Ascondo, J.; Martín-López, A.; Iturricastillo, A.; Granados, C.; Garate, I.; Romaratezabala, E.; Martínez-Aldama, I.; Romero, S.; Yanci, J. Analysis of the Barriers and Motives for Practicing Physical Activity and Sport for People with a Disability: Differences According to Gender and Type of Disability. *Int. J. Environ. Res. Public Health* **2023**, *20*, 1320. [CrossRef]
43. Grimshaw, J.M.; Hróbjartsson, A.; Lalu, M.M.; Li, T.; Loder, E.W.; Mayo-Wilson, E.; McGuinness, L.; McDonald, S.; Stewart, L.A.; Thomas, J.; et al. Pravila PRISMA 2020. *Med. Flum.* **2021**, *57*, 444–465. [CrossRef]

44. Lefebvre, C.; Glanville, J.; Briscoe, S.; Littlewood, A.; Marshall, C.; Metzendorf, M.-I.; Noel-Storr, A.; Rader, T.; Shokraneh, F.; Thomas, J.; et al. *Searching for and Selecting Studies*; Wiley Online Library: New York, NY, USA, 2019.
45. Page, M.J.; McKenzie, J.E.; Bossuyt, P.M.; Boutron, I.; Hoffmann, T.C.; Mulrow, C.D.; Shamseer, L.; Tetzlaff, J.M.; Akl, E.A.; Brennan, S.E.; et al. Declaración PRISMA 2020: Una guía actualizada para la publicación de revisiones sistemáticas. *Rev. Española Cardiol.* **2021**, *74*, 790–799. [CrossRef]
46. Dlugonski, D.; Joyce, R.J.; Motl, R.W. Meanings, motivations, and strategies for engaging in physical activity among women with multiple sclerosis. *Disabil. Rehabil.* **2012**, *34*, 2148–2157. [CrossRef]
47. Henderson, K.A.; Bedini, L.A. "I have a soul that dances like tina turner, but my body can't": Physical activity and women with mobility impairments. *Res. Q. Exerc. Sport* **1995**, *66*, 151–161. [CrossRef]
48. Odette, F.; Israel, P.; Li, A.; Ullman, D.; Colontonio, A.; Maclean, H.; Locker, D. Barriers to Wellness Activities for Canadian Women with Physical Disabilities. *Health Care Women Int.* **2003**, *24*, 125–134. [CrossRef]
49. Ortiz Cárdenas, J.P.; Perdomo Vargas, I.R.; Garzón Patrana, G.; Vargas Reyes, J.D. Percepción de factores que inciden en la participación y competencia de mujeres atletas en Para Powerlifting. *Educ. Física y Cienc.* **2021**, *23*, e191. [CrossRef]
50. Rauch, A.; Fekete, C.; Cieza, A.; Geyh, S.; Meyer, T. Participation in physical activity in persons with spinal cord injury: A comprehensive perspective and insights into gender differences. *Disabil. Health J.* **2013**, *6*, 165–176. [CrossRef]
51. Richardson, E.V.; Smith, B.; Papathomas, A. Collective stories of exercise: Making sense of gym experiences with disabled peers. *Adapt. Phys. Act. Q.* **2017**, *34*, 276–294. [CrossRef] [PubMed]
52. Rimmer, J.H.; Rubin, S.S.; Braddock, D. Barriers to exercise in African American women with physical disabilities. *Arch. Phys. Med. Rehabil.* **2000**, *81*, 182–188. [CrossRef] [PubMed]
53. Tavares, E.; Coelho, J.; Rogado, P.; Correia, R.; Castro, C.; Fernandes, J.B. Barriers to Gait Training among Stroke Survivors: An Integrative Review. *J. Funct. Morphol. Kinesiol.* **2022**, *7*, 85. [CrossRef] [PubMed]
54. MacEachern, S.; Forkert, N.D.; Lemay, J.F.; Dewey, D. Physical Activity Participation and Barriers for Children and Adolescents with Disabilities. *Int. J. Disabil. Dev. Educ.* **2022**, *69*, 204–216. [CrossRef]
55. Barbosa-Granados, S.; Urrea-Cuellar, A. Influencia del deporte y la actividad física en el estado de salud físico y mental. *Katharsis* **2018**, *25*, 141–160. [CrossRef]
56. Aranda, R.M. Physical activity and quality of life in the elderly. A narrative review. *Rev. Habanera Cienc. Med.* **2018**, *17*, 813–825.
57. Mendoza, E.V.V.; Cano, A.G.B.; Chasipanta, W.G.A.; Navarrete, L.R.P.; Ipiales, E.N.P.; Frómeta, E.R. Programa de actividades físico-recreativas para desarrollar habilidades motrices en personas con discapacidad intelectual. *Rev. Cuba. Investig. Biomed.* **2017**, *36*, 1–13.
58. Velasco-Benítez, C.A.; Reyes-Oyola, F.A. Niveles de actividad física, calidad de vida relacionada con la salud, autoconcepto físico e índice de masa corporal: Un estudio en escolares colombianos. *Biomédica* **2018**, *38*, 451–452. [CrossRef] [PubMed]
59. Harwood, C.G.; Keegan, R.J.; Smith, J.M.J.; Raine, A.S. A systematic review of the intrapersonal correlates of motivational climate perceptions in sport and physical activity. *Psychol. Sport Exerc.* **2015**, *18*, 9–25. [CrossRef]
60. Monforte, J.; Úbeda-Colomer, J.; Pans, M.; Pérez-Samaniego, V.; Devís-Devís, J. Environmental barriers and facilitators to physical activity among university students with physical disability-a qualitative study in Spain. *Int. J. Environ. Res. Public Health* **2021**, *18*, 464. [CrossRef]
61. Gobierno de España. REAL DECRETO 1363/2007, de 24 de Octubre, por el que se Establece la Ordenación General de las Enseñanzas Deportivas de Régimen Especial. 2007; pp. 45945–45960. Available online: https://www.boe.es/eli/es/rd/2007/10/24/1363 (accessed on 20 April 2023).
62. López González, S.P. El derecho humano a la educación. *Derecho Glob. Estud. Sobre Derecho y Justicia* **2016**, *2*, 10–11. [CrossRef]
63. Ginis, K.A.M.; West, C.R. From guidelines to practice: Development and implementation of disability-specific physical activity guidelines. *Disabil. Rehabil.* **2021**, *43*, 3432–3439. [CrossRef]
64. Wright, A.; Roberts, R.; Bowman, G.; Crettenden, A. Barriers and facilitators to physical activity participation for children with physical disability: Comparing and contrasting the views of children, young people, and their clinicians. *Disabil. Rehabil.* **2019**, *41*, 1499–1507. [CrossRef]
65. Campos Izquierdo, A. Los profesionales de la actividad física y el deporte como elemento de garantía y calidad de servicios. *Cult. Cienc. y Deport.* **2007**, *3*, 51–57. [CrossRef]
66. Fernandes, J.B.; Fernandes, S.B.; Almeida, A.S.; Vareta, D.A.; Miller, C.A. Older adults' perceived barriers to participation in a falls prevention strategy. *J. Pers. Med.* **2021**, *11*, 450. [CrossRef]
67. Reina, R. Propuesta de intervención para la mejora de actitudes hacia personas con discapacidad a través de actividades deportivas y recreativas. *Lect. Educ. Física y Deport.* **2003**, *59*, 7.
68. Dashper, K. "It's a Form of Freedom": The experiences of people with disabilities within equestrian sport. *Ann. Leis. Res.* **2010**, *13*, 86–101. [CrossRef]
69. Hinrichsen, F.I.M.; Aros, A.F.M.; Miranda, F.H. Transcultural translation and adaptation of the questionnaire for children «Barriers and facilitators of sports in children with physical disabilities (BaFSCH)» for use into Spanish in Chile. *Retos* **2021**, *44*, 695–701. [CrossRef]
70. Gómez, B.; González, A.; Pasten, E.; Concha-Cisternas, Y. Sports family climate and the level of physical activity in adolescents. *Retos* **2022**, *45*, 440–445. [CrossRef]

71. Vaquero Solís, M.; Tapia Serrano, M.Á.; Cerro Herrero, D.; Sánchez Miguel, P.A. Importancia del rol familiar en la práctica de actividad física e IMC de escolares adolescentes. *Sport. Sci. J. Sch. Sport. Phys. Educ. Psychomot.* **2019**, *5*, 408–422. [CrossRef]
72. Sanz-Martín, D.; Ruiz-Tendero, G.; Fernández-García, E. Relación entre la práctica de actividad física y el apoyo social percibido de los adolescentes de la provincia de Soria. *Sport TK-Revista Euroam. Ciencias del Deport.* **2021**, *10*, 29–35. [CrossRef]
73. Lubans, D.R.; Sylva, K.; Morgan, P.J. Factors associated with physical activity in a sample of British secondary school students. *Aust. J. Educ. Dev. Psychol.* **2007**, *7*, 22–30.
74. López Alvarado, M.C.; De Andrés, S.; Gonzalez Martín, R. Discapacidad: Estigma y concienciación. *Comun. e Cid. Rev. Int. Xorn. Soc.* **2007**, *1*, 202–223.
75. Carrasco, L.F.; Martín, N.; Molero, F. Stigma consciousness and quality of life in persons with physical and sensory disability. *Int. J. Soc. Psychol.* **2013**, *28*, 259–271. [CrossRef]
76. Iáñez, A. Cuerpo y modernidad. El procesos de estigmatización en las personas con diversidad funcional física. *Trib. Abierta* **2009**, *2009*, 105–122.

MDPI
St. Alban-Anlage 66
4052 Basel
Switzerland
www.mdpi.com

Journal of Functional Morphology and Kinesiology Editorial Office
E-mail: jfmk@mdpi.com
www.mdpi.com/journal/jfmk

www.ingramcontent.com/pod-product-compliance
Lightning Source LLC
Chambersburg PA
CBHW062054220926
51850CB00010B/2767
* 9 7 8 3 7 2 5 8 0 5 8 4 6 *